THE AMENDING OF
THE FEDERAL
CONSTITUTION

Da Capo Press Reprints in

AMERICAN CONSTITUTIONAL AND LEGAL HISTORY

GENERAL EDITOR: LEONARD W. LEVY
Claremont Graduate School

THE AMENDING OF
THE FEDERAL
CONSTITUTION

BY LESTER B. ORFIELD

Foreword by
HENRY M. BATES

DA CAPO PRESS • NEW YORK • 1971

A Da Capo Press Reprint Edition

This Da Capo Press edition of
The Amending of the Federal Constitution
is an unabridged republication of the first edition
published in Ann Arbor and Chicago in 1942.

Library of Congress Catalog Card Number 70-147790
SBN 306-70094-8

Copyright, 1942, by University of Michigan

Published by Da Capo Press
A Division of Plenum Publishing Corporation
227 West 17th Street, New York, N.Y. 10011
All Rights Reserved

Manufactured in the United States of America

MICHIGAN LEGAL STUDIES

———

THE AMENDING
OF THE
FEDERAL CONSTITUTION

MICHIGAN LEGAL STUDIES

———

Discovery Before Trial
George Ragland, Jr.

Torts in the Conflict of Laws
Moffatt Hancock

The Amending of the Federal Constitution
Lester B. Orfield

Review of Administrative Acts
Armin Uhler

THE AMENDING OF
THE FEDERAL
CONSTITUTION

by

LESTER BERNHARDT ORFIELD

PROFESSOR OF LAW, UNIVERSITY OF NEBRASKA

———

Foreword

by

HENRY M. BATES

Ann Arbor
THE UNIVERSITY OF MICHIGAN PRESS

———

Chicago
CALLAGHAN & COMPANY

1942

PUBLISHED UNDER THE AUSPICES OF THE UNIVERSITY OF MICHIGAN LAW
SCHOOL (WHICH, HOWEVER, ASSUMES NO RESPONSIBILITY FOR THE VIEWS
EXPRESSED) WITH THE AID OF FUNDS DERIVED FROM GIFTS TO THE UNIVERSITY
OF MICHIGAN BY WILLIAM W. COOK

To my Parents,
Andrew Christian
and
Alpha Bennett Orfield,
Who early impressed upon me the
Nobility of Scholarship

Foreword

PROJECTS to amend the Constitution of the United States have poured in an almost unceasing stream upon the nation ever since the beginning of our national history. Most of these have had slight intrinsic importance, and for that reason and because backed by little popular approval nor by strong pressure groups, they have not been given official life by Congress or the States. Only twenty-one of these proposals have been adopted in the century and a half of our life as a nation. But the acutely transitional character of the last quarter of a century has stimulated more general discussion and more intensive study of our constitutional system than had heretofore taken place since the decade or two following the adoption of the Articles of Confederation. The shattering impact of World War Number One and its aftermath, and the even more profound dislocations caused by the present war have inevitably induced intense study of the organic features of our constitutional scheme as well as of such other provisions as those relating to civil liberties. From these changes in the conditions of life of the nation and possibly still more from changed and changing theories as to the objectives of government, has come the tendency to revise and modify our constitutional arrangement, which is fairly certain to produce many definite proposals to amend the Constitution in the near future.

There has been much less study of the Amending Clause of the Constitution than of any other of its important provisions. Consequently, there is comparatively little material of an official sort relating to the process of amending. There have been strangely few amendments. It is apparent from a study of the debates in the Constitutional Convention and contemporary discussion in the States, that our much publicized "founding fathers" anticipated that the Amending Clause would be employed far more often than has proved to be the case. While most of the twenty-one amendments which are now part of our Constitution have been frequently involved in litigation in both Federal and State Supreme Courts, that litigation has been concerned chiefly with the content of the amendments and not with the manner of their adoption. During the last five years, questions regarding the validity of the methods actually adopted have come with greater frequency than at any prior time in our history. That frequent amendment of the Constitution has been avoided, whatever the reasons therefor, is probably a most fortunate circumstance for the country. To have amended the Constitution frequently during the first century of our national existence might have resulted in the addition of some hastily conceived and unwise changes creating new problems and defects and tending to reduce our whole constitutional structure to the level of ordinary legislation.

Nevertheless, the pressure from recent changes in our national life and others which will inevitably develop, would seem likely to increase the demand for constitutional amendments, particularly when the present world-wide and revolutionary war has wreaked its complete vengeance upon society. If present governmental tendencies in this country continue to advance in the direction they are now taking, it is reasonably certain that bills will be introduced in Congress, the purpose of which is to create new boards, commissions or other offices, granting new authority and still further extending governmental regulatory power or control, especially in the fields of commerce, industrial relations, agriculture and taxation. Already there has been an enormous extension of governmental administration into fields which had heretofore been regarded as strictly private and insulated from governmental interference by the Due Process Clause in both the Fifth and Fourteenth Amendments. But with the decision of *Munn v. Illinois*, 94 U. S. 113, the old strictly limited category of public utilities and other businesses subject to public regulation was demonstrated to be utterly inadequate and illogical. The concept of businesses charged with a public interest, which had lain relatively dormant since Sir Mathew Hale's time, was revived and became the justification for an extension of governmental activity which shocked and frightened a great many people whose sincere beliefs concerning political and economic matters, or whose selfish interest, had made them the partisans of an extreme laissez faire theory of government. And recent decisions of the Supreme Court, especially several since the First World War, have opened the way for repeated and successful attacks upon the economic and political theories of John Stewart Mill and his followers in this country. It is not easy to find any logical and permanent limit beyond which the doctrines with regard to businesses charged with public interest may not be carried to sustain public regulation and perhaps control.

For a half century at least, the United States and the several States have been greatly enlarging the field of administrative law and action. Until recently Congress has been restrained by a rigid and historically unsound conception of due process of law, which has now been greatly modified if indeed not wholly rejected by the Supreme Court.

Important decisions of the Court during the last five years have all but destroyed the heretofore prevailing view that administrative proceedings must be conducted in accordance with certain implicit requirements, not unlike those which dictate judicial procedure. The same decisions have come near to establishing the power of administrative commissions and officers to exercise so-called quasi-judicial functions without review by the courts, but complete finality of determination by administrative functionaries has not been declared by the courts, and agitation for constitutional amendment to bring about that finality is not improbable.

Theories and even sentimental notions about state sovereignty and the Reserved Powers Clause of the Tenth Amendment had imposed other restrictions upon the exercise of the police power of the States and unduly restrained the exercise of the so-called implied powers of Congress. There had been a gradual invasion of the supposed field of reserved rights through a slowly enlarging conception of the scope of the interstate commerce power of Congress. Recent decisions of the Court have practically discarded the old and very unsatisfactory test of the direct or indirect effect upon interstate commerce by the application and enforcement of both state and congressional legislation concerned with industrial and business functioning. This, of course, has opened the door wider for both state and federal regulation of business. But the door is not yet as wide open as some think it should be, and it is far too wide open to accord with the views and opinions of a probably small minority at the present time. That minority, however, may after a time develop new strength and find new opportunity, say from an increasing popular fear of totalitarian government, to impose restraints, with the probable result of a demand for constitutional amendment.

As to the scope of the commerce power of Congress, opinions continue to differ greatly. And so, the vexing question whether state legislation interferes with or usurps the power given to Congress, and the converse of that question whether Congressional legislation is in reality regulation of interstate commerce, or whether it goes beyond such regulation and affects the exercise of state police powers, and interferes with legal intra-state commerce, are bound to arise and to be vigorously debated. So it is with respect to some areas in the field of taxation.

The specific grants of authority have left the extent of the President's power far from clear. Thus the bitter controversy raging about our relationship to the present war has made it painfully clear that the clause making the President the Commander-in-Chief of the Army and Navy, those conferring the power over foreign relations, and the general grant of executive power, make it entirely possible for the President to make war in effect or bring on war, even though the power to declare war is given to Congress exclusively. If a President, however wisely, were so to exercise his clearly granted power as to bring us into war, and if the Congress were opposed to his policy and refused to make adequate appropriations and other arrangements for carrying on the war, the consequences obviously might be disastrous.

There are many other unsettled areas of national power concerning the executive and other departments, and, while probably it is fortunate that the Constitution makers refrained from making many specific grants, and from making any disposition of some areas of power not falling clearly within any of the three great departments of government, it seems probable that there may be a demand for making, clarifying or re-arranging some of the distributions of power in this and other fields. How many are the possibilities of clash of views, how many important matters are still undetermined, are made very clear by Professor E. S. Corwin's book recently published, entitled "The President, Office and Powers." This book is based upon an exhaustive, analytical and historical study of the Presidency, and is one of the most important contributions to the understanding of American government made in many years. It gives expression to a few interpretations and some views with which the writer, at least, does not wholly agree, but the book as a whole is thoroughly sound and penetrating.

Doubtless the stream of criticism of our judicial department will continue. Criticism of our courts is inevitable, and, if it is not accompanied by maladroit efforts to weaken the foundations of the judicial system, criticism is healthful. Already many proposals to amend Article Two of the Constitution have been made and doubtless many more will be made in the future.

By no means all of the possible defects or deficiencies indicated in the foregoing pages are likely to require or be accorded constitutional amendment. They have been suggested merely as illustrative of the fact that at any time we may have the beginning of a more determined and systematic attempt to amend the Constitution; and this makes Professor Orfield's book particularly timely. Professor Orfield has made an exhaustive study of all of the materials available for consideration of his subject. His book presents a comprehensive picture of constitutional amendment as provided for and developed during the century and a half of our national existence. The author presents a statement of what has happened and of judicial and other official opinions relating to the Amending Clause. He has said comparatively little by way of argument for any particular theory relating to the various steps in procedure. To have restricted his treatment of the subject in this manner, seems to the writer a wise decision. The important thing at the present time is to have an accurate, fair and wholly non-partisan presentation of the subject. Various steps in procedure can best be investigated and the existing ones perhaps improved upon by separate studies of each step, or of groups of related steps. A reader of Professor Orfield's book would do well to examine Everett S. Brown's book "The Ratification of the Twenty-First Amendment to the Constitution of the United States," and also Professor Brown's article on the same subject in the "American Political Science Review" XXIX (Dec. 1935) 1005–1017.

Professor Orfield has made a valuable contribution to a most important subject.

HENRY M. BATES

Preface

MOST treatises on constitutional law dispose of the federal amending clause in summary fashion. The commentators have thought fit to stress chiefly the division of authority between the federal government and the states. They have attached a high degree of significance to the dogma of separation of powers. A great deal of attention has been devoted to the doctrines of judicial review, the supremacy of the Federal Constitution, and the Bill of Rights. The taxation and the commerce clauses have come in for their full share of consideration. In recent years extensive studies have been made of the due process clause of the Fourteenth Amendment. As a result, the amendment clause has almost been lost sight of. No monograph on Article Five has been published prior to the present book. Yet when one stops to realize that the subjects just referred to have to do only with the existing distribution of powers, and that the operation of the amending power may bring about a complete reshuffling of the Constitution, it becomes obvious that one is dealing with a power of a higher grade and of more potential importance than any other power provided for in the Constitution. As John W. Burgess says:

"A complete constitution may be said to consist of three fundamental parts. The first is the organization of the state for the accomplishment of future changes in the constitution. This is usually called the amending clause, and the power which it describes and regulates is called the amending power. This is the most important part of a constitution. Upon its existence and truthfulness, i.e., its correspondence with real and natural conditions, depends the question as to whether the state shall develop with peaceful continuity or shall suffer alternations of stagnation, retrogression and revolution. A constitution, which may be imperfect and erroneous in its other parts, can be easily supplemented and corrected, if only the state be truthfully organized in the constitution; but if this be not accomplished, error will accumulate until nothing short of revolution can save the life of a state." [1]

One may approach the study of the amending clause from at least three different points of view: from that of constitutional law, from that of jurisprudence and legal philosophy, and from that of political science and legislation. From the standpoint of constitutional law the genesis and justiciability of the power may be considered; the procedure of amendment may be examined in detail; and the scope of the amending power may be analyzed. From the point of jurisprudence, the relation of the amending power to the concept of sovereignty may be developed. Finally, from the standpoint of political science and legislation, the reform of the amending process itself may be made the basis of investigation.

The writer has experienced considerable difficulty and hesitation with respect to the use of the expression "federal amending power." Closely analyzed, "power" admits of several meanings. It may mean the capacity to amend, the composite body which does the amending, or even the process of amending. Ambiguity at least as to title has been sought to be avoided by calling this book "The Amending of the Federal Constitution." The writer is indebted to Dean E. Blythe Stason of the University of Michigan Law School for valuable suggestions with respect to the problem of terminology.

This book was begun by the writer as the holder of a Research Fellowship in the University of Michigan Law School during the year 1928–1929. The writer there was fortunate in having the advice and assistance of Dean Henry M. Bates.

---

[1] 1 BURGESS, POLITICAL SCIENCE AND COMPARATIVE CONSTITUTIONAL LAW (1891) 137.

Professor Edwin D. Dickinson, now Dean of the School of Jurisprudence of the University of California, offered some suggestions as to the topic of sovereignty. Full responsibility is assumed by the writer, however, for all statements and conclusions. The writer first became interested in the federal amending process as a student in the classes of Professor Henry Rottschaefer of the University of Minnesota Law School.

All but one of the chapters were published in 1930, 1931 and 1932 in various law reviews, all of which have graciously consented to the reprinting. These reviews were the Illinois Law Review, Iowa Law Review, Michigan Law Review, Minnesota Law Review, Nebraska Law Bulletin, and the North Carolina Law Review. All of these articles have since been revised and brought up to date and a new chapter has been added. Special attention has been given to the far-reaching 1939 decisions by the Supreme Court of the United States and to recent suggestions for changing the amending process.

Gratitude is due to the University of Minnesota Law School for the use of its library during the summer of 1939, and to the University of Southern California Law School for similar use in the summer of 1940. Sincere appreciation is felt to Miss Katherine Kempfer for editing the manuscript in its latest form. It would be impossible to overrate the value of suggestions made by her. She has given freely of her time and first rate ability at analysis. The writer is deeply indebted to Dean Emeritus Henry M. Bates for writing the introduction, as well as for encouragement in the revision and publication of this book.

Lester B. Orfield

Lake Minnetonka, Minnesota
    September 2, 1941

Table of Contents

Table of Cases

ARTICLE FIVE
THE CONSTITUTION
OF THE UNITED STATES

"The Congress, whenever two thirds of both Houses shall deem it necessary, shall propose Amendments to this Constitution, or on the Application of the Legislatures of two thirds of the several States, shall call a Convention for proposing Amendments, which, in either Case, shall be valid to all Intents and Purposes, as Part of this Constitution, when ratified by the Legislatures of three fourths of the several States, or by Conventions in three fourths thereof, as the one or the other Mode of Ratification may be proposed by the Congress; Provided that no Amendment which may be made prior to the Year one thousand eight hundred and eight shall in any Manner affect the first and fourth Clauses in the Ninth Section of the first Article; and that no State, without its Consent, shall be deprived of its equal Suffrage in the Senate."

CHAPTER I

The Genesis of Article Five

THE idea of amending the organic instrument of a state is peculiarly American. Although many of our political and legal institutions take their origin from English and occasionally Continental conceptions, such is not the case in the fundamental matter of altering the constitution. The idea of a written constitution was developed at a late stage of Western civilization, and the United States, not Europe, took the lead. The doctrine of popular sovereignty had an especially strong appeal to the inhabitants of the colonies in the latter half of the eighteenth century. The people were sovereign: it followed that they could make a constitution. Corollary to this, of course, they could revise and amend the document which they had adopted.

The first written charters or constitutions providing for their amendment appear to have been the charters of the Colony of Pennsylvania, which was the only colony to make such provision.[1] Eight of the state constitutions during the period between the declaration of independence and the meeting of the Constitutional Convention of 1787 contained amendment clauses.[2] Even more important, the Articles of Confederation, defective as they were, made provision for their alteration. It was almost inevitable, therefore, that when the Constitutional Convention assembled some plan of revision would be presented.

The Constitutional Convention assembled on May 14, 1787, and at the meeting of May 29, Randolph presented

[1] 2 POORE, THE FEDERAL AND STATE CONSTITUTIONS, COLONIAL CHARTERS, AND OTHER ORGANIC LAWS OF THE UNITED STATES, 2d ed. (1878) 1518, 1527, 1531, 1536.

[2] For detailed consideration of these laws, see Martig, "Amending the Constitution," (1937) 35 MICH. L. REV. 1253–1255.

I

the first plan for a new constitution in the form of fifteen resolutions.[3] The thirteenth declared that provision should be made for amendment of the constitution whenever thought necessary and that the assent of the national legislature should not be required. Charles Pinckney presented a proposed draft of a constitution at the same meeting.[4] Article sixteen of his draft set forth that if the legislatures of two-thirds of the states should apply for a convention to amend the constitution, the national legislature should call one; or, in the alternative, Congress by a two-thirds vote of each house might propose, and two-thirds of the legislatures might adopt. Both drafts were referred to the committee of the whole house.

On June 5, the convention discussed Randolph's resolution.[5] Pinckney expressed doubt as to the propriety or need of an amendment clause. Gerry defended it, however, on the grounds that such a new and difficult experiment required periodical revision, that the opportunity for such revision would stabilize the government, and that "Nothing had yet happened in the states where the provision existed to prove its impropriety." Randolph's resolution was again brought up on June 9.[6] Several members thought it not a necessity; they furthermore thought it improper to dispense with the consent of Congress. Mason was of the opinion that the provision was necessary, since the Constitution, like the Articles of Confederation, would prove defective. It would be better to provide for amendments in any easy constitutional way than to rely on chance and violence. He was opposed to having Congress participate in the process since it might abuse its power and refuse to give its assent to changes desired. The resolution

---

[3] ELLIOT, DEBATES ON THE ADOPTION OF THE FEDERAL CONSTITUTION, 2d ed. (1937 facsimile of 1836 ed.) 127–128. Volume 5 is a revised edition of Madison's diary of the debates.

[4] Ibid. 129–132.

[5] Ibid. 157.

[6] Ibid. 182.

was unanimously adopted, but the clause dispensing with the consent of Congress was postponed for further discussion.

A long interval now occurred during which the convention appears to have ignored or overlooked the question of an amending clause. Randolph's original resolution, except as to congressional participation in amending,[7] seems to have been the basis of action until August 6, when Rutledge delivered the report[8] of the committee of detail, to which the resolution had been referred. Article nineteen of the committee's draft provided that Congress should call a convention on the application of the legislatures of two-thirds of the states. There was no discussion of the report until August 30, when Gouverneur Morris suggested that Congress be permitted to call a convention whenever it chose.[9] But the convention unanimously agreed to the article as reported by the committee.

The most serious and detailed discussion did not occur until the last week of the convention.[10] On September 10, Gerry moved to reconsider article nineteen. The Constitution, he asserted, would be paramount to the state constitutions. Under the article, two-thirds of the states could obtain a convention, "a majority of which can bind the Union to innovations that may subvert the state constitutions altogether." He asked whether such a state of affairs should be brought about. Hamilton seconded Gerry's motion, but with a different motive than the latter. He did not object to the result described by Gerry and contended that it was no worse to subject the people of the United States to "the major voice" than to so subject the people of a particular state. He desired an easier mode of amendment than that provided in the Articles of Confederation, and regarded article nineteen as

[7] Ibid. 190, 351, 376.
[8] Ibid. 376–381.
[9] Ibid. 498.
[10] Ibid. 530–532.

inadequate in accomplishing this. Like Gouverneur Morris, he proposed that Congress be given a free hand in calling a convention.

"The state legislatures will not apply for alterations, but with a view to increase their own powers. The national legislature will be the first to perceive, and will be most sensible to the necessity of amendments; and ought also to be empowered, whenever two thirds of each branch should concur, to call a convention. There could be no danger in giving this power, as the people would finally decide in the case."[11]

James Madison also supported the motion for reconsideration. The language concerning the calling of a convention was too vague. It was not clear how the convention would be formed, nor by what rules it would transact business, nor what force its acts would have. The motion to reconsider was thereupon passed, nine states favoring and one opposing. Sherman moved that Congress be permitted to propose amendments to the states, but that "no amendments shall be binding until consented to by the several states." Wilson moved to insert "two thirds of" before the words "several states" in Sherman's proposal. This failed by a five to six vote, but a later motion by Wilson to insert instead "three fourths of" was adopted.

Madison then moved to postpone the amended proposition in order to consider a proposal of his own, worded much like the present Article Five providing for proposal of amendments by Congress either on a two-thirds vote of each house or on application of the legislatures of two-thirds of the states, and ratification by the legislatures or conventions of three-fourths of the states. Hamilton seconded the motion. This proposal meant a significant change in the entire scheme. Instead of permitting amendment by a single convention, the plan made necessary the participation of the legislatures or conventions of the states. At this point Rutledge stated that he would

[11] Ibid. 531.

never agree to an amending power "by which the articles relating to slaves might be altered by the states not interested in that property, and prejudiced against it."[12] A proviso was then added to Madison's plan to meet this objection, and his amended proposition was adopted by a vote of nine to one.

Five days later, as the convention was about to conclude its labors, the amendment clause was reported as Article Five by the committee of style and arrangement.[13] Sherman feared that "three fourths of the states might be brought to do things fatal to particular states; as abolishing them altogether, or depriving them of their equality in the Senate." He therefore thought it reasonable that the limitations on the amending power should be enlarged so as to provide "that no state should be affected in its internal police, or deprived of their equality in the Senate."

Mason believed that the proposed method of amending the constitution was "exceptionable and dangerous." Both modes required action by Congress immediately or ultimately; hence no amendment of the proper kind could be obtained by the people if the government became oppressive, as he believed would be the case. Gouverneur Morris and Gerry then moved to amend the article so as to require a convention on the application of two-thirds of the states, in order to obviate this objection. Madison pointed out in response that he did not see why Congress would not be as much obligated to propose amendments applied for by two-thirds of the states, as to call a convention on a similar application. He was not unalterably opposed to providing for a convention, but thought that difficulties might arise as to the form and quorum, matters which should be avoided in constitutional regulations. The motion for a convention was, however, unanimously adopted. Sherman moved to amend

[12] Ibid. 532.
[13] Ibid. 551–552.

Article Five so as to require ratification of amendments by all
state legislatures or conventions instead of three-fourths of
them, but his motion failed, seven to three. Gerry moved
to amend so as to allow ratification only by the state legislatures and not by state conventions as an alternative method,
but this failed, ten to one.

One last attempt was made to limit the amending body.
Sherman, in accordance with his previously expressed idea,
moved to annex at the end of the article a clause that "no state
shall, without its consent, be affected in its internal police,
or deprived of its equal suffrage in the senate."[14] Madison
objected that if such special provisos were added every state
would insist on them, for their boundaries, exports, and other
matters. Sherman's motion then failed, eight to three, the
small states, Connecticut, New Jersey, and Delaware voting
for it. He then moved to strike out Article Five altogether,
and this motion also failed, by an eight to two vote. Gouverneur Morris moved to annex the simple proviso, as it now
appears in Article Five, "that no state, without its consent,
shall be deprived of its equal suffrage in the Senate." And
as Madison concisely reports it, this motion, "being dictated
by the circulating murmurs of the small states, was agreed
to without debate, no one opposing it, or on the question,
saying no." At this same meeting the entire Constitution as
amended was accepted by the convention, and ordered to be
engrossed.[15] Two days later on Monday, September 17, the
engrossed Constitution was read and signed, and the convention adjourned.[16]

[14] Ibid. 552.

[15] Ibid. 553.

[16] Ibid. 553–567. For an account of the adoption of the Constitution by the
states, see Martig, "Amending the Constitution," (1937) 35 MICH. L. REV.
1253 at 1261–1266.

CHAPTER II

Judicial Review of Validity of Amendments

A. JUSTICIABILITY

TO one not particularly familiar with constitutional law the notion of a court's passing on the legality of a constitutional amendment might seem strange. To him it would perhaps seem correct that the courts should unquestionably assume the validity of the Constitution and its amendments as an irreducible minimum in the decision of cases. To a Continental lawyer accustomed to a legal system in which the courts may not declare invalid even a statute, the idea of a court's determining whether a constitutional amendment is valid or not would seem astonishing. Even one familiar with American constitutional law might well have had some doubts before the litigation over the legality of the Eighteenth and Nineteenth Amendments.

Prior to the decisions in the 1920's, the only instance in which the Supreme Court of the United States had passed on the legitimacy of an amendment to the federal Constitution had arisen more than a century before in the case of *Hollingsworth v. Virginia*,[1] as to the adoption of the Eleventh Amendment. In that case the attorney general of the United States, in defending the legality of the amendment, made no attempt to show that the matter was a political question, and the court did not discuss the issue. The case can therefore be cited only to the effect that the court and the parties assumed it to be a legal question. The court, moreover, passed only on the legality of the procedure of amendment, and not on the content of the amendment itself. In the later and much

[1] (1798) 3 Dall. (3 U. S.) 378.

cited case of *Luther v. Borden,*[2] the Supreme Court declared
in dictum that the question of validity of the adoption of
an amendment was a political question. This case attracted
great attention and was widely cited in the state decisions, so
that many came to have the view that the question was political. Last of all, inasmuch as the courts have not assumed to
pass on the constitutionality of the Constitution itself, there is
some logic in arguing that, since an amendment becomes as
much a part of the Constitution as any other part of it (in
fact repeals any part inconsistent with it), the legality of an
amendment is no more open to attack than that of the Constitution itself.

It may be laid down dogmatically that the constitutionality
of the Constitution itself is a political question.[3] In the first
place it would seem a contradiction in terms to raise such a
question, except in reference to the matter of its having been

[2] (1849) 7 How. (48 U. S.) 1 at 39. Taney, C. J., said: "In forming the
constitutions of the different States, after the Declaration of Independence, and
in the various changes and alterations which have since been made, the political
department has always determined whether the proposed constitution or amendment was ratified or not by the people of the State, and the judicial power has
followed its decision." As late as 1888 it was asserted that this case "is still
the law of the federal courts" in Smith v. Good, (C. C. R. I. 1888) 34 Fed.
204 at 208.

[3] Luther v. Borden, (1849) 7 How. (48 U. S.) 1; Smith v. Good, (C. C. R. I.
1888) 34 F. 204; Brickhouse v. Brooks, (C. C. Va. 1908) 165 F. 534; State v.
Starling, (1867) 15 Rich. L. (S. C.) 120; Koehler v. Hill, (1883) 60 Iowa
543, 14 N. W. 738, 15 N. W. 609; Miller v. Johnson, (1892) 92 Ky. 589, 18
S. W. 522, constitution held valid although the convention which had been
elected to draft it made several changes in it after it had been voted on by the
people of the state; Taylor v. Commonwealth, (1903) 101 Va. 829, 44 S. E.
754, constitution upheld though it had never been submitted to popular vote;
Carpenter v. Cornish, (1912) 83 N. J. L. 696, 85 A. 240, affirming 83 N. J. L.
254, 83 A. 31; O'Neill, J., dissenting in Foley v. Democratic Parish Committee,
(1915) 138 La. 220, 70 So. 104. See the statement in Brittle v. People, (1873)
2 Neb. 198 at 210: "When, however, a State government has been formed, and
the State admitted to the Union with a given constitution, courts must recognize,
and are as fully bound by, the fact as the merest citizen; and I submit, with all
respect, that we can as well dispute the validity of the United States Constitution, because the convention framing it, disregarding all instructions limiting
its members to making amendments to the old articles of confederation, assumed
to make an entirely new frame of government, as we can inquire into any supposed irregularities or illegalities which may have entered into the construction
of our own."

validly adopted according to the previously existing constitution. Where the existing constitution has come into operation through a revolution, obviously a very dangerous problem would arise if the courts should attempt to pass on the validity of the new constitution. Where the new constitution has not been the result of a revolution, a new government has not begun to function under the new constitution, the people have not acquiesced, and the old courts continue to operate, they could declare the new constitution void.[4] Where a new government, executive and legislative, had taken their oaths under the new constitution, or even where a new government had commenced to operate under the new constitution and there was popular acquiescence, it would still perhaps be logically possible for the old courts to declare the new constitution invalid. But where the courts, as well as the other branches of the government, are operating under the new constitution, it seems inconceivable that they could pass on the validity of the instrument which is their creator. In theory, the court might decide the new constitution was invalid. But this would be tantamount to a declaration that the court itself no longer exists, since it was the creature of the constitution. The futility of the proceeding would make such a decision unlikely. As an actual fact such a court might continue to exist if the other departments of government accepted and enforced the decision, but this would seem to be a case of usurpation.

From the fact that the courts cannot declare the existing constitution invalid, it follows that they cannot so declare

[4] Loring v. Young, (1921) 239 Mass. 349, 132 N. E. 65. The paucity of precedent on this point seems to have led to the broad view frequently asserted that the validity of a constitution is not assailable at any stage. In 15 L. R. A. 524, the commentator on Miller v. Johnson, (1892) 92 Ky. 589, 18 S. W. 522, points out that since there is no question of opposing governments or of the existence of the court, and since the adoption of a new constitution is in effect only an amendment of the old one and does not in fact upset the existing government, "it is difficult to see why the question of lawful adoption is not as much a judicial question in case of a new constitution as it is in the case of an amendment, eo nomine."

any part of it (exclusive of amendments)[5] except where the parts are in conflict, in which event the courts perhaps would speak of construing or harmonizing. In fact, to declare a part void would seem even less justifiable than to nullify the whole new constitution, for in recognizing part of a new constitution it must recognize its entire validity. Since the old constitution is no longer in existence, there is no authority on which it can predicate a declaration that a part of the new constitution is invalid.

The view that the courts may not declare the existing constitution or a part of it (exclusive of amendments) invalid has particular force as to the federal Constitution. In the case of the states, many of them have adopted wholly new constitutions in pursuance, in most cases, of the mode prescribed in the previous constitution. In such cases there is doubtless justification for the courts' passing on the validity of the new constitution, though as a matter of fact such cases have been very rare. But the Constitution of the United States was not adopted according to the mode prescribed in the Articles of Confederation. In other words, our existing constitution is the product of a revolution, bloodless though it was.[6] The

[5] Carpenter v. Cornish, (1912) 83 N. J. L. 696, 85 A. 240, affg. 83 N. J. L. 254, 83 A. 31. But this view seems to have been departed from in a number of Louisiana cases arising over the 1920 state constitution. Huff v. Selber, (D. C. La. 1925) 10 F. (2d) 236; Pender v. Gray, (1921) 149 La. 184, 88 So. 786; State ex rel. Hoffman v. Judge, (1921) 149 La. 363, 89 So. 215; State v. Jones, (1922) 151 La. 714, 92 So. 310. An earlier case, State v. American Sugar Refining Co., (1915) 137 La. 507, 68 So. 742, is partially explainable on the ground that the constitution then made no provision for a convention, that the people by popular vote adopted the legislative restrictions as to subject matter imposed on the convention, and that the constitution was never ratified by popular vote. O'Neill, J., dissented on the ground that if part of the constitution could be declared invalid, the whole might be. See also, Foley v. Democratic Parish Committee, (1915) 138 La. 220, 70 So. 104.

[6] Jameson says that "it is clear, that the act of disregarding the provisions of the 13th of the Articles of Confederation, was done confessedly as an act of revolution, and not as an act within the legal competence of either the people or the Convention, under the Constitution then in force." JAMESON, CONSTITUTIONAL CONVENTIONS, 4th ed. (1887), § 564, p. 596. Under Article Thirteen, Congress should have proposed and the legislatures of every state should have ratified the constitution. Technically, every step was complied with except that

Supreme Court and all the other federal courts are and always have been the creatures of the existing Constitution. Thus there has never been any court before whom its invalidity might be asserted. The federal courts have never assumed to pass on the validity of the original Constitution or any part of it, and have never admitted that it was the creature of revolution, though · the commentators have frequently pointed it out.

Passing from the question of judicial cognizance of the validity of the Constitution to that of an amendment thereto, it would not be illogical to expect somewhat the same treatment of the problem.[7] The adoption of a constitution and the adoption of an amendment certainly have many points in

ratification was by three-fourths of the states (though all eventually ratified), inasmuch as the Constitutional Convention sent the Constitution to Congress, which at the advisory direction of the convention transmitted it to the state legislatures, which in turn at the recommendation of the convention passed it on to the state conventions. The framing of an entirely new constitution in violation of the directions of Congress and the designating of the ratifying bodies have been asserted to be revolutionary, but if the Constitutional Convention and the state conventions be regarded as advisory bodies the only illegal step was ratification by less than a unanimous vote. The ground of necessity pleaded by Randolph seems a rather dubious legal justification. See also, 1 COOLEY, CONSTITUTIONAL LIMITATIONS, 8th ed. (1927) 9; 1 BURGESS, POLITICAL SCIENCE AND COMPARATIVE CONSTITUTIONAL LAW (1891) 98; McCulloch v. Maryland, (1819) 4 Wheat. (17 U. S.) 316 at 403.

Professor Powell has stated: "At one time I inclined toward the view that the Constitution is still unconstitutional and that from the lawyer's standpoint we should still be operating under the Articles of Confederation which provided for a perpetual union that could not be changed without the consent of Congress and the legislatures of all the states. I have since modified that view. While the Constitution was ratified in state conventions rather than in state legislatures as the Articles of Confederation prescribed, the conventions were called by the state legislatures and so may be regarded as having lawful authority delegated by the legislatures. I now think that all irregularities were cured when North Carolina and Rhode Island finally ratified and that the Constitution then became constitutional though it had not been constitutional previously. Of course, Rhode Island's concurrence was coerced by threats of economic pressure, but she still concurred." Powell, "Changing Constitutional Phases," (1939) 19 BOST. U. L. REV. 509 at 511–512.

[7] In Smith v. Good, (C. C. R. I. 1888) 34 F. 204, it is asserted that both questions are political; while in Loring v. Young, (1921) 239 Mass. 349, 132 N. E. 65, it is stated that both are judicial, Luther v. Borden, (1849) 7 How. (48 U. S.) 1, being distinguished on the ground that in that case two rival governments were arrayed against each other in armed conflict.

common. In both there is the exercise of the highest sovereign power of the state. The adoption of an amendment is the adoption of a constitution in little. It is conceivable that over a long period of time a constitution might be so altered as to bear little resemblance to the original document. Looked at from one point of view, an amendment is of even greater import than the original provisions of the constitution since it automatically repeals all clauses inconsistent with it.[8] It may even repeal a Supreme Court decision.[9] Looked at from a practical standpoint, however, the chief difference is seen to be that an amendment does not produce so comprehensive and so serious an effect on the existing frame of government. The courts are left relatively free to see that the prescribed constitutional mode of alterations is complied with.

1. *Validity of Procedure of Adoption*

At the outset it should be noted that as a matter of logic a distinction might be taken between the justiciability of matters of procedure on the one hand and matters of substance on the other hand. By matters of procedure are meant questions as to whether amendments were properly proposed or properly ratified or both. Has an amendment been proposed or ratified according to the methods expressly or impliedly specified in Article Five? By matters of substance are meant, assuming that the proper procedure for amending has been followed, questions as to the content of the amendment proper. Are there limitations as to the type of subject which may be dealt with by constitutional amendment, or if not, are there

---

[8] Johnson v. Tompkins, (C. C. Pa. 1833) Baldw. 571 at 598, F. Cas. No. 7416; Osborn v. Nicholson, (C. C. Ark. 1870) 1 Dill. 219, F. Cas. No. 10595; University v. McIver, (1875) 72 N. C. 76; Grant v. Hardage, (1913) 106 Ark. 506, 153 S. W. 826.

[9] The Eleventh, Fourteenth and Sixteenth Amendments operated to nullify previous decisions. Such would also be the effect of the child labor amendment. The Eleventh Amendment operated retroactively.

limitations as to how certain subjects may be treated by constitutional amendment? The Supreme Court need not treat these two problems alike, and the two types of validity will be discussed separately. The justiciability of matters of procedure of adoption will first be discussed.

If the Constitution made specific provision for the submission of the question of the validity of amendments to a designated tribunal, it might perhaps be asserted that their validity is not a question for the ordinary courts,[10] though even in that case the exclusion of the courts has been doubted.[11] Article Five, however, is silent, so that there is much reason to assert that the validity of amendments, like so many other controversies which may arise over the interpretation of the Constitution, is a legal question.[12] The theory of the courts in claiming the power to adjudicate amendments is doubtless the same as that back of the power to declare laws unconstitutional. The Supreme Court may set aside any unconstitutional act of Congress or of the President, and reverse its own and the decisions of the lower courts where the interpretation was erroneous. From this it follows that where there is a failure to

[10] Worman v. Hagen, (1893) 78 Md. 152, 27 A. 616. In State v. Swift, (1880) 69 Ind. 505, two judges dissenting, it appears that the court assumed the validity of a statute interpreted to allow the governor to ascertain the adoption of the amendment; in Rice v. Palmer, (1906) 78 Ark. 432, 96 S. W. 396, there is dictum that a statute could establish a special tribunal for the purpose. Jameson is of the view that Congress alone has the power to pass on amendments except in suits between individuals. JAMESON, CONSTITUTIONAL CONVENTIONS, 4th ed. (1887) 626–627.

[11] McConaughy v. Secretary of State, (1909) 106 Minn. 392, 119 N. W. 408. But this seems improper since the courts, as well as the other departments of government, are bound by the Constitution.

[12] In practice, Congress has several times in effect decided on the meaning of Article Five. In resolutions it has asserted that the approval of an amendment by the President is unnecessary (see infra, chap. III, note 30), that two-thirds of a quorum of each house of Congress is the majority required for proposing amendments [SENATE JOURNAL, 1st Cong., 1st sess. (Sept. 9, 1789), p. 77], that the Fourteenth Amendment was ratified [(1868) 15 Stat. L. 708–711], and that states may not withdraw their ratifications [(1868) 15 Stat. L. 706, 708].

comply with the regular mode of amendment prescribed in Article Five, the courts may regard the procedure as null and void.

Hollingsworth v. Virginia,[13] as mentioned above, seems to have been the first case, either national or state, in which the validity of an amendment was passed on. But, as there stated, no attempt was made to show that the issue was a political one; the question, moreover, was simply one as to the procedure in adopting the amendment; and the court upheld the validity of the amendment. In 1836 a state case[14] on the subject maintained the right of the courts to inquire into the validity of amendments. But the opinion of the court was brief, and like the prior federal case upheld the validity of the amendment. In 1849 the federal Supreme Court asserted in dictum that the question was political.[15] Until the recent cases on the Eighteenth[16] and Nineteenth[17] Amendments, this was the only pronouncement of the court on the subject, so that if there had been no intervening circumstances the court might have adhered to its view in that case. However, in the meantime there had been constantly increasing litigation in the state courts over the validity of amendments. In 1854 the Alabama court in *Collier v. Frierson*[18] asserted that it was a justiciable question and held an amendment invalid. The case is notable for the fact that it is the first and only case before 1880 holding an amendment unconstitutional. In 1856 the Mississippi Supreme Court held the question a judicial one.[19] In 1864, however,

[13] (1798) 3 Dall. (3 U. S.) 378. See note 1, supra.

[14] State v. McBride, (1836) 4 Mo. 303.

[15] Luther v. Borden, (1849) 7 How. (48 U. S.) 1.

[16] National Prohibition Cases, (1920) 253 U. S. 350, 40 S. Ct. 486, 588.

[17] Leser v. Garnett, (1922) 258 U. S. 130, 42 S. Ct. 217.

[18] (1854) 24 Ala. 100.

[19] Green v. Weller, (1856) 32 Miss. 650.

the Maryland court took the view that it was a political question.[20] In 1876 the Minnesota court regarded it as judicial.[21]

Up to 1880 only about seven cases had arisen in which the validity of an amendment was attacked in the courts. Up to 1890 about twenty such cases had arisen. But since that date a large number of cases have been decided. The state decisions have been virtually unanimous to the effect that the question is judicial, and the state courts now exercise supervision over every step of the amending process.[22] *Luther v. Borden*[23] was discussed by many of the courts, and the limited holding of that case was precisely defined.

What then should be the position of the courts as to amendment of the federal Constitution? That the question has been an open one even up to recent times is indicated by the cases which have arisen. In the first case which arose, *Hollingsworth v. Virginia*,[24] the Supreme Court in 1798 passed on the procedure of amendment with respect to a proposal by Congress and held that the President need not concur in the proposal of an amendment. But no one raised the point that

[20] Miles v. Bradford, (1864) 22 Md. 170. The same view has since been taken in State v. Swift, (1880) 69 Ind. 505, power of political department inferred from a statute; Beck, J., dissenting in Koehler v. Hill, (1883) 60 Iowa 543 at 568, 14 N. W. 738, 15 N. W. 609; Van Syckel, J., dissenting in Bott v. Board of Registry, (1897) 61 N. J. L. 160, 38 A. 848; McCulloch, J., dissenting in Rice v. Palmer, (1906) 78 Ark. 432, 96 S. W. 396, pointing out that if the question is judicial the validity of an amendment is never definitely settled.

[21] Dayton v. St. Paul, (1876) 22 Minn. 400.

[22] (1939) 53 HARV. L. REV. 134; (1940) 24 MINN. L. REV. 393 at 402.

[23] (1849) 7 How. (48 U. S.) 1. In that case two rival governments were in armed conflict; the validity of a constitution, not an amendment, was in issue, and the opinion was therefore dictum; federal jurisdiction was involved as to the validity of a state constitution, and not of a federal amendment; the constitution of Rhode Island provided no mode of amendment. There are dicta in a few cases that when the amendment relates to the existence, power or functions of the courts, the question is political. Koehler v. Hill, (1883) 60 Iowa 543, 14 N. W. 738, 15 N. W. 609; State ex rel. McClurg v. Powell, (1900) 77 Miss. 543, 27 So. 927.

[24] (1798) 3 Dall. (3 U. S.) 378.

the issue was a political one; and it should be noted that the court upheld the amendment involved. The opinion was a brief one of only five lines. In 1849 the Supreme Court in a dictum in the famous case of *Luther v. Borden*[25] stated that the question was a political one. In *White v. Hart*[26] the Supreme Court in dictum intimated that the validity of the Civil War Amendments was a political question. In *Dodge v. Woolsey*[27] Mr. Justice Campbell in a dissenting opinion referred with approval to the doctrine of political questions as laid down in *Luther v. Borden*. In *Smith v. Good*[28] a federal circuit judge, in passing on a controversy involving the validity of an amendment to a *state* constitution, held the controversy to be a political one and stated that the case of *Luther v. Borden* was still controlling in the federal courts, and that it had been followed in *White v. Hart*. Thus the cases arising in the nineteenth century seem to have regarded the question as a political one.

It was in the first one-third of the twentieth century that support for the view that the issue should be regarded as a judicial one received its greatest impetus, though some of the cases involved substance rather then procedure. In 1905 a lower federal court held that the validity of an amendment to a *state* constitution was a judicial question.[29] In 1910 a lower federal court passed on the validity of the Fifteenth Amendment, seeming to have assumed that the validity of the substance of an amendment involved a judicial question.[30] This latter case was offset by a lower federal court decision as to the validity of the Eighteenth Amendment that only the

[25] (1849) 7 How. (48 U. S.) 1. The facts are given in note 23, supra.

[26] (1871) 13 Wall. (80 U. S.) 646.

[27] (1885) 18 How. (59 U. S.) 331 at 373. This case did not involve the validity of an amendment.

[28] (C. C. R. I. 1888) 34 F. 204.

[29] Knight v. Shelton, (C. C. Ark. 1905) 134 F. 423.

[30] Anderson v. Myers, (C. C. Md. 1910) 182 F. 223, affd. Myers v. Anderson, (1915) 238 U. S. 368, 35 S. Ct. 932.

political department can declare an amendment void for violating alleged limitations as to substance.[31] Thus up to 1920 there were no decisions by the Supreme Court itself squarely passing on the justiciability of amendments. In fact, between 1798 and 1920 the validity of no federal amendment was passed upon by the Supreme Court. In 1920 in *Hawke v. Smith*[32] the Supreme Court passed on a question of ratification by the state legislatures and concluded that the states could not restrict the ratifying power by providing for a binding popular referendum. The decision, it is to be noted, is aimed at the acts of the states and not those of Congress. The court did, however, construe the meaning of the phrase "legislatures" in the federal Constitution rather than the phrase as it appeared in the resolution of Congress proposing the amendment.

In the same year came the *National Prohibition Cases*,[33] in which the Supreme Court upheld the validity of the Eighteenth Amendment against arguments of unconstitutional content and improper procedure of adoption. The solicitor general argued that both of these questions were political. The procedural question involved the meaning of "two-thirds of both Houses" in the proposal of an amendment by Congress.[34] The Supreme Court failed to develop any doctrine as to just what questions it was deciding, or of its own power. Hence the decision is somewhat dubious as a precedent. In *Dillon v. Gloss*,[35] decided a year later, the court seemed more clearly to review the extent of the powers of Congress under Article Five with respect to fixing the time limit for ratification, but the court was not very explicit as to its own powers. In 1922, in *Leser v. Garnett*,[36] the court again seems

---

[31] Feigenspan v. Bodine, (D. C. N. J. 1920) 264 F. 186.

[32] (1920) 253 U. S. 221, 40 S. Ct. 495.

[33] (1920) 253 U. S. 350, 40 S. Ct. 486, 588.

[34] See infra, chap. III, at note 28.

[35] (1921) 256 U. S. 368, 41 S. Ct. 510.

[36] (1922) 258 U. S. 130, 42 S. Ct. 217.

inferentially to have given comfort to the doctrine of political question. After arguing only by analogy to the Fifteenth Amendment, the court declared that the subject of the Nineteenth Amendment was within the amending power. But as to the argument that two of the states had not ratified properly, the court gave the broad answer that "official notice to the Secretary, duly authenticated, that they had done so was conclusive upon him, and, being certified to by his proclamation, is conclusive upon the courts."[37] Thus in effect the court treated the state acts and the acts of the secretary of state as involving the doctrine of political question.

In 1931 after almost a decade the court in *United States v. Sprague*[38] did not try to distinguish the question before it from that in *Leser v. Garnett*. The court ruled that Congress could select the method of ratification, whether by state legislatures or by state conventions. The language of the court is such as to induce the belief that the court regarded the amending process as generally justiciable.

There was an interval of eight years without any decisions on the amending clause. Then came the decisions in 1939 involving the ratification of the child labor amendment.[39] The court laid down a doctrine that some steps in the amending process involved political questions. It should be carefully noted that it did not hold all questions concerning the amending process to be political. The effect of the previous rejection by a state of an amendment was held to involve a political

[37] Ibid., 258 U. S. at 137. ROTTSCHAEFER, CONSTITUTIONAL LAW (1939) 399, states: "It should be noted that the conclusive effect of the official notice to, and the certification thereof by, the Secretary is based on certain assumptions. How far a court would reach its own independent conclusion on the matters thus assumed cannot be definitely stated." See also Quarles, "Amendments to the Federal Constitution," (1940) 26 A. B. A. J. 617 at 618. Mr. Quarles, however, states that the *proposal* of an amendment is a political question.

[38] (1931) 282 U. S. 716, 51 S. Ct. 220.

[39] Coleman v. Miller, (1939) 307 U. S. 433, 59 S. Ct. 972; Chandler v. Wise, (1939) 307 U. S. 474, 59 S. Ct. 922.

question. The interval of time in which the states might ratify an amendment was also held to involve a political question.[40] Thus it is only as to these two questions that the court definitely decides that no justiciable question is involved. The court came to no conclusion as to the justiciability of the question whether a lieutenant governor of a state was such a part of the legislature that he could cast a deciding vote when the state senate was evenly divided. The court gave as its reason that the court was equally divided, although nine judges heard the case.[41] The Kansas Supreme Court had apparently regarded all three of the above issues as justiciable,[42] and the Kentucky Court of Appeals had inferentially regarded the first two as justiciable.[43] The majority opinion thus seems to leave untouched the apparent doctrine of the earlier cases that certain procedural questions were justiciable.

The difficulties in deciding how long the states should have to ratify, particularly where there has been a considerable period of no action at all followed by widespread action, doubtless justified the court in treating the question of time as a political one. A proper review of whether Kansas had ratified the child labor amendment would entail "an appraisal of a great variety of relevant conditions, political, social and economic, which can hardly be said to be within the appropriate range of evidence receivable in a court of justice."[44] It should be noted, however, that just such an

[40] Two of the justices, McReynolds and Butler, seemed to dissent on the issue of lapse of time. Presumably they concurred in the view that the effect of prior rejection by a state was a political question. See note, (1939) 48 YALE L. J. 1455 at 1457.

[41] It is therefore suggested in (1939) 48 YALE L. J. 1455 that the court "sawed a justice in half." But McReynolds, J., was absent at the last conference of the court held on June 3. (1939) 28 GEO. L. J. 199 at 200, note 7.

[42] Coleman v. Miller, (1937) 146 Kan. 390, 71 P. (2d) 518; see opinion by Mr. Justice Black, (1939) 307 U. S. 433 at 456, 59 S. Ct. 972.

[43] Wise v. Chandler, (1937) 270 Ky. 1, 108 S. W. (2d) 1024.

[44] Coleman v. Miller, (1939) 307 U. S. 433 at 453, 59 S. Ct. 972.

appraisal has been made in the multitudinous cases involving due process.[45] On the other hand, the difficulties as to the effect of rejection were not so great, although admittedly the theorists were badly divided. The court might well have held, as the solicitor general argued, that states could constitutionally reverse their former acts of rejection or ratification until such time as three-fourths of them had ratified. Perhaps, however, that question was deemed too closely linked with the time allowable for ratification. The court indicated two reasons for regarding the question of the effect of a prior rejection as involving a political question: (1) historical precedent in the efforts made by New Jersey and Ohio to withdraw their ratifications of the Fourteenth Amendment, Congress in effect declaring their withdrawals abortive;[46] and (2) the absence of any basis in either Constitution or statute for judicial interference. But neither reason is strongly convincing.[47] With respect to the first, it seems an unusual approach for the body recognized as having the power to review acts of Congress to adopt and rely on an act of Congress as precedent, particularly since the act of Congress was passed in a period of unrest and since the court had had no opportunity to pass on its validity. With respect to the second reason, it should be observed that there were no stronger constitutional or statutory bases for the decisions rendered in previous cases arising concerning the amending process.

Making the effect of a prior rejection a political question results in greater uncertainty as to the status of an amendment. On the general problem of justiciability it should be remembered also that the state courts have frequently and by the great weight of authority held that they may pass

[45] Moore and Adelson, "The Supreme Court: 1938 Term, II," (1940) 26 Va. L. Rev. 697 at 709; (1939) 39 Col. L. Rev. 1232 at 1235–1236; (1940) 24 Minn. L. Rev. 393 at 404.

[46] (1868) 15 Stat. L. 708.

[47] (1940) 24 Minn. L. Rev. 393 at 399–400.

upon the validity of the procedure of amending the state constitutions, even though there be no express basis therefor. From the point of view of orderly amending procedure it is doubtful that the doctrine of political question should be extended to other procedural steps. If orderly procedure is essential in the enactment of ordinary statutes, should it not be even more so as to the adoption of important and permanent constitutional amendments? Such orderly procedure might call for compliance with certain fundamental prerequisites without emphasizing small details.

In *Coleman v. Miller*,[48] four of the members of the Supreme Court felt that a far more sweeping doctrine of political questions should be laid down. Mr. Justice Black in an opinion concurred in by Mr. Justice Roberts, Mr. Justice Frankfurter and Mr. Justice Douglas, thought that Congress possesses "exclusive power over the amending process," that neither "state nor federal courts can review that power," and that "whether submission, intervening procedure or Congressional determination of ratification conforms to the commands of the Constitution, calls for decisions by a 'political department' of questions of a type which this Court has frequently designated 'political.' "[49] No question can get into the courts. "The process itself is 'political' in its entirety, from submission until an amendment becomes part of the Constitution, and is not subject to judicial guidance, control or interference at any point."[50] In the companion case of *Chandler v. Wise*,[51] Mr. Justice Black and Mr. Justice Douglas state that "we do

[48] (1939) 307 U. S. 433, 59 S. Ct. 972.

[49] Ibid., 307 U. S. at 459, 457.

[50] Ibid., 307 U. S. at 459.

[51] (1939) 307 U. S. 474 at 478, 59 S. Ct. 992. For a criticism of this view, see Quarles, "Amendments to the Federal Constitution," (1940) 26 A. B. A. J. 617. It is pointed out that the Constitution does not expressly or impliedly except the amending process from the judicial power of the federal courts, whereas it inferentially does except the processes of impeachment, election of Congressmen, expulsion of Congressmen, and suits against the United States by citizens of another state.

not believe that state or federal courts have any jurisdiction to interfere with the amending process."

The view that the amending process involves essentially. political issues has been urged by a number of writers. Albert E. Pillsbury, former Attorney General of Massachusetts, argued in 1909 that the scope of the amending power is a political question.[52] Wayne B. Wheeler argued in 1920 that the validity of the Eighteenth Amendment was a political question.[53] Professor Oliver P. Field in 1924 pointed out that courts had developed the doctrine of political questions where there was a "lack of legal principles for the courts to apply in their consideration of cases involving certain types of subject matter."[54] Melville Fuller Weston set forth a doctrine of political questions in 1925 particularly with respect to the adoption and amendment of constitutions.[55] Walter F. Dodd in 1931 was one of the most recent writers on the subject.[56]

2. *Validity of Substance*

It has just been seen that even under the most recent decisions some questions of procedure in amendment are justici-

[52] Address, (1909) 16 ME. ST. BAR. ASSN. PROC. 17 at 26.
[53] "The Constitutionality of the Constitution is not a Justiciable Question," (1920) 90 CENT. L. J. 152.
[54] "The Doctrine of Political Questions in the Federal Courts," (1924) 8 MINN. L. REV. 485 at 513. Professor Field did not suggest application of the doctrine to the federal amending process. His article is cited as authoritative by Chief Justice Hughes in Coleman v. Miller, (1939) 307 U. S. 433 at 455, 59 S. Ct. 972.
[55] "Political Questions," (1925) 38 HARV. L. REV. 296 at 304, 307. This article was also cited as authoritative in Coleman v. Miller, supra. Compare Finkelstein, "Judicial Self-Limitation," (1924) 37 HARV. L. REV. 338, and "Further Notes on Judicial Self-Limitation," (1925) 39 HARV. L. REV. 221 at 234.
[56] "Judicially Non-Enforceable Provisions of Constitutions," (1931) 80 U. PA. L. REV. 54 at 89. See also Yawitz, "The Legal Effect under American Decisions of Alleged Irregularities in the Adoption of a Constitution or Constitutional Amendment," (1925) 10 ST. LOUIS L. REV. 279 at 283; note (1932) 27 ILL. L. REV. 72; (1938) 26 KY. L. J. 364; page 5 of brief of the Solicitor General of the United States as amicus curiae in Coleman v. Miller, (1939) 307 U. S. 433, 59 S. Ct. 972; (1939) 39 COL. L. REV. 1232 at 1235; Moore and Adelson, "The Supreme Court: 1938 Term, II," (1940) 26 VA. L. REV. 697 at 707–709.

able. But there may be difficulties other than procedural ones. Will the courts inquire into the substance of an amendment, or is that a political question? Most of the cases have involved the question of the validity of procedure. It was not until 1920 that the Supreme Court passed on the substance of an amendment. The court ruled, in the *National Prohibition Cases*,[57] that there were no defects of substance in the Eighteenth Amendment. The following year the Nineteenth Amendment was attacked as improper in substance and the court expressly discussed the question of substance,[58] whereas no reasoning was set out in the *National Prohibition Cases*. Back in 1915 when the content of the Fifteenth Amendment was attacked, the court completely ignored that argument in its decision.[59] In 1931 the Supreme Court inferentially refused to allow an attack on the substance of an amendment when it held that all amendments were subject to ratification by state legislatures if Congress so chose.[60] In the light of the recent decisions on the child labor amendment, it may be that the court now regards the substance of an amendment as presenting a political question. That would from a practical point of view be a defensible position since no limitations on substance have yet been found, and it is unlikely that any will ever be found.[61]

Relatively few attacks have been made on the substance of amendments in the state courts. Apparently the first case in which this question was directly raised was that of *Livermore v. Waite*[62] by the California court in 1894. That court

[57] National Prohibition Cases, (1920) 253 U. S. 350, 40 S. Ct. 486.

[58] Leser v. Garnett, (1922) 258 U. S. 130, 42 S. Ct. 217.

[59] Myers v. Anderson, (1915) 238 U. S. 368, 35 S. Ct. 932.

[60] United States v. Sprague, (1931) 282 U. S. 716, 51 S. Ct. 220.

[61] See infra, chap. IV.

[62] (1894) 102 Cal. 113, 36 P. 424. The court suggests that the power of the legislature to propose amendments is much less than that of a convention, and that a convention is subject only to the Constitution of the United States. The distinction appears unsound, however, as a convention is merely a legal agent of the state for the purpose of amendment, just as the legislature is. The court also contends that an amendment which if adopted would be in-

held that an amendment was void in substance because certain of its provisions were to become operative at the will of certain officials mentioned in it, although it was regularly voted on by the people. Neither the federal nor the state constitution imposed such a restriction and it seems that it was one discovered by the California courts. Two years later the Missouri court took the opposite view in a case involving similar facts.[63] Where the constitution is silent as to the scope of an amendment, the view of the state courts appears to be that the courts may not pass on the character of the amendment.[64] Where the state constitution contains limitations on the scope of amendments, logically the courts should have power to determine whether the content is proper.[65] Limitations on the scope of amendments should be found within the amending clause, and the other articles of the constitution should not be viewed as limitations. Thus the bill of rights and the amending clause are themselves subject to alteration unless expressly forbidden to be altered. Most state constitutions contain no such limitations, however, and the problem therefore seldom

operative, or contingent on the acts of a group of individuals, is invalid. But if the people have imposed no such limitations, there would seem to be no good reason why such an amendment may not be proposed.

[63] Edwards v. Lesueur, (1896) 132 Mo. 410, 33 S. W. 1130. But in State ex rel. Halliburton v. Roach, (1910) 230 Mo. 408, 130 S. W. 689, an amendment was held void as being legislative in character, and also because it was operative for only ten years; but in dictum the court said that a proposed prohibition amendment would be valid, since prohibition was subject to permanent as well as temporary regulation. This decision was probably a political one. Professor Rottschaefer says its position is indefensible. ROTTSCHAEFER, CONSTITUTIONAL LAW (1939) 398.

[64] State v. Swift, (1880) 69 Ind. 512; Prohibitory Amendment Cases, (1881) 24 Kan. 700; State ex rel. Cranmer v. Thorson, (1896) 9 S. D. 149, 68 N. W. 202; People ex rel. Elder v. Sours, (1903) 31 Colo. 369, 74 P. 167; Frantz v. Autry, (1907) 18 Okla. 561, 91 P. 193; Louisiana Ry. & Navigation Co. v. Madere, (1909) 124 La. 635, 50 So. 609; State ex rel. Greenlund v. Fulton, (1919) 99 Ohio St. 168, 124 N. E. 172; Switzer v. State ex rel. Silvey, (1921) 103 Ohio St. 306, 133 N. E. 552, suggesting that a federal amendment may be invalid for indefiniteness; Browne v. City of New York, (1925) 241 N. Y. 96, 149 N. E. 211.

[65] The Alabama constitution, article 18, § 284, forbids the change of representation in the legislature on any other than a population basis.

arises, as the doctrine of implied limits on the nature of amendments has not been adopted by the state courts.

The Constitution of the United States contains one express restriction on the nature of amendments. No state may be deprived of its equal suffrage in the Senate without its consent. Prior to 1808 no amendment could be made abolishing the slave trade, or imposing a direct tax without apportionment. Since that date, unless the courts adopt the view that there are implied limitations, the only criterion of character an amendment has had to meet is that it must not violate the equal suffrage clause. The absence of any limitations as to form or substance is shown in the cases of the Eleventh and the Eighteenth Amendments. The Eleventh Amendment operated retroactively. The Eighteenth Amendment by its own provision was not to go into effect until a year after its ratification, and was to be inoperative unless ratified within seven years after its submission by Congress to the states.[66] Though, as has been seen, the Eighteenth and Nineteenth Amendments were attacked as void in substance, the contentions were rejected.[67] Since no implied limitations as to scope are likely to be laid down and since the only limitation on content is the equal suffrage clause and that is really a limitation on the method of ratification rather than on the substance of amendments, there would seem to be no great dangers arising out of the view that a political question is here involved. Arguably, however, the Supreme Court cases on substance might be interpreted as meaning simply that there are no limitations on the substance of amendments. On that view it would not be necessary to assert that conformance to limitations is a political question.

[66] See Dillon v. Gloss, (1921) 256 U. S. 368, 41 S. Ct. 510; Druggan v. Anderson, (1925) 269 U. S. 36, 46 S. Ct. 14.

[67] National Prohibition Cases, (1920) 253 U. S. 350 at 386, 40 S. Ct. 486; Leser v. Garnett, (1922) 258 U. S. 130, 42 S. Ct. 217.

The question of justiciability has now been treated both as to the validity of the procedure of adoption and the validity of substance. It would seem of value to summarize the state of the law after the 1939 decisions. First, as to procedure it may be said that certain phases of procedure are political and certain are justiciable questions. The effect of a state's previous rejection of an amendment upon its later approval involves a political question.[68] The time interval after submission of an amendment in which states may ratify also involves a political question. On the other hand, neither expressly nor impliedly overruled[69] are earlier holdings that the following involve justiciable questions: (1) the meaning of "two-thirds of both Houses" in the proposal of an amendment by Congress; (2) whether Congress has the power of selecting ratification by legislatures rather than by conventions; (3) the necessity of the President's approval of the proposal of an amendment; and (4) the meaning of "legislatures" ratifying federal amendments with respect to compulsory popular referenda. Undecided is the question whether a lieutenant governor of a state is such a part of the legislature that he may cast a deciding vote when the state senate is evenly divided. Second, as to the justiciability of the substance of an amendment, possibly though not probably unaffected are decisions as to the Eighteenth and Nineteenth Amendments holding inferentially that the problem is justiciable.

With respect to the proper procedure required as a result of the doctrine of political question, it would seem the following is called for: a proper party plaintiff must first prosecute a suit to determine whether the matter involved is justi-

---

[68] Probably there would be the same result as to the effect of a prior ratification. (1939) 13 So. CAL. L. REV. 122 at 124.

[69] Moore and Adelson, "The Supreme Court: 1938 Term, II," (1940) 26 VA. L. REV. 697 at 707–709. The majority of the court carefully distinguished Dillon v. Gloss, (1921) 256 U. S. 368, 41 S. Ct. 510; four justices wished to overrule it. See also (1940) 24 MINN. L. REV. 393 at 399.

ciable, and if it is not justiciable he must appeal to Congress.[70] If the question is found to be a political one, there would seem to be no very effective or regular methods of enforcing the procedure Article Five seems to demand. Thus political prestige rather than legal right may become the more dominant influence.

The doctrine of political question raises a number of questions, the answers to which cannot easily be predicted. Where a political question is found to be involved as to a certain procedural step in a given case, what are the powers of the Secretary of State of the United States? May he promulgate the adoption of the amendment only under the formal express permission conferred by Congress, or may he do so unless Congress forbids promulgation? Is a two-thirds vote of Congress necessary to allow or to prevent promulgation of the amendment? May Congress decide the political question before three-fourths of the states have ratified? If it does, may it later, but before three-fourths have ratified, change its position? May Congress decide, with respect to a particular amendment, that a state once having rejected may later ratify, and then decide differently with respect to a different amendment?

B. PROCEDURAL QUESTIONS

It has been seen that at least some questions of the legality of the procedure of adoption of an amendment to the federal Constitution are justiciable. If the court had held that all questions concerning the amending process are political, obviously no one could raise the question of validity in the courts. But since the court regards some questions as justiciable, the problem immediately arises as to how the validity of an amendment may be attacked.

[70] (1940) 24 MINN. L. REV. 393 at 406.

1. *Proper Forum*

It would seem feasible to raise the question of the validity of ratification by a particular state in the courts of that state as well as in the federal courts. One case reached the United States Supreme Court by writ of error to the Supreme Court of the state of Ohio to review a decree of the latter court.[71] Another case reached the Supreme Court by writ of error to the Court of Appeals of Maryland to review a judgment of the latter court.[72] In each of these cases state courts passed on the validity of amendments to the federal Constitution. In each of them the proceeding was by a citizen and voter, or citizens and voters, of a state against its public officers. No question as to the jurisdiction of the state courts or as to the availability of the relief prayed, if a case were made out for the granting of such relief, was raised.

2. *Time of Attack*

It will be conceded that the validity of an amendment, if justiciable at all, can be attacked after its promulgation and when it is sought to be put into effect. But must the plaintiff wait until then to bring suit or may he sue before ratification? In an early case a federal trial court refused to permit attack on the validity of an amendment prior to adoption.[73] However, the state courts have permitted attacks on an amendment proposed by Congress even though it has not as yet been ratified by three-fourths of the states.[74] This practice was impliedly approved by the Supreme Court when it refused jurisdiction upon other grounds of an appeal from an

[71] Hawke v. Smith, (1920) 253 U. S. 221, 40 S. Ct. 495.

[72] Leser v. Garnett, (1922) 258 U. S. 130, 42 S. Ct. 217.

[73] State of Ohio ex rel. Erchenbrecher v. Cox, (D. C. Ohio, 1919) 257 F. 334.

[74] Wise v. Chandler, (1937) 270 Ky. 1, 108 S. W. (2d) 1024; Coleman v. Miller, (1937) 146 Kan. 390, 71 P. (2d) 518. In Hawke v. Smith, (1920) 253 U. S. 231, 40 S. Ct. 495, the Supreme Court reviewed an Ohio case where the validity of the Nineteenth Amendment was attacked prior to adoption.

attack in a state court on the Child Labor Amendment after only twenty-eight states had ratified.[75] Arguably an employer of child labor might have a sufficient special interest to attack the child labor amendment, and yet not be able to show that the injury is clear and immediate.[76] In the first place, thirty-six states might never ratify. In the second place, the child labor amendment does not abolish child labor, but merely authorizes Congress to do so. Moreover, technically an injunction as to certifying by one state would be useless, since it is the action of three-fourths of the states and not the certifying notice that marks the adoption of an amendment.[77]

Another theory which may bar relief is that of the doctrine of separation of powers.[78] That doctrine prevents interference with legislative processes. For instance, no injunction lies against an administrative official who is submitting to the electorate a proposed amendment to a state constitution.[79]

[75] Coleman v. Miller, (1939) 307 U. S. 433, 59 S. Ct. 972.

[76] (1937) 37 COL. L. REV. 1201. No irreparable injury was found in State of Ohio ex rel. Erchenbrecher v. Cox, (D. C. Ohio, 1919) 257 F. 334.

[77] United States ex rel. Widenman v. Colby, (App. D. C. 1920) 265 F. 998, affirmed (1921) 257 U. S. 619, 42 S. Ct. 169.

[78] (1937) 37 COL. L. REV. 1201; State of Ohio ex rel. Erchenbrecher v. Cox, (D. C. Ohio, 1919) 257 F. 334 (Eighteenth Amendment); Clements v. Roberts, (1921) 144 Tenn. 129, 230 S. W. 30 (Nineteenth Amendment).

[79] State ex rel. Cranmer v. Thorson, (1896) 9 S. D. 149, 68 N. W. 202; People ex rel. O'Reilly v. Mills, (1902) 30 Colo. 262, 70 P. 322. Cf. Ellingham v. Dye, (1912) 178 Ind. 336, 99 N. E. 1. See also Frantz v. Autry, (1907) 18 Okla. 561 at 603–611, 91 P. 193; Threadgill v. Cross, (1910) 26 Okla. 403, 109 P. 558; State ex rel. Byerley v. State Board of Canvassers, (1919) 44 N. D. 126, 172 N. W. 80; State ex rel. Marcolin v. Smith, (1922) 105 Ohio St. 570, 138 N. E. 881; McAlister v. State ex rel. Short, (1923) 95 Okla. 200, 219 P. 134; Hamilton v. Secretary of State, (1924) 227 Mich. 111, 198 N. W. 843. But see Wells v. Bain, (1873) 75 Pa. St. 39; Hatch v. Stoneman, (1885) 66 Cal. 632, 6 P. 734; Livermore v. Waite, (1894) 102 Cal. 113, 36 P. 424; Edwards v. Lesueur, (1896) 132 Mo. 410 at 441, 33 S. W. 1130; People ex rel. Attorney General v. Curry, (1900) 130 Cal. 82, 62 P. 516; Holmberg v. Jones, (1901) 7 Idaho 752, 65 P. 563; State ex rel. Halliburton v. Roach, (1910) 230 Mo. 408, 130 S. W. 689, two judges dissenting; State ex rel. Hay v. Alderson, (1914) 49 Mont. 387, 142 P. 210; Tax Commission Case, (1923) 68 Mont. 450, 219 P. 817; State ex rel. Linde v. Hall, (1917) 35 N. D. 34, 159 N. W. 281, which seems not to have been followed in State ex rel. Byerley v. State Board of Canvassers, supra.

Arguably the same theory should apply where the federal secretary of state is the defendant.[80] Hence to attack the validity of an amendment it is thought necessary to await its apparent ratification. The difficulty of the plaintiff if he does so wait is that he will run into the objection that the courts will not go behind the secretary of state's promulgation of ratification. It has been argued that the validity of ratification of an amendment as distinct from the substance of an amendment may not be attacked after the secretary of state's proclamation of its adoption.[81] It has also been stated that an irregularity of Congress in proposing an amendment cannot be attacked prior to adoption, as for instance by an action to enjoin the governor of a state from submitting an amendment to the legislature, but only after its promulgation and when it is sought to put it into effect.[82] That seems sound policy as preventing too free attack on amendments, and as giving proper weight to the fact that it was Congress that was acting.

With respect to the remedy of injunction, it should be noted that it might be sought at any of a number of stages: (1) against the submission of an amendment to the state by the Secretary of State of the United States; (2) against submission by the governor to the legislature or state convention; (3) against legislative officers certifying action by the legislature; (4) against certification of ratification by the governor; (5) and against certification by the Secretary of State of the United States. No case has arisen as to submission by the United States Secretary of State to the state. It is true that after Congress has proposed an amendment, the secretary of state sends a copy thereof to each governor, and the gov-

---

[80] Nor would mandamus lie against the secretary of state to compel announcement of the rejection of an amendment, since the statute under which he acts imposes no such duty on him, (1818) 3 Stat. L. 439; (1934) 5 U. S. C. § 160.

[81] Brief for Appellant, p. 2, in Wise v. Chandler, (1937) 270 Ky. 1, 108 S. W. (2d) 1024.

[82] ROTTSCHAEFER, CONSTITUTIONAL LAW (1939) 388, citing State of Ohio ex rel. Erchenbrecher v. Cox, (D. C. Ohio, 1919) 257 F. 334.

ernor in turn transmits it to the legislature. But the Constitution is silent as to these two steps, which are based simply on statute. It would therefore seem that they might be omitted as unnecessary. Since the two steps are not legally significant, injunction would be refused as futile. With respect to submission by the governor to the legislature, it has been held in a lower federal case that no injunction lies to attack an irregularity of Congress in proposing.[83] With respect to legislative officers certifying action by the legislature, the Supreme Court of Kansas refused relief by way of mandamus.[84] The Kentucky state court allowed injunction and a declaratory judgment with respect to certification by the governor to the Secretary of State of the United States.[85] With respect to injunction against certification by the secretary of state, no injunction should lie, and it has been refused,[86] since the Constitution calls for no act by the secretary of state, the final act being the approval by three-fourths of the states.

In favor of permitting attack before adoption by three-fourths of the states is the view that procedural difficulties in framing constitutional questions should be minimized in the interests of efficiency and certainty.[87] To refuse relief seems technical. To grant it makes for speed. The opposing argument is that constitutional decisions should be few in

[83] State of Ohio ex rel. Erchenbrecher v. Cox, (D. C. Ohio, 1919) 257 F. 334.

[84] Coleman v. Miller, (1937) 146 Kan. 490, 71 P. (2d) 518.

[85] Wise v. Chandler, (1937) 270 Ky. 1, 108 S. W. (2d) 1024. Since the governor had already mailed the certificate of ratification to the secretary of state (subsequent to the filing of the bill for injunction and issuance of the restraining order, but prior to the service thereof), it is hard to see how either an injunction or a declaratory judgment would accomplish anything. (1937) 37 Col. L. Rev. 1201. It was argued in the case that since, under the doctrine of Leser v. Garnett, (1922) 258 U. S. 130, 42 S. Ct. 217, the validity of inoperative ratifications might not be assailed after promulgation by the federal secretary of state, the proper time to attack was at the time the governor was about to send in notice of ratification.

[86] Fairchild v. Hughes, (1922) 258 U. S. 126, 42 S. Ct. 274.

[87] Comments, (1937) 47 Yale L. J. 148; (1932) 41 Yale L. J. 1195; Fraenkel, "Constitutional Issues in the Supreme Court, 1935 Term," (1936) 85 U. Pa. L. Rev. 27 at 78.

number, postponed as long as possible, and rendered only if necessary.[88]

3. *Proper Party Plaintiff*

The right of a party to raise the issue of validity of an amendment should be determined by the same theories that are applied to other constitutional issues. In a case arising in the federal courts it was held that the general right of a citizen to have the federal government administered according to law, and to prevent waste of public moneys was not a basis for a suit to decide whether a federal amendment about to be adopted was valid.[89] But a private individual whose interests of person or property have been injured, or are threatened with injury, by the enforcement of legislation the validity of which depends upon the validity of a constitutional amendment, should have the right to raise the issue in a proceeding to which he is a party.

Members of the Kansas legislature assailed the validity of the ratification of the child labor amendment by an original proceeding in mandamus in the Kansas Supreme Court to enjoin further proceedings, and to compel the secretary of state of Kansas to erase the indorsement that the resolution had passed the senate and to indorse on the resolution a statement that it did not pass. Petitioners also sought to restrain the officers of the legislature from signing the resolution, and the secretary of state from authenticating and delivering it

[88] Comments, (1937) 47 YALE L. J. 148; (1936) 45 YALE L. J. 649 at 670–671; (1936) 46 YALE L. J. 255 at 268 ff.; Frankfurter, "A Note on Advisory Opinions," (1924) 37 HARV. L. REV. 1002.

[89] Fairchild v. Hughes, (1922) 258 U. S. 126, 42 S. Ct. 274. This case did not decide that such a party could not attack in the *state* courts. See also, notes (1937) 37 COL. L. REV. 1201; (1937) 24 VA. L. REV. 194; comments, (1937) 47 YALE L. J. 148; (1939) 48 YALE L. J. 1455; and article by Moore and Adelson, "The Supreme Court: 1938 Term, II," (1940) 26 VA. L. REV. 697 at 706.

to the governor. The Kansas Supreme Court denied a writ of mandamus but stated that the right of the plaintiffs to sue was itself clear.[90] The United States Supreme Court granted certiorari and though it upheld the action of the legislature it agreed, four judges dissenting, that the parties had a right to sue.[91] This holding is probably consistent with earlier cases.[92] The holding is also in accord with the theory of most state courts recognizing any citizen's interest.[93] The Wyoming court has held that a taxpayer might sue to enjoin an election as to repeal of the Eighteenth Amendment, although the injunction was refused in the particular case since the election was legal.[94] In Iowa a recent statute authorized injunctions against the submission of amendments to state constitutions. Any taxpayer might sue. The governor and secretary of state could be enjoined from submitting the amendment. Thus Iowa is the first state to allow the judicial determination of the validity of a constitutional amendment before its adoption.[95]

In Kentucky, where a suit was brought by individual citizens and members of the legislature to enjoin certification of ratification to the secretary of state by state officials, no ques-

[90] Coleman v. Miller, (1937) 146 Kan. 390, 71 P. (2d) 518. Petitioners were 21 members of the Kansas senate, 20 of whom voted against the resolution, and 3 members of the house.

[91] Coleman v. Miller, (1939) 307 U. S. 433, 59 S. Ct. 972. For the views of the four judges dissenting as to jurisdiction, see the opinion by Frankfurter, J., 307 U. S. at 464–470. See also (1939) 39 COL. L. REV. 1232; cf. (1937) 47 YALE L. J. 148 at 150; (1937) 24 VA. L. REV. 194 at 195.

[92] Hawke v. Smith, (1920) 253 U. S. 221, 40 S. Ct. 475; Leser v. Garnett, (1922) 258 U. S. 130, 42 S. Ct. 217 (suits by citizens and electors); Moore and Adelson, "The Supreme Court: 1938 Term, II," (1940) 26 VA. L. REV. 697 at 707. Compare (1939) 39 COL. L. REV. 1232 at 1233–1234.

[93] (1937) 47 YALE L. J. 148; (1933) 43 YALE L. J. 340 at 341; Ellingham v. Dye, (1912) 178 Ind. 336, 99 N. E. 1; Zoercher v. Alger, (1930) 202 Ind. 214, 172 N. E. 186, 907.

[94] Spriggs v. Clark, (1932) 45 Wyo. 62, 14 P. (2d) 667, noted (1933) 18 CORN. L. Q. 278, (1933) 1 GEO. WASH. L. REV. 271 and (1933) 10 N. Y. U. L. Q. REV. 395.

[95] Comment, (1932) 17 IOWA L. REV. 250.

tion of the plaintiff's capacity to sue was raised, for the defendant had failed to file a special demurrer.[96] When the Kentucky case came to the United States Supreme Court, the Solicitor General of the United States, in his brief for the United States as *amicus curiae,* conceded that the case was properly before the court.[97] He pointed out that the petitioners (defendants in the state court) were public officers performing federal functions and were seeking to sustain the validity of the act of ratification. Hence decisions holding that public officers may not invoke the jurisdiction of the court in their official capacity to challenge the constitutionality of state acts were not in point. The case, moreover, was not academic. To prevent official notice of the action of the state from reaching the Secretary of State of the United States interfered with the amending process. Official notice from the state is conclusive on the federal secretary of state as to the procedural validity of the ratification, and the proclamation by the federal secretary of state is conclusive on the courts in that regard. Moreover, the orderly receipt of official notice aids in avoiding confusion and uncertainty.

The solicitor general was more dubious in the Kansas case, since the petitioners (plaintiffs in the state court) were public officers attacking the validity of the claimed ratification. But he went on to point out that at least two of the petitioners were members of the state legislature when the amendment was previously rejected and had voted for rejection. Hence their suit might be regarded as an effort on their part to pro-

---

[96] Wise v. Chandler, (1937) 270 Ky. 1, 108 S. W. (2d) 1024. The Kansas and Kentucky cases seem to be the first cases involving attacks on federal amendments by legislators. (1939) 28 GEO. L. J. 199 at 201. Possibly in reality legislators were given a standing to sue because they take part in the amending process. Or possibly jurisdiction was taken to make possible a decision on the merits.

[97] But he admitted that if the case had been first brought in a federal court it would properly have been dismissed on the ground that the complainants had no sufficient legal interest. Brief, p. 34.

tect and vindicate their votes as against what was asserted to be a spuriously countervailing act.

The Supreme Court, in ruling on the Kentucky case, concluded that it was without jurisdiction on certiorari to review the action of the Kentucky court directing the clerk of the court to give official notice to the secretary of state of rejection of the child labor amendment, since after the governor forwarded the certificate of ratification there no longer existed a controversy.[98] The case had become moot. That is to say, while the petitioners might be proper parties, there must still be a controversy. The writ of certiorari was therefore dismissed. The court thought that the state court had jurisdiction up to the time of forwarding the certification of ratification. After such forwarding "there was no longer a controversy susceptible of judicial determination."[99] Justices Black and Douglas concurred on the ground that neither the state nor federal courts "have any jurisdiction to interfere with the amending process."[100] Justices McReynolds and Butler thought that the Kentucky judgment should be affirmed.

The Supreme Court, in ruling on the Kansas case, concluded that the members of the Kansas Senate who voted against ratification of the child labor amendment, and who claimed that their votes were sufficient to prevent ratification, had such an interest in mandamus proceedings begun by them and other legislatures questioning the validity of the legislative action as to give the United States Supreme Court jurisdiction to review on certiorari the adverse decision of the Kansas Supreme Court even though they would not have had standing to sue initially in the federal courts.[101] The Kansas

[98] Compare Chase v. Billings, (1934) 106 Vt. 149, 170 A. 903.

[99] Chandler v. Wise, (1939) 307 U. S. 474 at 477–478, 59 S. Ct. 992.

[100] Ibid., 307 U. S. at 478.

[101] Moore and Adelson, "The Supreme Court: 1938 Term, II," (1940) 26 VA. L. REV. 697 at 706.

court had likewise treated the legislator's interest as sufficient to justify it in entertaining and deciding federal questions raised. The decision of the Kansas court was affirmed. Four of the judges thought that the petitioners had no standing to sue; that there was no controversy before the court. These four judges, in an opinion by Mr. Justice Frankfurter, thought it immaterial that such petitioners were given standing to sue in the Kansas Supreme Court. Such petitioners had no more standing than other citizens of Kansas or even of other parts of the United States. Every United States citizen was equally interested in whether or not the child labor amendment was still alive. Clearly such petitioners would have no standing to sue in a federal court. The federal courts are not bound by state court rulings as to the petitioners' standing.[102] Petitioners' rights of voting in the Kansas legislature were merely political rights undeserving of protection. Justice Butler, in a dissenting opinion concurred in by Justice McReynolds, did not deny that the petitioners could sue.

The present chapter indicates the difficulties encountered in attacking the validity of an amendment to the federal Constitution. If the Supreme Court is not ready to apply the doctrine of political questions to all phases of the amending process, as four members of the court wish, it will apply it to some phases of the amending process and what such phases are remains largely uncertain. Even if the court finds a justiciable question presented, the court may find that the case was brought in the wrong court, or that it was brought at too early a stage in the amending process, or that it was not brought by a proper party plaintiff, or that there was no controversy.

---

[102] A more logical line of reasoning would seem to be as follows: a majority of the court hold that the effect of a prior rejection and the time interval for ratification are not justiciable questions. Such a holding means that they are not justiciable in either state or federal courts. Mr. Justice Black's opinion brings this out clearly. Moreover, since the issues are "exclusively federal questions and not state questions," as pointed out by the Chief Justice, Coleman v. Miller, 307 U. S. 433 at 438, 59 S. Ct. 972, the holding as to justiciability binds the state courts. See comment, (1939) 48 YALE L. J. 1455 at 1456, note 4.

CHAPTER III

The Procedure for Amending the Federal Constitution

A. EXCLUSIVENESS OF CONSTITUTIONAL MODES

ONE of the basic questions which may arise concerning the validity of a constitutional amendment, and the one which has most frequently arisen, is whether the proper procedure was followed in its adoption. The Constitution in Article Five makes express provision as to the mode of procedure, and resort must therefore first be had to it. Two methods of proposal and two of ratification are designated. Proposal may be by a two-thirds vote of each house of Congress, or by application of the legislatures of two-thirds of the states to Congress for the call of a national convention. Ratification may be by the state legislatures or by specially called state conventions, as Congress may choose, a favorable vote by three-fourths of the states being required in either case. From these express provisions it reasonably follows that the indicated methods are exclusive, and the courts have so declared.[1]

Revolution as a mode of changing the Constitution would thus be unlawful. In fact, it seems inconsistent to speak of revolution and law in the same breath, for supposedly one of the essential characteristics of the conception of law is order and regular procedure. Jameson defines a revolution as "a political act or acts done in violation of law, or without law."[2] A century and a half ago, and for that matter a good deal

[1] Hawke v. Smith, (1920) 253 U. S. 221, 40 S. Ct. 495; ROTTSCHAEFER, CONSTITUTIONAL LAW (1939) 8.

[2] JAMESON, CONSTITUTIONAL CONVENTIONS, 4th ed. (1887) 101.

later, it was common for the courts to refer to the right of revolution as a legal right, and not to distinguish it as a political or ethical right. Our revolt from England and the irregular procedure in the adoption of our Constitution resulted in stamping the judicial mind with a tolerant attitude toward revolution. Both, while perhaps justifiable politically and morally, were not so from a juridical viewpoint. For many years the courts and the commentators either tacitly affirmed the right, or used vague language capable of varying interpretations.[3] In several state constitutions the bill of rights expressly declared that the people at all times had a right to alter and amend the constitution.[4] But for over a century the states, as well as the nation, have lived under constitutions in most cases regularly adopted and amended. As a result the courts look askance at the idea of revolution, and expressly refer to it as illegal.[5] Hence, alteration in the constitution not secured by constitutional methods would be in-

[3] In Wells v. Bain, (1873) 75 Pa. 39 at 47, the following modes of altering the Constitution are indicated: "1. The mode provided in the existing constitution. 2. A law, as the instrumental process of raising the body for revision and conveying it to the powers of the people. 3. A revolution." For discussion of this case, see Shenton, "The 'Sovereign' Convention of 1873," (1935) 22 PA. B. A. Q. 171. See also Fuller, "Political Questions," (1925) 38 HARV. L. REV. 296 at 305.

[4] Madison proposed an amendment to be prefixed to the Constitution providing "That the people have an indubitable, inalienable, and indefeasible right to reform or change their Government, whenever it may be found adverse or inadequate to the purposes of its institution." AMES, THE PROPOSED AMENDMENTS TO THE CONSTITUTION (1897) 185.

[5] "No heresy has ever been taught in this country so fraught with evil, as the doctrine that the people have a constitutional right to disregard the constitution, and that they can set themselves above the instrumentalities appointed by the constitution for the administration of law. It tends directly to the encouragement of revolution and anarchy." Koehler v. Hill, (1883) 60 Iowa 543 at 616.

"The Society has, it is true, the physical power to override its own restrictions. But such an act would almost certainly be illegal, because in violation of the letter of the law. Even were the whole people, by unanimous action, to effect organic changes in modes forbidden by the existing organic law, it would be an act of revolution." JAMESON, CONSTITUTIONAL CONVENTIONS, 4th ed. (1887) 599.

"The legal assumption that sovereignty is ultimately vested in the people affords no legal basis for the direct exercise by the people of any sovereign power whose direct exercise by them has not been expressly or impliedly reserved." ROTTSCHAEFER, CONSTITUTIONAL LAW (1939) 8.

valid, although sought by a large section of the people. The principle that the people are sovereign does not mean that they can change the constitution except as provided therein.

As a result of the express provisions of Article Five, the federal Constitution has always been free from the difficulty existing in the case of the early state constitutions, which in several instances made no provision whatever for amendment or revision.[6] In those cases, it was held that the legislature had an implied power to call a convention for revision, after a popular vote on the question, but that the legislature itself had no power to propose amendments.[7] Where the constitution provided for amendment by legislative proposal and did not expressly negative any other mode, the legislature might call a convention; but where the constitution provided for changes by a convention, it appeared that the legislature could not propose amendments. The early constitutions were either silent on the subject, or permitted revision in only one of the two ways just referred to. The earliest mode was revision by convention. Later some of the Southern states developed the legislative mode. Article Five embodies both modes, so that there can be no doubt of the authority to make use of either method. The subsequent state constitutions have in most cases copied the federal plan, which was the first to provide for both modes. In the event of a repeal of the amendment clause, perhaps Congress might, on analogy to the procedure in the case of early state constitutions, call a convention, but could not itself propose amendments. On the other hand, perhaps even its power to call a convention might be doubtful, inasmuch as the powers of the Congress must be expressly or impliedly conferred by the Constitution.[8]

[6] Dodd, The Revision and Amendment of State Constitutions (1910) 44-45.

[7] Ibid.

[8] Where there is no amending clause in the constitution of a nation, the general view is "that it is to be considered as tacitly understood, that amendment may be made either by the ordinary legislative method, or by the same power by which the constitution was originally adopted." This was the opinion given

B. PROPOSAL OF AMENDMENTS

1. *Proposal by National Convention*

One of the two modes of proposing a federal amendment is by constitutional convention, a method corresponding to the original organization which proposed the Constitution itself. Congress, at the request of two-thirds of the state legislatures, is to call a convention. It is thus to be noted that Congress may not call a convention on its own initiative apart from state action. In this respect Congress resembles the state legislatures, which generally are not authorized to call a convention without a previous popular vote. When it is remembered that a state legislature has all powers not forbidden it by the state or national constitution, while Congress has only the powers expressly or impliedly conferred by the Constitution, it seems clear that Congress has no power in the absence of a request by the state legislatures. Revision of the Constitution by a convention is thus left to the initiative of the states. All that Congress can do in bringing about a convention is of a purely advisory character, as by resolution inviting the state legislatures to apply for a convention.

It must not be assumed, however, that Congress is a mere ministerial cog in the call of a convention. The convention does not come about through the mere act of the state legislatures. It is necessary that Congress act upon their applications. It would appear to be the constitutional duty of Congress to issue the call when requested.[9] A simple majority of

by Italian jurists as to alterations of the Italian constitution, which is silent on the subject. WILLOUGHBY, THE NATURE OF THE STATE (1928) 215. See also ROTTSCHAEFER, CONSTITUTIONAL LAW (1939) 9.

[9] This seems to have been the early view. See Speech of Representative Samuel Lyman on March 14, 1796, in 1 BENTON, ABRIDGEMENT OF THE DEBATES OF CONGRESS (1857) 659. The debates at the Constitutional Convention show that this mode was provided because of the fear that the federal government might become oppressive and refuse to initiate amendments desired by the states. Iredell in his argument before the North Carolina Convention asserted that the duty was mandatory. 4 ELLIOT, DEBATES ON THE ADOPTION OF THE FEDERAL CONSTITUTION, 2d ed. (1937 facsimile of 1836 ed.) 178.

Congress could issue it, and it is probable that the approval of the President is unnecessary.[10] But suppose that Congress would refuse. Since Congress is one of the three coordinate branches of the government, there would seem to be no valid method of coercing it to make the call. While the federal courts may declare acts of Congress invalid, they may not do so until the act has been passed. Viewed negatively, there is no valid method of preventing Congress from passing an unconstitutional act. Viewed affirmatively, there is no method of coercing Congress into performing its constitutional duty at any time.[11] The Constitution specifically provides that Congress shall reapportion the number of representatives in the lower house every ten years. Yet it is a well-known fact that reapportionment which ought to have been made in 1920 was not then made. A further difficulty is that Congress seemingly is left some discretion in the matter, as probably it is in the hands of Congress to decide when two-thirds of the state legislature have made the request. This would seem to follow from the 1939 decision leaving to Congress the power to fix the time for ratification and the effect of prior rejections.[12] A clear case is of course possible should two-thirds of the states all at one time request a convention for an identical purpose, and little discretion would seem to be left to Congress. In all likelihood, however, a much wider range of discretion will be left to Congress, since the probability of simultaneous requests for a single purpose seems remote.

A question, then, which may face either Congress or the courts is, when have two-thirds of the legislatures made application for the call of a convention? The issue may arise as to the time each individual state makes its request. Must the requests be simultaneous or approximately so? The answer would seem to be that the time relation between the action

---

[10] Supra, chap. II, at note 24.

[11] Dodd, "Judicially Non-Enforcible Provisions of Constitutions," (1932) 80 U. Pa. L. Rev. 54 at 82.

[12] Coleman v. Miller, (1939) 307 U. S. 433, 59 S. Ct. 972.

of each legislature must be reasonably approximate. The call would seem to outlive the particular Congress to which it is addressed. But it would seem unreasonable that, for example, the request of a legislature in 1800 should be joined to a request in another state in 1825, and these to requests in 1850 and 1900, to constitute the necessary two-thirds. The maximum life of a request should not be more than a generation. Perhaps the most perfect analogy is to be found in the length of time allowed for the ratification of amendments by the state legislatures.[13]

A closely related problem is whether the requests must seek a convention for identical purposes. Should two-thirds of the legislatures ask a convention for the purpose of a general revision or for the same specific purpose, there would be no difficulty. But when one legislature desires a convention for one purpose, as to prohibit polygamy, another legislature for another purpose, as to adopt the initiative and referendum, and a third legislature for a general purpose, there is some doubt whether the prerequisite for a call has been met. The better view would seem to be that the ground of the applications would be immaterial, and that a demand by two-thirds of the states would conclusively show a widespread desire for constitutional changes.

It may be pertinent to inquire whether or not a convention is now impending. The question is not wholly speculative, inasmuch as some of the opponents of the Eighteenth Amendment have asserted that two-thirds, or almost that number, of the state legislatures have made the necessary request. Until 1930 there had been no systematic study of the instances where state legislatures had petitioned Congress to call a convention.[14] In 1901 several legislatures petitioned for a convention

---

[13] Infra, subdivision C.

[14] See study by Senator Tydings of Maryland, S. Doc. 78, 71st Cong., 2d sess. (1930). The best discussion seems to be that by Wheeler, "Is a Constitutional Convention Impending?" (1927) 21 ILL. L. REV. 782.

to consider an amendment for the popular election of Senators, and by 1909 twenty-six states had petitioned for that purpose. The adoption of the Seventeenth Amendment would perhaps destroy the effect of these petitions. Eighteen states have requested a convention to punish polygamy. Twelve states have petitioned with reference to amendments on other subjects. In 1899 Texas and in 1911 Wisconsin petitioned for a convention without indicating its purpose. All in all, from 1901 to 1926 thirty-two different states, or the necessary two-thirds, petitioned for a convention. The requests have been over a considerable length of time, so that it seems proper to conclude that there is no sufficient basis for the call of a convention.[15] The repeal of the Eighteenth Amendment fortifies this view.

Assuming that a proper request for the call has been made and that Congress is willing to issue the call, a number of issues would still remain unsettled. When and where could the convention meet? How would the delegates be elected? Would they represent the states or the people as an aggregate? The debates of the Constitutional Convention throw no light on these problems. Logically it would seem that Congress could regulate all these matters. In the first place, Congress is the general legislative body of the nation. Moreover under Article Five Congress is vested with three distinct powers: to propose amendments, to call a convention when requested by two-thirds of the states, and to designate the mode of ratification (as, e. g., whether by state conventions).[16] The 1939

[15] Where a legislature merely petitions Congress to submit an amendment, it would seem improper to regard this as an application for a convention. See Report by New York State Bar Association Committee, 74 CONG. REC. (1931) 2924 at 2926, and (1931) 17 A. B. A. J. 143.

[16] "As a rule the Constitution speaks in general terms, leaving Congress to deal with subsidiary matters of detail as the public interests and changing conditions may require; and Article V is no exception to the rule." Dillon v. Gloss, (1921) 256 U. S. 368, 41 S. Ct. 510. It would seem, however, that Congress could not add additional burdens to the constitutional procedure for amending the Constitution. See Hamilton v. Secretary of State, (1924) 227 Mich, 111, 198 N. W. 843.

decisions of the United States Supreme Court indicate a tendency to give wide powers to Congress. It might reasonably be argued that under its power to call a convention it has implied authority to fix the time and place of meeting, the number, manner, and date of the election of delegates, and that it also may determine whether the delegates shall represent the states or the nation at large. If the precedent of the Constitutional Convention were followed, the call would be addressed to the states, and would leave to them the method of selecting delegates; and the convention would vote by states.

Perhaps the most important question concerning a convention is as to the extent of its powers. Could it propose a wholly new constitution? Article Five says that Congress "shall call a convention for proposing amendments." If this rule were interpreted literally, it might be argued that the convention could not propose an entirely new constitution in the form of a single document superseding the existing Constitution. But there would seem to be no lawful reason why the convention could not propose what was the equivalent of a new constitution in the form of separate amendments.[17] The organization and peculiar mandate from the people of a convention would seem to warrant the belief that it may revise the Constitution at its discretion. The courts should be slow to adopt a construction which would permit a new constitution only by revolution. The precedent of instructions by Congress as to the scope of its action and the violation thereof by the Constitutional Convention can, however, scarcely be cited, as the convention had no legal standing under the Articles of Confederation. Where the states apply for a convention for general purposes, it would seem that the convention would be free to draft a new document. But even though the application

[17] Mr. Stone, Representative from Maryland in the First Congress, doubted that the amending power extended to the making of a new constitution. ANNALS OF CONGRESS, 1st Cong., 1st sess. (1789) 739; Platz, "Article Five of the Federal Constitution," (1934) 3 GEO. WASH. L. REV. 17 at 24, 46.

were for a limited purpose, it would seem that the state legislatures. would have no authority to limit an instrumentality
set up under the federal Constitution.[18] In reality, the right of
the legislatures is confined to applying for a convention, and
any statement of purposes in their petitions would be irrele-
vant as to the scope of powers of the convention. Inasmuch
as Congress issues the call simply on the basis of the application of the state legislatures, there would seem to be no war
rant for an attempt by Congress to limit the changes proposed.[19] The primary and in fact the sole business of the convention would be to propose changes in the Constitution. In
this sphere the only limitation on it would seem to be Article
Five.

A very serious disturbance might be created if the convention should go beyond its constituent functions and attempt to
legislate. An analysis of the fundamental nature of a convention would seem to exclude such a power. The earliest
view seems to have been that a convention was absolute.[20] The

[18] In 1903 the California legislature adopted the following resolution. "And
the request of and consent to, the calling and holding of such convention as
hereby made and given, is limited to the consideration and adoption of such
amendments to said Constitution as herein mentioned and no other." Cal. Stat.
(1903) 683.

[19] Wells v. Bain, (1874) 75 Pa. 39; Woods' Appeal, (1874) 75 Pa. 59.
In State ex rel. McCready v. Hunt, (1834) 2 Hill. L. (S. C.) 1, it was held
that acts of the convention on subjects not mentioned in the legislative call
were valid only if ratified by the people. The Louisiana cases have taken the
view that the convention is confined to the subjects specified. Huff v. Selber,
(D. C. La. 1925) 10 F. (2d) 236; State v. American Sugar Refining Co.,
(1915) 137 La. 407, 68 So. 742. The 1920 convention was forbidden to alter
the existing provisions as to limits on the indebtedness of the state and its
political subdivisions, the tenure and salary of officers, and the location of the
state capital.

[20] DODD, THE REVISION AND AMENDMENT OF STATE CONSTITUTIONS (1910),
chap. III. A recent case leaning in that direction is Baker v. Moorhead, (1919)
103 Neb. 811, 174 N. W. 840, holding that the general rule that provisions of
a constitution will be construed as mandatory, rather than directory, does not
apply with the same strictness to the provisions for constitutional conventions,
as it applies to other clauses of the constitution, even that providing for amendments, on the ground that the constitution makers of one generation do not in-
tend to prevent later generations from exercising their "sovereign right" to alter
the constitution.

convention was sovereign and subject to no restraint. On the other hand, Jameson, whose views have been most frequently cited in decisions, viewed a convention as a body with strictly limited powers, and subject to the restrictions imposed on it by the legislative call.[21] A third and intermediate view is that urged by Dodd—that a convention, though not sovereign, is a body independent of the legislature; it is bound by the existing constitution, but not by the acts of the legislature, as to the extent of its constituent power.[22] This view has become increasingly prevalent in the state decisions. Accepting this view, it would seem that no restrictions can be placed on the scope of its constituent activity, but that its acts beyond this function would be void.[23] Hence a convention would have no power to interfere with the President or Congress or the states, except of course as the provisions of the proposed constitution might do. It probably could not appropriate money except where Congress failed to act.[24] The Constitutional Convention referred the matter of salaries to Congress. After all it seems that there need be no fear of usurpation by a convention. In the first place, it is limited to the business of altering the Constitution. In the second place, its power in this respect is further limited, for it may merely propose, not adopt, changes. In the third place, the convention not only has no power to adopt, but also has no power to provide for ratification. The latter power is left to Congress. Under the proposed Wadsworth-Garrett amendment the convention would be authorized to refer its proposals to the state legis-

[21] JAMESON, CONSTITUTIONAL CONVENTIONS, 4th ed. (1887) §§ 382–389.

[22] DODD, THE REVISION AND AMENDMENT OF STATE CONSTITUTIONS (1910) 73, 77–80; HOAR, CONSTITUTIONAL CONVENTIONS (1917) 91.

[23] Ex parte Birmingham & Atlantic Ry. Co., (1905) 145 Ala. 514, 42 So. 118; Opinion of the Justices, (1889) 76 N. H. 612, 85 A. 781. The convention may not fix the date when amendments shall go into effect, but if the legislature authorizes, and the people acquiesce, its action is valid. See Hawkins v. Filkins, (1866) 24 Ark. 286.

[24] Platz, "Article Five of the Constitution," (1934) 3 GEO. WASH. L. REV. 17 at 47.

latures or state conventions, as it chose, in the same manner that Congress may now act.

What is the precise nature of the control to which a convention would be subject? Clearly it would be bound by the Constitution, since under our legal system there is no organ of government not subject to the Constitution. Congress's control would seem to be limited to fixing the date and place of elections and meeting, and to determining the mode of representation, whether by states or by the nation. The state legislatures would have no control over the convention whatever. The convention should not be hindered from selecting its own officers, fixing its own rules of procedure, passing on the qualifications and election of its members, and from proposing any alterations it chooses.[25] While in existence it is a separate arm of the nation, coordinate with Congress in its sphere. A more doubtful question is whether the courts might enjoin the convention. As to mere irregular procedure this is doubtful, particularly since the convention merely proposes while the states accept or reject; but if the convention went beyond its constituent functions, and sought to perform executive or legislative acts, perhaps the courts might intervene. The courts could probably pass on the legality of amendments proposed by the convention after they had been adopted by the states. Its proposals would stand on no different footing than amendments proposed by Congress. A nice problem might be raised if Congress should issue a call, and an attempt should be made to enjoin the election of delegates on the ground that the applications of the state legislatures for the call were insufficient. The state decisions, however, have held that the courts will not supervise conventions, nor anticipate their action when assembled.[26] On the principle that the courts

[25] Goodrich v. Moore, (1858) 2 Minn. 49.

[26] Frantz v. Autry, (1907) 18 Okla. 561, 91 P. 193; but see Wells v. Bain, (1873) 75 Pa. 39, which asserts Jameson's view that a convention is not a coordinate branch of the government.

will not enjoin the acts of a coordinate branch of the government, the courts would probably refuse to intervene in the case of a federal convention.

2. *Proposal by Congress*

The second method of proposing an amendment is by a two-thirds vote of each House of Congress. Under the Articles of Confederation, Congress alone could propose amendments, but only a majority vote was required. This mode is of particular importance inasmuch as every amendment thus far adopted, as well as proposed, has been initiated in this manner. Since all but five amendments proposed by Congress have been adopted by the states, proposal seems to have been the most critical step in the amending process. Something like three thousand propositions to amend have been offered to Congress, and only twenty-six have emerged successfully.

A proposition to amend is generally offered in the form of a joint resolution, though on occasion the form of a bill has been employed. At this point it may be well to note that when Congress is engaged in the amending process it is not legislating. It is exercising a peculiar power bestowed upon it by Article Five. This article for the most part controls the process; and other provisions of the Constitution, such as those relating to the passage of legislation, have but little bearing.[27] As it is couched in general terms as to the mode of proposal, it appears that considerable discretion is left to Congress. In practice, after the proposition has been introduced and read twice, it is referred to a committee, generally the committee on the judiciary, unless there is a committee on the subject to which the amendment refers. If the resolution is important and many favor it, it is referred to a select committee. Most

[27] But Professor Rottschaefer states that Congress could prescribe rules for ratification by state conventions and that in doing so, it would be exercising power under Article One. ROTTSCHAEFER, CONSTITUTIONAL LAW (1939) 387.

amendments die in committee. Next the amendment may be reported and discussed but not voted on. If fortunate, it may be voted on, and either passes or fails. Amendments may be proposed in Congress at any time and in any number, and there is no requirement that an amendment deal only with one subject. In this respect the process is much freer than that provided in the constitutions of many of the states. Nor is there any requirement that the amendment be entered on the journals of each house of Congress, nor passed by more than one Congress. The state constitutions generally contain a substantial number of regulations on the legislative procedure of amendment, and a large number of cases arise on such subjects as entry on the legislative journals and publication in the newspapers of the proposed amendment.

As a result of the broad phrasing of Article Five, there has been but little litigation concerning the legality of the procedure of Congress in proposing amendments. One question which has arisen is what is meant by "two-thirds of both Houses." The question was first raised as to the adoption of the Twelfth Amendment. It has been contended that it means two-thirds of the entire membership. Congress in practice interpreted it to mean two-thirds of a quorum of each house, and many amendments, including some of the first ten, have thus been proposed. The Supreme Court upheld this interpretation.[28] Article Five also provides that amendments shall be

[28] National Prohibition Cases, (1920) 253 U. S. 350, 40 S. Ct. 486, 588; State of Ohio ex rel. Erchenbrecher v. Cox, (D. C. Ohio, 1919) 257 F. 334; Jebbia v. United States, (C. C. A. 4th, 1930) 37 F. (2d) 343; semble, Missouri Pacific Ry. Co. v. Kansas, (1919) 248 U. S. 276, 39 S. Ct. 93; Green v. Weller, (1856) 32 Miss. 650. The two-thirds vote is required only on the final passage of the resolution; the amendment, while being considered, may be amended by a majority vote. Apparently the absence of representation in Congress, through secession or otherwise, is no bar to a proposal, as the Fourteenth Amendment was submitted by a Congress in which only twenty-five out of thirty-six states were represented. When the Fifteenth Amendment was proposed it was argued in the Senate that there was no authority to propose as three states were still excluded from membership. CONG. GLOBE, 40th Cong., 3d sess. (1869) 711. The function of selecting the mode of ratification would seem to be apart from that of proposing an amendment, and it might be argued

proposed whenever Congress "shall deem it necessary." When the validity of the Eighteenth Amendment was at-tacked, its opponents asserted that Congress had not shown that it deemed it necessary. The Supreme Court pointed out, however, that there had been no such express declaration in any previous resolution of amendment.[29] The earliest question to arise was whether the approval of the President was necessary. The Attorney General, in arguing the case, pointed out that the amending process was unique in its nature and not legislative, and also that a two-thirds instead of a majority vote was required to pass a proposal. The Supreme Court in a concise opinion thought it obvious that the President's approval was unnecessary.[30]

that only a majority vote is required. But Congress has always performed both functions in a single resolution. Perhaps the call of a convention would require only a majority vote.

[29] National Prohibition Cases, (1920) 253 U. S. 350, 40 S. Ct. 486, 588; Feigenspan v. Bodine, (D. C. N. J. 1920) 264 F. 186.

[30] Hollingsworth v. Virginia, (1798) 3 Dall. (3 U. S.) 378; see also Hawke v. Smith, (1920) 253 U. S. 221 at 229, 40 S. Ct. 495. In spite of the early decision of the point, there seem to have been some doubts as to the necessity of the President's approval. JAMESON, CONSTITUTIONAL CONVENTIONS, 4th ed. (1887) §§ 556–561. In 1803 a motion in the Senate to submit the Twelfth Amendment to the President was defeated. In 1861 the President signed the Corwin amendment without anyone's protesting. President Lincoln inadvertently signed the Thirteenth Amendment, but immediately notified Congress, and the Senate adopted a motion that his approval was unnecessary and not a precedent. In submitting the Fourteenth Amendment to the states, President Johnson informed Congress that he was acting in a purely ministerial capacity. The President has signed no subsequent amendments. President John Quincy Adams was of the view that the President should not even suggest amendments to Congress. At present resolutions of amendment are printed in the statutes as signed by the Speaker of the House and the President of the Senate, and attested to by the clerk of the House and the Secretary of the Senate.

Some state decisions have distinguished between the proposal and the submission of an amendment, and assert that the governor must approve the latter. Hatch v. Stoneman, (1885) 66 Cal. 632, 6 P. 734. This has not been the practice of Congress, which has always performed both acts in a single resolution. Jameson is of the view that both the submission of a state amendment and the call of a state convention are legislative. JAMESON, CONSTITUTIONAL CONVENTIONS, 4th ed. (1887) 576. But it seems doubtful that the President's approval would be required if Congress were to call a convention, particularly as the call arises at the application of the state legislatures. The same reasoning would seem to apply to an attempted distinction between the proposal and the selection of the mode of ratification, whether by legislatures or conventions.

Several important speculative questions might arise in connection with the powers of Congress. Could Congress propose an entirely new constitution in the form of an amendment? Though such action would be extraordinary, there would seem to be no legal reason why it could not. Article Five contains no limit as to the number and nature and separability of amendments. It might perhaps be asserted that a general revision is more appropriate by a convention, particularly since this alternative mode is expressly provided, but this would seem a question of policy rather than of law, and no limitation should be implied. The Constitution itself makes no distinction between proposals by Congress and by a convention, since provision is for a "Convention for proposing amendments." Since a convention would probably have full powers to propose and since Congress probably has the same powers as a convention, it would seem that Congress could probably propose a whole new constitution. No one has yet been able to draw a satisfactory line between amendment and revision, and it is doubtful that the courts would attempt to do so. An Indiana case, however, appears to hold that a legislature may not propose a wholly new constitution.[31]

Suppose Congress should attempt to withdraw an amendment after it had been proposed.[32] This question was directly

[31] Ellingham v. Dye, (1912) 178 Ind. 336, 99 N. E. 1. But in that case the legislature failed to go through the form of legislative proposal under the amending clause. In Root's brief in the National Prohibition Cases, (1920) 253 U. S. 350, 40 S. Ct. 486, 588, it is contended that the power of Congress to propose is not so great as that of a convention. See also Livermore v. Waite, (1894) 102 Cal. 113, 36 P. 424. In Switzer v. State ex rel. Silvey, (1921) 103 Ohio St. 306 at 317, 133 N. E. 552, the court puts this query: "What would be said of a proposed amendment to the federal constitution, if bearing the proper label 'amendment' which this proposal does not do, it suggested merely that it proposed to abandon the present written constitution and adopt the 'English' or the 'Chinese Plan' of government, instead of the American 'Federal' plan? Could it logically be held that such proposal fell within the word 'amendment' as contemplated in the federal constitution?"

[32] JAMESON, CONSTITUTIONAL CONVENTIONS, 4th ed. (1887) 634; BURDICK, THE LAW OF THE AMERICAN CONSTITUTION (1922) § 19. Perhaps it would be improper for one House of Congress to withdraw its proposal after the other House had acted, and possibly even before. In Crawford v. Gilchrist, (1912)

raised in 1864 when Senator Anthony proposed to repeal the joint resolution submitting the Corwin amendment.[33] In such a case the analogy of a state legislature's attempting to withdraw its ratification of an amendment would seem apposite.[34] The practice has been to regard such a withdrawal as ineffectual. The theory apparently is that each affirmative step in the passage of an amendment is irrevocable. If Congress had first rejected and then passed the proposition, its action would be proper, since negative action is viewed as no action at all. From a strictly logical viewpoint it would seem that Congress could withdraw an amendment before three-fourths of the states had ratified. The amendment has no legal effect until adopted. It is a mere *res nullius*. Yet on the basis of convenience it may be replied that confusion would be introduced if Congress were permitted to retract its action. It may also be argued that when Congress has proposed, its work is done, since Article Five limits it to proposing, and leaves the matter of adoption up to the states. Both of these arguments are rather technical, and possibly on the basis of the 1939 cases the Supreme Court would regard the question as a political one.[35]

The questions of the power of Congress to provide that ratification should be only by legislatures elected subsequently to the proposal by Congress and its power to regulate the rules of procedure of the legislatures in ratifying amendments[36] are discussed in the section on ratification by state legislatures.

64 Fla. 41, 59 So. 963, one house of the state legislature was allowed to withdraw its consent to a proposed state amendment after the other house had consented. Cockrell, J., dissenting, pointed out that when the Civil War Amendments were ratified, the legislatures were not allowed to withdraw their ratifications.

[33] S. J. R. 25, CONG. GLOBE, 38th Cong., 1st sess. (1864) 522.

[34] See this chapter, infra, p. 70 et seq.

[35] Coleman v. Miller, (1939) 307 U. S. 433; 59 S. Ct. 972; (1940) 24 MINN. L. REV. 393 at 396.

[36] See infra, p. 63 et seq.

Suppose the Congressional procedure of proposing an amendment was defective in some respect. Would such defect be cured by ratification by the states? One writer asserts that the Supreme Court would have to find the amendment invalid.[37] There are some cases involving amendment of state constitutions which hold that the defect would be cured.[38]

C. RATIFICATION OF AMENDMENTS

1. *Ratification by State Conventions*

The second great step in the amending process is ratification by the states.[39] One method of such ratification is by state conventions. The first amending clause proposed at the Constitutional Convention provided for this mode of ratification exclusively. The Constitution itself was adopted by such conventions. The fact of ratification by such conventions was early asserted to prove the national, rather than the federal, character of the Constitution. This mode of ratification may therefore be described as the national method, and that by the state legislatures as the federal. The framers of the Constitution doubtless expected that the method would be used, but so far every amendment except one has been referred to the state legislatures.[40] Attempts had sometimes been made to use the method even before it was used as to the Twenty-First Amendment. At the time of proposal of the Thirteenth and

[37] Platz, "Article Five of the Federal Constitution," (1934) 3 GEO. WASH. L. REV. 17 at 31.

[38] (1922) 35 HARV. L. REV. 593.

[39] The selection of the mode is left up to Congress. As has been pointed out, the question seems distinct from that of the content of the amendment itself. Both have always been provided for in the resolution of amendment.

[40] Ratification by conventions might become useful if a state should abolish its legislature and adopt the initiative and referendum for all legislation. See the suggestion of Parker, J., dissenting in State ex rel. Mullen v. Howell, (1919) 107 Wash. 167, 181 P. 920. But the state would lose its vote unless Congress provided for ratification by conventions. It would seem that Congress could not provide for ratification in some states by conventions and in others by the legislatures.

Fifteenth Amendments it was sought to secure such a submission. In connection with the latter amendment it was argued that gerrymandering prevailed in many of the states and that Congress could regulate the selection of the convention so that they would truly represent the people. Furthermore it was pointed out that the previous amendments, especially the first twelve, restricted only the national government, while this amendment curtailed the power of the states. Therefore the people should have an opportunity to pass upon it. In reply it was stated that Congress had never used the method because it was dilatory, expensive, and generally unwise.

The claim has been made that the Eighteenth and Nineteenth Amendments should have been ratified by conventions on the ground that they took away power from the states and interfered with personal liberty.[41] There is nothing in Article Five, however, which gives any greater validity to ratification by conventions than by the state legislatures. Certainly the language of the article makes no distinction, and there seems no reasonable basis to imply one. The question has been adjudicated in the recent case of *United States v. Sprague*,[42] which went to the Supreme Court. In this case the Eighteenth Amendment was assailed on the ground that it should have been ratified by conventions because it conferred "new direct powers over individuals" and was not simply a change in the

---

[41] JESSUP, THE BILL OF RIGHTS AND ITS DESTRUCTION BY ALLEGED DUE PROCESS OF LAW (1927) 71; Marbury, "The Nineteenth Amendment and After," (1920) 7 VA. L. REV. 1 at 5; Root's brief in the National Prohibition Cases, (1920) 253 U. S. 350, 40 S. Ct. 486, 588. In Ex parte Kerby, (1922) 102 Ore. 612, 205 P. 279, it was held that the power to amend the state constitution through legislative proposal with a subsequent popular vote was equally broad as that by the constitutional initiative, including the right to alter the bill of rights. That the Eighteenth Amendment should have been ratified by state conventions is the chief contention of Smith, "Is Prohibition Constitutional?" (1929) 4 PLAIN TALK 415.

[42] (1931) 282 U. S. 716, 51 S. Ct. 220, noted (1932) 27 ILL. L. REV. 72, (1931) 29 MICH. L. REV. 777, (1931) 79 U. PA. L. REV. 807 and Creekmore, "The Sprague Case," (1931) 3 MISS. L. J. 282.

machinery of the federal government. It was pointed out that the Constitution itself, which surrendered up liberties of the people, was ratified by conventions. Finally it was urged that the Tenth Amendment re-enforced this view and cured any doubts.[43] The trial court rejected all these views, yet held the Eighteenth Amendment unconstitutional on a theory of "political science" and a "scientific approach to the problem of government."[44] The United States Supreme Court in up-holding the Eighteenth Amendment rejected all these theories.

Conventions, like legislatures, are mere agents of the people. Much criticism of the amending process has arisen in recent years on the ground that the people do not participate. The difficulties of changing Article Five so as to permit of such participation seem very great, but it should never be forgotten that there is always the possibility of ratification by conventions if Congress so chooses.

Perhaps the nearest approach until the last decade to a possible controversy over the legality of ratification by conventions was in the case of the Corwin amendment. This amendment was submitted by Congress to the state legislatures. An Illinois convention, which had been convened to change the state constitution, on its own initiative voted on the amendment and accepted it. As only two other states ratified it, the effect of its action never got into the courts. But since Congress is vested with the power to select the mode of ratification, and had here chosen the other mode, it would seem that the action of the convention was null and void.[45]

[43] Bacon, "How the Tenth Amendment Affected the Fifth Article of the Constitution," (1930) 16 VA. L. REV. 771.

[44] United States v. Sprague, (D. C. N. J. 1930) 44 F. (2d) 967 at 982, 984. Oddly enough, the trial court, though criticising the Supreme Court for its holding in the National Prohibition Cases, (1920) 253 U. S. 350, 40 S. Ct. 486, 588, that the court could pass on the substance of amendments, held that certain amendments must be ratified by conventions.

[45] AMES, THE PROPOSED AMENDMENTS TO THE CONSTITUTION (1897) 286. Fullerton, J., dissenting in State ex rel. Mullen v. Howell, (1919) 107 Wash.

Another question of great importance is, in case ratification by conventions is provided for, what body can regulate their election and procedure? Since Congress is given several powers under the amending clause, among which is the power to determine that ratification shall be by conventions, it might reasonably be argued that it has the power to prescribe the date and mode of their election.[46] When the Constitution itself was adopted, the state legislatures appear to have controlled these matters. Congress simply referred the Constitution to the state legislatures with the recommendation that they pass it on to conventions to be called in each state.

Up to 1933 no amendments had been submitted to conventions. The first twenty amendments had been ratified by legislatures. When the Twenty-First Amendment was proposed there was considerable discussion as to whether Congress should call the conventions, and as to whether Congress should lay down the rules for conventions with respect to qualifications of electors, protection against fraud and irregularities, and election by districts or at large. Mr. James M. Beck, formerly solicitor general, claimed that Congress had no power to regulate such conventions in any respect.[47] Former Attorney General A. Mitchell Palmer asserted that Congress had such power and that its power was exclusive.[48] But he later advised Congress to regulate a few matters and leave the rest to the states.[49] Senators Hebert and Lewis and Rep-

167 at 199, 181 P. 920, uses as *reductio ad absurdum* the conclusion that conventions could ratify, although Congress selected the legislative mode, if the constitutional methods of ratification were not exclusive.

[46] ". . . Congress is plainly given the power to submit such a proposal to conventions in the several states, and to provide the manner of electing delegates to, and the calling of, such conventions, all of which could be readily done by Congress wholly apart from state constitutional and statutory law." Parker, J., dissenting in State ex rel. Mullen v. Howell, (1919) 107 Wash. 167 at 196, 181 P. 920. Jameson is of the view that the state legislatures would issue the calls for conventions. JAMESON, CONSTITUTIONAL CONVENTIONS, 4th ed. (1887) 61, 153.

[47] 76 CONG. REC. (1932) 124–130.

[48] 76 CONG. REC. (1932) 130.

[49] NEW YORK TIMES, Jan. 2, 1933, p. 8, col. 1.

resentative Sumners thought that Congress might regulate, while Senators Bratton (now United States Circuit Judge) and Walsh were of the opposite opinion.[50] The writers were also divided. Howard Lee McBain,[51] Ralph T. Martig[52] and Professor Dowling[53] thought that Congress could regulate. Professor Rottschaefer, writing in 1939, has taken the same view.[54] Former Secretary of State Bainbridge Colby in 1938 likewise expressed that opinion.[55] Historical evidence to show that Congress may call state conventions is cited in a recent article by Abraham C. Weinfeld.[56] Other writers have denied the power, for example, Alexander Lincoln,[57] former Attorney General William D. Mitchell,[58] and Herbert S. Phillips,[59] and Federal Judge William Clark.[60] In 1937 Representative Wadsworth introduced a bill to regulate ratifying conventions in several respects.[61] Election was to be at large, within five years after proposal, and the time of convention meeting was fixed.

In favor of Congressional regulation several arguments may be made. If Congress could not control, ratification by

[50] 76 CONG. REC. (1932) 4153, 4152–4153, 4163, 4148–4150; see Weinfeld, "Power of Congress over State Ratifying Conventions," (1938) 51 HARV. L. REV. 473 at 474.

[51] McBain, "Or by Conventions," NEW YORK TIMES, Dec. 11, 1932, § IV, p. 1:7.

[52] "Amending the Constitution," (1937) 35 MICH. L. REV. 1253 at 1273–1274, 1284; see also (1934) 2 GEO. WASH L. REV. 216; (1933) 7 ST. JOHN'S L. REV. 375.

[53] "A New Experiment in Ratification," (1933) 19 A. B. A. J. 383 at 387.

[54] CONSTITUTIONAL LAW (1939) 392.

[55] HEARINGS ON S. J. RES. 134, 75th Cong., 3d sess. (1938) 60.

[56] "Power of Congress over State Ratifying Conventions," (1938) 51 HARV. L. REV. 473 at 476–488.

[57] "Ratification by Conventions," (1933) 18 MASS. L. Q. 287.

[58] "Methods of Amending the Constitution," (1932) 25 LAWY. & BANKER 265.

[59] "Has the Congress Power Under Article V of the Constitution to Call and Regulate the Holding of Ratifying Conventions Independent of State Legislatures?" (1933) 6 FLA. S. B. A. J. 573.

[60] HEARINGS ON S. J. RES. 134, 75th Cong., 3d sess. (1938) 21–25.

[61] H. R. 299, 75th Cong., 1st sess. (1937).

convention would be at the mercy of the state legislatures, hence this method of ratification would be almost the same as legislative ratification. Although the Twenty-First Amendment was rapidly ratified, other amendments might be long delayed if the regulation of conventions was left to the state legislatures. Ratification by state conventions is a federal function, as is ratification by state legislatures.[62] Under Article One, section 4, Congress may regulate the election of United States Senators and Representatives. Even though reasoning from the premise that a legislature must be what was a legislature at the time of the drafting of the Constitution, a convention must be what a convention then was, not all conventions were even then called by the states.

When the Twenty-First Amendment was submitted, Congress after considerable debate was silent as to the calling of conventions. In 1933 forty-three states passed laws providing for the holding of conventions to ratify the Twenty-First Amendment.[63] The only states not passing statutes were Georgia, Kansas, Louisiana, Mississippi, and North Dakota. Pursuant to such statutes, conventions were held in 1933 in thirty-eight states. Thirty-seven conventions ratified, the only rejection occurring in South Carolina. In North Carolina, the electorate voted for convention delegates, but against holding a convention. In Montana, Nebraska, Oklahoma, and

---

[62] The Supreme Court of North Carolina has recently advised that a state constitutional provision as to calling a convention to amend the state constitution did not apply to state conventions to amend the federal Constitution. Opinion of the Justices, (1933) 204 N. C. 806, 172 S. E. 474. The United States Supreme Court has held that state constitutions may not fetter state legislatures in the ratification of federal amendments. Leser v. Garnett, (1922) 258 U. S. 120, 42 S. Ct. 217. See also the opinion of Judge Parker, dissenting, in State ex rel. Mullen v. Howell, (1919) 107 Wash. 167 at 196, 181 P. 920, quoted in note 46, supra.

[63] BROWN, RATIFICATION OF THE TWENTY-FIRST AMENDMENT TO THE CONSTITUTION OF THE UNITED STATES (1938) 515; see also article by the same author on the same subject, (1935) 29 AM. POL. SCI. REV. 1005–1017. The state convention records and laws are set out in detail in the volume by Brown, a book indispensable to the student of ratification of federal amendments by state conventions.

South Dakota provision was made for the choice of convention delegates in the next year, 1934.[64] The number of delegates varied from 329 in Indiana to 3 in New Mexico.[65] In only six conventions were there more than a hundred delegates.

The states, in providing for conventions, inferentially recognized the power of Congress to deal with the subject. The Supreme Court of Ohio ruled that when Congress fails to act, the state legislatures may call conventions.[66] Twenty one state laws provided that if Congress later acted as to the organization of state conventions, then the state statute was superseded. Only New Mexico framed a statute denying the power of Congress to act.[67]

The scope of the power of state conventions would seem to be reasonably clear. They have the exclusive power of the states to ratify amendments proposed to them by Congress. They are not at liberty to go outside their constituent functions, however, so as to interfere with the state or national governments. What was said of the powers of a national convention applies almost completely to state conventions with the sole exception that the function of the former is to propose and the latter to ratify. In passing on the amendment, the conventions have the same powers and disabilities as the state legislatures have.[68] The same time limits and the same right to reject and later to ratify would seem to govern.[69] While these conventions are state instrumentalities in some respects, their powers with respect to ratification are derived from Article Five, so that they may also be looked upon as federal agencies. Doubtless the states might empower such

[64] Brown, Ratification of the Twenty-First Amendment (1938) 5.
[65] Ibid. 516.
[66] State ex rel. Donnelly v. Myers, (1933) 127 Ohio St. 104, 186 N. E. 918.
[67] Brown, "The Ratification of the Twenty-First Amendment," (1935) 29 Am. Pol. Sci. Rev. 1005 at 1008–1009.
[68] See in general, Jameson, Constitutional Conventions, 4th ed. (1887) chap. VI.
[69] See infra, p. 70 et seq.

conventions to perform strictly state functions in addition to their functions of ratification. The Illinois convention which attempted to ratify the Corwin amendment was sitting as a state constitutional convention.

The most striking characteristic of the conventions which ratified the Twenty-First Amendment was their lack of true deliberation.[70] The question arose whether the state legislatures could so regulate the conventions as to strip them of their deliberative character, as by providing for a popular referendum which should be binding on the convention. The Alabama Supreme Court advised that no deliberation was necessary and that a popular referendum might be made binding.[71] The Alabama legislature passed a bill over the governor's veto providing for such referendum. The Maine Supreme Court advised that deliberation was essential.[72]

In favor of the view that deliberation is not necessary, it may be pointed out that Congress has already deliberated, whereas a convention to amend the state constitution must take that preliminary step;[73] and that the language of *Hawke v. Smith*,[74] speaking of "deliberative assemblages" was immediately followed by the statement that such bodies "would voice the will of the people." Moreover, legislative action was involved there, and legislative action is naturally deliberative,

---

[70] Brown, Ratification of the Twenty-First Amendment (1938) 5.

[71] In re Opinion of the Justices, (1933) 226 Ala. 565, 148 So. 107, noted (1933) 47 Harv. L. Rev. 130, (1934) 28 Ill. L. Rev. 709, (1933) 18 Minn. L. Rev. 70.

[72] In re Opinion of the Justices, (1933) 132 Me. 491, 167 A. 176, noted in (1934) 2 Geo. Wash. L. Rev. 216. There are decisions which go even farther and reject a popular referendum as to a state statute providing machinery for the selection of members of conventions to ratify a federal amendment and for conducting such conventions. State ex rel. Donnelly v. Myers, (1933) 127 Ohio St. 104, 186 N. E. 918; State ex rel. Tate v. Sevier, (1933) 333 Mo. 662, 62 S. W. (2d) 895. That this view is extreme is pointed out by Rottschaefer, Constitutional Law (1939) 391; (1934) 1 U. Chi. L. Rev. 498; (1934) 34 Col. L. Rev. 168.

[73] Dowling, "A New Experiment in Ratification," (1933) 19 A. B. A. J. 383.

[74] (1920) 253 U. S. 221 at 227, 40 S. Ct. 495.

at least to some extent. It may also be pointed out that the fact that the conventions which ratified the Constitution were deliberative is not conclusive, since there were no facilities for taking a popular vote in the early days.[75] The meaning of "conventions" was vague in the early days.[76] Finally it may be argued that certification by the state and proclamation by the secretary of state of ratification by three-fourths of the states bar any attack on the deliberative character of the conventions.[77] But, prior to the proclamation by the secretary of state, possibly the proper state officials might be enjoined from certifying the results of a pledged convention.

2. *Ratification by State Legislatures*

As has been indicated, the other method of ratification is by the state legislatures. This was the method of ratification used in amending the Articles of Confederation, and gives peculiar prominence to the states as such. The usual course of procedure is that after Congress has proposed an amendment, the secretary of state sends a copy thereof to the governor of each state. The governor of each state in turn submits it to the legislature. These two steps, it is to be noted, are not mentioned in the Constitution, but are based simply on statute or practice.[78] Even though both of them were omitted, it would therefore seem that the amendment could not be attacked for such omission. The only substantial requirements demanded by the Constitution are that there be a two-thirds

[75] McPherson v. Blacker, (1892) 146 U. S. 1 at 36, 13 S. Ct. 3.

[76] (1934) 28 ILL. L. REV. 709.

[77] Leser v. Garnett, (1922) 258 U. S. 130, 42 S. Ct. 217.

[78] State of Ohio ex rel. Erchenbrecher v. Cox, (D. C. Ohio, 1919) 257 F. 334. Some state legislatures attempted to ratify the Fifteenth Amendment upon telegraphic information without waiting for the official copy. This would seem to be valid where the legislature acts on the basis of correct information. Thus Nevada's ratification before an official copy reached the state seems to have been good. See MATHEWS, LEGISLATIVE AND JUDICIAL HISTORY OF THE FIFTEENTH AMENDMENT (1909) 57.

vote of each house of Congress in its favor and that it be ratified by three-fourths of the state legislatures. In this respect Article Five resembles the chief prerequisites for the amendment of a state constitution: the vote of the constitutionally designated majority of the legislature and the approval of the constitutional majority of the voters.[79] It would seem then that a state legislature could proceed at once after Congress has proposed.

To determine the legality of the acts of the state legislature in ratifying, one must first inquire into the nature of the function of the legislature in performing the act of ratification. As in the case of Congress, resort must first be had to Article Five. The entire extent of the power of the legislature is to be found in that article, and anything in the state constitution to the contrary is void.[80] Thus the legislature may be placed in the unusual position of having violated its own rules of procedure and the state constitution, though this is not theoretically incorrect since the Constitution of the United States is supreme and the legislature is free to violate the state constitution whenever it is inconsistent with the federal Constitution. The legislature in ratifying an amendment is not exercising a legislative function, just as Congress, when it proposes, is not legislating.[81] The state decisions also hold that

[79] See the opinion of Brewer, J., later a member of the federal Supreme Court, in Prohibitory Amendment Cases, (1881) 24 Kan. 700.

[80] The present Missouri constitution forbids the legislature's adopting any amendment to the federal Constitution impairing the right of local self-government. Mo. Const. (1875), art. 2, §3. The West Virginia constitution declares it the duty of the state government to guard the state from federal encroachments upon its "internal government and police." W. Va. Const. (1872), art. 1, §2. A Missouri constitutional convention proposed an amendment to the state bill of rights forbidding ratification of any amendment affecting "the individual liberty of the people of the United States."

[81] Mr. Justice Day, writing the opinion of the court in Hawke v. Smith, (1920) 253 U. S. 221 at 229, 40 S. Ct. 495, stated: "Ratification by a state of a constitutional amendment is not an act of legislation within the proper sense of the word. It is but the expression of the assent of the State to a proposed amendment."

The Maine court in Opinion of the Justices, (1919) 118 Me. 544 at 546—

when the legislature proposes an amendment to the state constitution it is not legislating. The provisions of the state constitution and the rules of the legislature as to the passage of statutes, bills, and other forms of legislation are not controlling in the adoption of an amendment. The legislature in ratifying is exercising a ministerial or constituent function; the ratifying process is equivalent to a roll call of the states. The courts have asserted that the legislature acts as a federal agent, and exclusively under the federal Constitution.[82]

Bearing in mind that Article Five is the source of the state legislature's authority, one may proceed to inquire what is the extent of this authority. In the first place, which legislature as regards time may ratify? Article Five makes no express provision, but it would seem that the legislature existing at the time of the proposal by Congress or any later legislature existing during the pendency of the amendment may pass on it. Congress probably could not forbid such action.[83] Any pro-

---

547, 107 A. 673, stated: "Here again, the State Legislature in ratifying the amendment, as Congress in proposing it, is not, strictly speaking, acting in the discharge of legislative duties and functions as a law making body, but is acting in behalf of and as representatives of the people as a ratifying body under the power expressly conferred upon it by Article V. The people through their Constitution might have clothed the Senate alone, or the House alone, or the Governor's Council, or the Governor, with the power of ratification, or might have reserved that power to themselves to be exercised by popular vote. But they did not." *Contra:* (1938) 18 Bost. U. L. Rev. 169 at 173.

[82] This question is distinguishable from that in Haire v. Rice, (1907) 204 U. S. 291, 27 S. Ct. 281, in which it was held that when Congress designates a state legislature as an agency for carrying out a federal purpose, the legislature must act in subordination to the state constitution since that is the source of its powers. Similarly the state is engaged in ordinary law making when it regulates the election of Representatives in Congress, hence the governor's veto is effective. Smiley v. Holm, (1931) 285 U. S. 355, 52 S. Ct. 397, noted (1932) 17 Corn. L. Q. 466; (1932) 27 Ill. L. Rev. 445; (1932) 30 Mich. L. Rev. 969, 1337; (1932) 16 Minn. L. Rev. 850. In the amending process, the state legislatures derive their authority directly from Article Five, which supersedes anything inconsistent therewith in the state constitutions. This seems to be the answer to the theory advanced by Brown, "The Sixteenth Amendment to the United States Constitution," (1920) 54 Am. L. Rev. 843 at 849, that the Sixteenth Amendment is void because some of the legislatures ratifying had no power to impose an income tax.

[83] In the case of the Fourteenth and Fifteenth Amendments, efforts were made to provide that ratification should only be by legislatures elected subsequently to

vision of the state constitution forbidding the existing legislature from doing so would seem to be unconstitutional. As a matter of fact, in the case of the Nineteenth Amendment the existing Tennessee legislature proceeded to ratify although the state constitution definitely provided that ratification must be by a subsequently elected legislature.[84] When it is recalled that every amendment has so far been acted upon by existing legislatures, there can seem little doubt of the propriety of this procedure. It would also seem that a special session of the legislature would have the power to ratify.[85]

Another question is whether Congress or the states may regulate the rules of procedure of the legislatures in ratifying amendments. The constitutionality of Congressional regula-

the proposal by Congress. See chap. VI, p. 189, infra. It was argued that Congress had this power by necessary implication. In reply it was argued that the Constitution referred to the then existing legislatures and any later legislatures during the pendency of the amendment. Moreover, all previous amendments had been ratified by the existing legislatures. The proposed Wadsworth-Garrett amendment expressly provides for ratification by subsequently elected legislatures only. See chap. VI, p. 189 et seq.

[84] The Tennessee Attorney General rendered an opinion that this was valid. (1920) 24 LAW NOTES 81. Chapter 560 of the Acts of 1920 of Massachusetts declares it to be the policy of the state that the legislature should defer its action on federal amendments until a popular vote has been taken. A commission appointed by the governor of Virginia under an act of March 25, 1926, to study revision of the state constitution recommended that it be the policy of the state that only subsequently elected legislatures act on federal amendments. Former Governor Alfred Smith of New York in his January 4, 1928, message urged an amendment to the state constitution "that no future amendments to the federal Constitution be acted upon by the Legislature before referendum by State statute to the people." N. Y. LEG. DOC. (1928), No. 3, p. 90.

[85] The decision in People ex rel. Attorney General v. Curry, (1900) 130 Cal. 82, 62 P. 516, that a special session of the California legislature could not propose amendments to the state constitution unless the subjects thereof were specified in the proclamation calling the special session, seems erroneous, and was based on the theory that an amendment is a form of legislation. In Sweeney v. King, (1927) 289 Pa. St. 92, 137 A. 178, an opposite result was reached and the California decision was rejected. The child labor amendment was ratified in Kentucky by the legislature when in special session, although the governor's original proclamation did not mention the subject of ratification. His amended proclamation did so mention. The Alabama court advised that the legislature may not at a special session provide for a convention to pass on an amendment unless the subject is included in the governor's proclamation. In re Opinions of the Justices, (1933) 226 Ala. 168, 146 So. 407.

tion would seem exceedingly doubtful. The states cannot be coerced into adopting an amendment. If they choose to remain passive and never so much as discuss the amendment, there is nothing Congress can do to force them to act. Congress has done its work when it proposes, and the matter of adoption is for the states.[86] On the other hand, the state legislature is not bound by its ordinary rules of procedure in the ratification of an amendment. A federal amendment could not be invalidated for a breach of the rules, especially when they were of such a nature as to impede the adoption of an amendment. As a minimum power the state could provide for the time and place of meeting of the legislature, whether it should be bicameral or unicameral, the number and election of its members, its organization and officers. The state could perhaps even abolish its legislature altogether, at least as far as Article Five is concerned, although such action might be regarded as a failure to maintain a republican form of government. Ratification would then have to be by conventions, or the state would lose its voice in the amending process.

It would seem improper that a mere majority vote of the legislators taken in an individual poll at a time and place other than prescribed in the state constitution would be sufficient. On the other hand, there would seem to be some doubt

[86] One of the most detailed plans for regulating the legislatures is that proposed by Senator Morton as a result of the obstructive tactics in the Indiana legislature to hinder the adoption of the Fifteenth Amendment. AMES, THE PROPOSED AMENDMENTS TO THE CONSTITUTION (1909) 291. On the sixth legislative day of the meeting of any state legislature, each house was to proceed at noon to act upon any amendment proposed; except that the legislature must not have taken any action on the amendment at any of its previous sessions. If a majority of the members of each house voted for it, it passed. If no conclusive action was taken the first day, the houses were to meet at the same hour each subsequent day until such action had been taken. In case of resignation, withdrawal, or refusal to qualify of a minority of either house, such action would not affect the passage of the amendment. The governor was to forward certified copies of the action of each house to the President of the United States. This bill, like any other proposed regulation of the action of the state legislature, would seem to have no warrant in the terms of Article Five, but, failing of passage, no issue was raised.

that the state constitution could prescribe an excessive majority for its adoption. Article Five is silent as to the majority of votes required in the state legislatures, so that it is not clear what majority is necessary and whether Congress or the states could determine what the majority shall be. Perhaps a simple majority of a quorum of each house is sufficient.[87] The two houses of the legislature will probably each vote separately on the amendment. A state may permit the vote of the lieutenant governor to count in favor of ratification when the senate would otherwise be equally divided.[88] The approval of the governor appears to be superfluous. In fact, even amendments to the state constitutions have only in exceptional instances required the signature of that official.[89]

[87] Leser v. Board of Registry, (1921) 139 Md. 46, 114 A. 840. When the Fifteenth Amendment was proposed, the Indiana constitution required a quorum of two-thirds of the legislature to transact business. The speaker of the House of Representatives ruled, however, that a majority of the total membership could act on the amendment. INDIANA HOUSE JOURNAL (1869) 602. See MATHEWS, LEGISLATIVE AND JUDICIAL HISTORY OF THE FIFTEENTH AMENDMENT (1909) 63. Dodd, "Amending the Federal Constitution," (1921) 30 YALE L. J. 321 at 344, is of the view that the state may determine the quorum.

[88] Coleman v. Miller, (1937) 146 Kan. 390, 71 P. (2d) 518; (1938) 18 BOST. U. L. REV. 169 at 173. The United States Supreme Court, being equally divided as to whether or not this was a political question, left the decision of the lower court undisturbed. Coleman v. Miller, (1939) 307 U. S. 433, 59 S. Ct. 972.

[89] In re Senate File No. 31, (1889) 25 Neb. 864, 41 N. W. 981; State ex rel. Morris v. Mason, (1891) 43 La. Ann. 590, 9 So. 776; State v. Dahl, (1896) 6 N. D. 81, 58 N. W. 418; Commonwealth ex. rel. Attorney General v. Griest, (1900) 196 Pa. St. 396, 46 A. 505; Warfield v. Vandiver, (1908) 101 Md. 78, 60 A. 538; Murphy Chair Co. v. Attorney General, (1907) 148 Mich. 563, 112 N. W. 127; State v. American Sugar Refining Co., (1915) 137 La. 407, 68 So. 742; People ex rel. v. Ramer, (1916) 62 Colo. 128, 160 P. 1032; Mitchell v. Hopper, (1922) 153 Ark. 515, 241 S. W. 10; (1931) 45 HARV. L. REV. 355. Fullerton, J., dissenting in State ex rel. Mullen v. Howell, (1919) 107 Wash. 167, 181 P. 920, asserts that the governor must sign a federal amendment when the constitution provides that legislative measures are subject to the approval of the governor. In Hatch v. Stoneman, (1885) 66 Cal. 634, 6 P. 734, and Clements v. Hall, (1921) 23 Ariz. 2, 201 P. 87, it is asserted that the governor must approve the submission as distinguished from the proposal. But in the case of a federal amendment the legislature ratifies and does not submit an amendment, so that such a distinction, at best a doubtful one, cannot be made. The governor of New Hampshire vetoed the Twelfth Amendment, but enough states ratified to make the state's ratification unnecessary. The governor of Arkansas vetoed the Sixteenth Amendment, yet the act of the state legislature

Other questions of procedure also arise. Under the rules of some states, measures passed are open to reconsideration within a prescribed period.[90] But where a federal amendment has passed, whether the vote of adoption is irrevocable is seemingly a "political question."[91] Question may also arise as to the form of ratification. In most states it has been by joint resolution, as in the case of its proposal by Congress, but there seems to be no objection to employing the form of a bill.[92]

was transmitted to the Secretary of State and Arkansas was counted as a ratifying state. When the Kentucky legislature rejected the Thirteenth Amendment the state governor refused to sign the resolution, as he regarded his approval as unnecessary. On the other hand, a state may require signature of the governor to a bill regulating the election of representatives in Congress. Smiley v. Holm, (1931) 285 U. S. 355, 52 S. Ct. 397.

[90] At the time the Nineteenth Amendment was submitted, under the rule of the Tennessee House of Representatives a member voting for a resolution might change his vote and move to reconsider. This suspends the passage of the measure for two parliamentary days or until a new vote is taken. A move to reconsider the Nineteenth Amendment was immediately made in the house after the legislature had accepted it, but the governor had sent in the ratification, although on reconsideration the house rejected it.

In West Virginia the rules of the senate provided that after a measure is defeated and a motion to reconsider is lost, it cannot be reconsidered at that session. Although the senate had first rejected the amendment, it proceeded to ratify it despite the rule, and the ratification was sent in. But in Leser v. Board of Registry, (1921) 139 Md. 46, 114 A. 840, the court asserted that this resolution, although identical in language to the former one, came from the other house and hence was a different measure. In this case on appeal the Supreme Court held that the violations of legislative procedure in the two states were immaterial since two other states had later ratified and that official notice to the secretary of state, "duly authenticated," from the state legislatures was conclusive on the secretary of state, and being certified to by his proclamation is conclusive on the courts. Leser v. Garnett, (1922) 258 U. S. 130, 42 S. Ct. 217. The meaning of "duly authenticated" is not clear, since in many states there is no official who has the power to make a certificate of any action by the legislature which shall be conclusive on the courts. It perhaps means that the enrolled bill rule is to be applied to the action of the legislatures on amendments.

[91] Coleman v. Miller, (1939) 307 U. S. 433, 59 S. Ct. 972. The converse was there involved: Is a vote of rejection irrevocable? See (1939) 13 So. Cal. L. Rev. 122 at 124.

[92] There is a dictum in State ex rel. Mullen v. Howell, (1919) 107 Wash. 167, 181 P. 920, that the legislature may act by joint resolution, though the state constitution makes no provision therefor. Parker, J., dissenting on another point, says, 107 Wash. at 192, that the act of ratification would "be in substance identical in character, whether done by the legislature by a vote upon an informal motion, by a formal resolution, or by a formal bill as in the enactment

It would seem improper to attach conditions or reservations to the ratification. Article Five makes no provision for them, so that it appears that the legislature must accept or reject unconditionally. When the Constitution was ratified, serious attempts were made to impose conditions, but it was objected by such leaders as Hamilton and Madison that this would be equivalent to rejection, and as a result each state accepted the Constitution with no reservations, the obligation to adopt the Bill of Rights being wholly moral.[93]

The development of the initiative and referendum has resulted in attempts in some of the states to refer federal amendments to a popular vote.[94] The referendum laws have generally been couched in broad terms providing for a vote on all measures approved by the legislature. The Ohio constitution expressly provided for a referendum on federal amendments, so that the issue was squarely raised. Where there was merely a general referendum law, the courts sometimes avoided the question by deciding that a federal amendment was not a measure of the kind to be referred.[95] The Ohio

of ordinary state laws." Fullerton, J., in a dissenting opinion, asserts that a joint resolution is improper, and that an amendment must be passed in the manner provided for enacting laws under the state constitution.

[93] 1 HAMILTON, WORKS, Lodge ed. (1885) 463, 465; 1 BURGESS, POLITICAL SCIENCE AND COMPARATIVE CONSTITUTIONAL LAW (1891) 149; JAMESON, CONSTITUTIONAL CONVENTIONS, 4th ed. (1887) 629.

[94] In a recent case a state court held that a proposed initiative measure for a popular vote in the state on the question whether its congressmen should be requested to support an amendment repealing the Eighteenth Amendment was invalid on the ground that Article Five gives the people no direct voice in the amending process. Opinion of the Justices, (1928) 262 Mass. 603, 160 N. E. 439. There is a dictum in Ex parte Dillon, (1920) 262 F. 563, that Congress also could not permit a referendum.

[95] Whittemore v. Terral, (1919) 140 Ark. 493, 215 S. W. 686; In re Opinion of the Justices, (1919) 118 Me. 544, 107 A. 673; Herbring v. Brown, (1919) 92 Ore. 176, 180 P. 328; Prior v. Noland, (1920) 68 Colo. 263, 188 P. 729; Carson v. Sullivan, (1920) 284 Mo. 353, 223 S. W. 571; State v. Morris, (1920) 79 Okla. 89, 191 P. 364. Contra: State ex rel. Mullen v. Howell, (1919) 107 Wash. 167, 181 P. 920. See also Barlotti v. Lyons, (1920) 182 Cal. 575, 189 P. 282; Decher v. Vaughan, (1920) 209 Mich. 565, 177 N. W. 388.

Supreme Court held that a federal amendment was subject to referendum, but the matter was finally put at rest on appeal when the Supreme Court of the United States held the referendum unconstitutional.[96] When the framers of the Constitution provided for ratification by the state legislatures, they meant formal representative bodies who could not delegate these powers. Hence even though a state constitution gives the people a right to legislate, they are not to be regarded as the legislature for the purpose of ratifying a federal amendment.[97] Thus it appears definitely settled that the states have no authority to permit the people to participate directly in the amending process, but may perhaps call for an advisory vote before the legislature finally acts.[98] However, the legislature would have power to ratify either before or after such a vote, and the popular vote would have no binding force. A

Professor Noel T. Dowling believes that in the light of the recent cases of Coleman v. Miller, (1939) 307 U. S. 433, 59 S. Ct. 972, and Chandler v. Wise, (1939) 307 U. S. 474, 59 S. Ct. 992, Congress could provide that all amendments be submitted to state conventions, the delegates to be elected by popular vote and to be bound by a popular referendum on the amendment. Dowling, "Clarifying the Amending Process," (1940) 1 WASH. & LEE L. REV. 215 at 222.

[98] Hawke v. Smith, (1920) 253 U. S. 221, 40 S. Ct. 495; National Prohibition Cases, (1920) 253 U. S. 350, 40 S. Ct. 486, 588. Other cases taking the same view are: Ex parte Dillon, (D. C. Cal. 1920) 262 F. 563; Feigenspan v. Bodine, (D. C. N. J. 1920) 264 F. 186, and Barlotti v. Lyons, Decher v. Vaughan, semble Prior v. Noland (one judge dissenting), Re Opinion of the Justices, Carson v. Sullivan and State v. Morris, all cited supra, note 95. *Contra:* Hawke v. Smith, (1919) 100 Ohio St. 385, 126 N. E. 400, one judge dissenting; State ex rel. Mullen v. Howell, supra, note 95, four judges dissenting.

[97] The Supreme Court distinguished this case from Davis v. Hildebrant, (1916) 241 U. S. 565, 36 S. Ct. 708, which gave a broader meaning to the word "legislature" as used in Article I, sec. 4. In that case Congress had itself recognized the referendum as part of the legislative authority for the purpose of elections. The latter article allowed the state to legislate within the limitations therein named, but in the ratification of an amendment no legislation is required, and only an expression of assent is desired.

[98] The legislature may call for an advisory vote before finally acting. Parker, J., dissenting in State ex rel. Mullen v. Howell, (1919) 107 Wash. 167, 181 P. 920. But see note 94, supra. A referendum on the subject of repeal of the Eighteenth Amendment, the vote being advisory, is valid. Spriggs v. Clark, (1932) 45 Wyo. 63, 14 P. (2d) 667, noted (1933) 18 CORN. L. Q. 278, (1933) 1 GEO. WASH. L. REV. 271, (1933) 10 N. Y. U. L. Q. REV. 395.

ratification by the legislature would be valid despite rejection by a popular referendum. Ratification by a popular referendum, unaccompanied by legislative ratification, would have no legal effect.

A problem which has several times come up in practice is whether a legislature may change its action with respect to an amendment. One view with respect to ratification by state legislatures is that the first action by the legislature of a given state is conclusive and binds future legislatures, even though the first action was that of rejection. This view, which has received but small support, was taken in *Wise v. Chandler*[99] by the highest state court of Kentucky. It was argued that a convention ratifying a federal amendment could not change its action; hence rejection by a convention would be final; and that a state legislature had no greater power than a convention. It should be noted that treating both acceptance and rejection as conclusive is logically consistent and insures protection of minority rights.[100]

The Supreme Court of Kansas disagreed with the Kentucky court and held an original vote of rejection not conclusive, though stating an original vote of ratification would be conclusive.[101] The Kansas view is supported by Congressional practice as to the Thirteenth and Fourteenth Amendments,[102] and by the legal theory that the Constitution creates

[99] (1937) 270 Ky. 1, 108 S. W. (2d) 1024, noted or discussed (1938) 18 Bost. U. L. Rev. 169; (1937) 37 Col. L. Rev. 1201; (1937) 26 Geo L. J. 107 at 118; (1938) 6 Geo. Wash. L. Rev. 218; (1938) 26 Ky. L. J. 364; (1938) 22 Minn. L. Rev. 269; (1938) 17 Neb. L. Bull. 81; (1938) 11 So. Cal. L. Rev. 472; (1937) 24 Va. L. Rev. 194; (1937) 23 Wash. U. L. Q. 129; (1937) 47 Yale L. J. 148; Dowling, "Clarifying the Amending Process," (1940) 1 Wash. & Lee L. Rev. 215.

The same view was also taken by Cadwalader, "Amendment of the Federal Constitution," (1926) 60 Am. L. Rev. 389 at 393; Grinnell, "A 'Point of Order' on the Child Control Amendment," (1934) 20 A. B. A. J. 448, reprinted in (1934) 19 Mass. L. Q. No. 5, p. 22.

[100] (1938) 11 So. Cal. L. Rev. 472.

[101] Coleman v. Miller, (1937) 146 Kan. 390, 71 P. (2d) 518.

[102] (1938) 11 So. Cal. L. Rev. 472.

only a power to ratify and not a power to reject.[103] It is also supported on the ground of public policy in that less delay results and that it is less confusing than counting subsequent reversals.[104] To allow a rejection to be final is to make the amending process less deliberate. There might also be some difficulty as to the meaning of rejection, as for instance, is rejection by one house of the state legislature a rejection? However, this difficulty might be readily resolved by adopting the view that only an affirmative vote of rejection by both houses of the legislature is binding.

In declaring the adoption of the Fourteenth Amendment, Congress counted two states which had first rejected and then ratified. The Kentucky court sought to explain this by saying that the rejections should not count as rejections because they were by illegal governments.[105] But it by no means follows that an illegal government may not perform some valid acts, such as ratification of a federal amendment.[106] The Supreme Court has stated in a leading case:[107] "acts necessary to peace and good order among citizens . . . which would be valid if emanating from a lawful government, must be regarded in general as valid when proceeding from an actual, though unlawful government. . . ." Action on a constitutional amendment may be included within such acts.

A third possible view is that a state should be able to reject, despite prior ratification, before three-fourths of the

[103] Dodd, "Amending the Federal Constitution," (1921) 30 YALE L. J. 322; (1940) 24 MINN. L. REV. 393 at 395–396. In opposition it was argued to the Kentucky court that Van Devanter, J., had stated in Rhode Island v. Palmer (National Prohibition Cases), (1920) 253 U. S. 350 at 386, 40 S. Ct. 486, 588: "The referendum provisions of state constitutions and states cannot be applied, consistently with the Constitution of the United States, in the ratification or rejection of amendments to it." See also the view of Senator Garrett Davis, CONG. GLOBE, 41st Cong., 2d sess. (1870) 1479–1480.

[104] (1938) 11 SO. CAL. L. REV. 472.

[105] This distinction is approved in (1937) 24 VA. L. REV. 194.

[106] See (1937) 37 COL. L. REV. 1201 at 1203, note 21; (1938) 22 MINN. L. REV. 269.

[107] Texas v. White, (1868) 7 Wall. (74 U. S.) 700 at 733.

states had ratified.[108] Of course, such subsequent rejection could not come after three-fourths of the states had ratified. Under this view, both the Kentucky and the Kansas courts were in error as to the effect of prior ratification. Ratification should not be more final than rejection. Ratification by less than three-fourths of the states is ineffectual. Such is the theoretical approach. But there are even stronger practical arguments. It is more democratic to allow the reversal of prior action. A truer picture of public opinion at the final date of ratification is obtained. No great confusion is likely to result from such a rule.[109] Not to allow reversal of an acceptance may cause a cautious legislature not to act.[110]

It would seem to follow from the recent decision of the Supreme Court that the fact of rejection by more than one-fourth of the states does not bar ultimate ratification of an amendment if Congress deems the amendment still open for ratification. The view that rejection by more than a fourth of the states destroyed an amendment has been taken by the Kentucky Court.[111] The Kansas Court took the opposite view.[112] Since rejection by a single state was not conclusive, it logically followed that rejection by a group of states carried no greater weight. Thus the fact that twenty-one states had rejected the child labor amendment and notified the secre-

---

[108] Miller, "Amendment of the Federal Constitution," (1926) 10 MINN. L. REV. 185 at 188; (1938) 18 BOST. U. L. REV. 169; (1938) 22 MINN. L. REV. 269; (1938) 17 NEB. L. BULL. 81; (1937) 23 WASH. U. L. Q. 129; NICHOLAS MURRAY BUTLER, HEARINGS ON S. J. RES. 134, 75th Cong., 3d sess. (1938) 41–42; ROTTSCHAEFER, CONSTITUTIONAL LAW (1939) 395. The solicitor general in his brief in Coleman v. Miller at p. 26 admitted that ratification should be rescindable.

[109] (1938) 18 BOST. U. L. REV. 169.

[110] (1938) 11 SO. CAL. L. REV. 472.

[111] Wise v. Chandler, (1937) 270 Ky. 1, 108 S. W. (2d) 1024. It had earlier been claimed that rejection by more than one-fourth of the states would defeat the proposal until it was resubmitted to the states by Congress. Statement by Special Committee of the American Bar Association, "The Federal Child Labor Amendment," (1935) 21 A. B. A. J. 11 at 12; Grinnell, "A 'Point of Order' on the Child Control Amendment," (1934) 20 A. B. A. J. 448.

[112] Coleman v. Miller, (1937) 146 Kan. 490, 71 P. (2d) 518.

tary of state and four states had rejected without such notice did not destroy the amendment. That the present Article Five does not allow rejection by one-fourth of the states plus one to defeat the amendment permanently was to some extent indicated by the Wadsworth-Garrett Joint Resolution in 1926 proposing an amendment which would expressly permit one-fourth of the states plus one to kill the amendment. In the case of the Fourteenth Amendment ten states out of thirty-seven, or more than one-fourth, had rejected, yet Congress treated it as ratified.[113] Thus the prevailing view seems to be that a rejection is not final,[114] but there has as yet been no test of the finality of a ratification.

The Civil War created some new problems as to the amending process. The Fourteenth Amendment was proposed by Congress at a time when only twenty-five out of thirty-six states were represented in that body. Can Congress coerce the states into ratifying an amendment? The action of Congress in conditioning the readmission of some of the Southern States to representation in Congress on the acceptance of the Civil War Amendments was morally, if not legally, in the nature of coercion.[115] In normal times of peace such a method of

[113] FLACK, THE ADOPTION OF THE FOURTEENTH AMENDMENT (1908) c. 4.

[114] See discussion in (1940) 24 MINN. L. REV. 393 at 395. Professor Noel T. Dowling believes that much can be said for making it final. Dowling, "Clarifying the Amending Process," (1940) 1 WASH. & LEE L. REV. 215 at 222.

[115] Virginia, Mississippi, and Texas were required to ratify the Fifteenth Amendment as a condition precedent to readmission. Mathews says: "Since they ratified under duress, some question might be raised as to the validity of their ratifications." MATHEWS, LEGISLATIVE AND JUDICIAL HISTORY OF THE FIFTEENTH AMENDMENT (1909) 75. See also, VON HOLST, CONSTITUTIONAL LAW OF THE UNITED STATES, Mason translation (1887) 31, note; 2 CURTIS, CONSTITUTIONAL HISTORY OF THE UNITED STATES (1896) 161; 1 WILLOUGHBY, CONSTITUTIONAL LAW, 2d ed. (1929) 594.

"For some strange reason no one raised the contention that the Fourteenth Amendment was itself unconstitutional. Legislatures of Southern states under military government were chosen under regulations not of the state's own choosing, and their coerced ratification of the Amendment was deemed sufficient, although the states were not sufficiently restored to the Union to have representation in Congress." Powell, "Changing Constitutional Phases," (1939) 19 BOST. U. L. REV. 509 at 511.

amendment would doubtless be discredited. The Supreme Court has intimated in a dictum that the validity of the Civil War Amendments is a political question which may not be inquired into.[116] In case of a rebellion the question may also arise as to what is meant by three-fourths of the state legislatures. Does it mean simply three-fourths of the loyal states, or does it mean three-fourths of the whole number?[117] Since the Supreme Court has held that a state cannot take itself out of the Union, it would seem to mean three-fourths of the whole number.[118] This question might also arise when a new state has been admitted after the date of proposal. Logically it would seem that three-fourths of the number, including the new state, would be necessary. In the case of the Eleventh Amendment Secretary of State Pickering was doubtful, on account of the admission of Tennessee, whether three-fourths had ratified, but discovered that the required majority had done so before Tennessee was admitted.

The most recent of the Supreme Court decisions concern themselves with the question of the time limits for the ratifica-

[116] White v. Hart, (1871) 13 Wall. (80 U. S.) 646. But in Feigenspan v. Bodine, (D. C. N. J. 1920) 264 F. 186, it is asserted that the Thirteenth Amendment was not the "decision of war." In Leser v. Garnett, (1922) 258 U. S. 130, 42 S. Ct. 217, it is denied that the Fifteenth Amendment was illegally adopted.

[117] von Holst believes that "it must be recognized as an anomaly that states which were actually at the time neither full members of the Union, nor entitled to equal rights under it, voted upon an amendment to the constitution." VON HOLST, CONSTITUTIONAL LAW OF THE UNITED STATES, Mason translation (1887) 31, note. The Fourteenth Amendment was ratified by six de facto legislatures. Seward in his first proclamation of ratification, July 20, 1868, referred to these legislatures as "newly constituted and newly established bodies avowing themselves to be and acting as the legislatures, respectively" of the states. 15 Stat. L. 706 at 707; 1 WILLOUGHBY, CONSTITUTIONAL LAW, 2d ed. (1929) 594.

[118] This is the view in Calhoun v. Calhoun, (1870) 2 S. C. 283. The view of Burgess that the three-fourths majority should have been computed on the basis of the loyal states, and the Southern states then readmitted as "states" under the Constitution with the Fourteenth Amendment already a part of it, seems out of harmony with the theory of the Supreme Court. BURGESS, RECONSTRUCTION AND THE CONSTITUTION, 1866–1876 (1902) 202–206.

tion of amendments. Five amendments proposed by Congress never have been ratified by the states. Article Five makes no provision as to time. In 1789 with the first ten amendments, today known as the Bill of Rights, there was submitted one dealing with the compensation of members of Congress. In 1873 after Congress had passed the "salary grab act," the Ohio Senate passed a resolution purporting to ratify this amendment.[119] But as no other states ratified, the validity of this belated attempt was not litigated. The question was first litigated as to the ratification of the Eighteenth Amendment. In *Dillon v. Gloss*[120] the court held that Congress could prescribe a reasonable period and that a seven-year maximum period was not unreasonable. The argument of the court was that proposal and ratification are steps in a single process; that since amendments may be proposed only when deemed necessary, they must be presently disposed of; and that since ratification is but the expression of the people's assent, it must be sufficiently contemporaneous in all states to reflect the will of the people in all sections at relatively the same time. The limited character of the holding should be noted. There were four very old unratified amendments. The court did not assume to define a reasonable period. It held that Congress could fix a definite period for ratification under its power to designate the mode of ratification; but it could fix only a reasonable period. Seven years was a reasonable period. The court did not say that a period somewhat longer than seven years fixed by Congress would be unreasonable; nor did it lay down any rule as to the situation where Congress had fixed no period. Thus even though the child labor amendment remained unratified after fifteen years it was not clear before the recent decisions whether too long a period had expired.

[119] Ohio Laws (1873) 409.

[120] (1921) 256 U. S. 368, 41 S. Ct. 510.

The dictum in *Dillon v. Gloss* that the states should ratify during an interval when sentiment for the amendment really existed was not conclusive, since on one side there was the recent revival of interest while on the other side there was no interest during the years from 1927 to 1933.[121]

The child labor amendment was thought by the Kentucky Court,[122] and by a number of commentators,[123] to have been extinct because of the long period of failure to ratify by three-fourths of the states. The Supreme Court concluded, however, that a political question was involved, hence the matter was left in the hands of Congress.[124] Under the earlier rule Congress could prescribe a reasonable period when the amendment was proposed. Under the new rule Congress could prescribe such period at any later time.

Finally it remains to be inquired what it is that marks the conclusive adoption of an amendment. The secretary of state by statute is required to issue a proclamation of the ratification.[125] It might therefore be supposed that it is his act that completes the adoption. It has been held, however, that his action is unnecessary in this respect, and that it is the approval

---

[121] (1937) 47 YALE L. J. 148. ROTTSCHAEFER, CONSTITUTIONAL LAW (1939) 393, note 17, puts this question: "Quere as to the effect upon this issue of the fact that there was an intervening period during which the proposal had no relation to the then prevailing sentiments and felt needs, where the total period between the submission and purported ratification would be unreasonably long by any ordinary standard?"

[122] Wise v. Chandler, (1937) 270 Ky. 1, 108 S. W. (2d) 1024. *Contra:* Coleman v. Miller, (1937) 146 Kan. 390, 71 P. (2d) 518.

[123] Mitchell, "Methods of Amending the Constitution," (1932) 25 LAWY. & BANKER 265 at 267; (1938) 18 BOST. U. L. REV. 169 at 185.

[124] Coleman v. Miller, (1939) 307 U. S. 433, 59 S. Ct. 972; (1940) 13 So. CAL. L. REV. 122 at 124; (1940) 24 MINN. L. REV. 393.

[125] Rev. Stat. § 205; 8 U. S. C (1934) § 160: "Amendments to Constitution. Whenever official notice is received at the Department of State that any amendment proposed to the Constitution of the United States has been adopted, according to the provisions of the Constitution, the Secretary of State shall forthwith cause the amendment to be published, with his certificate, specifying the States by which the same may have been adopted, and that the same has become valid, to all intents and purposes, as a part of the Constitution of the United States."

by the last state to make up the three-fourths majority that makes the amendment law.[126] Article Five makes no mention of the secretary of state, and his proclamation is based purely on an act of Congress. When the state legislatures have completed their ratification, a certificate thereof is transmitted to the secretary of state. Suppose it be alleged that a state legislature has not actually ratified. Could the courts go back of the certificate of ratification and inquire into the legislative proceedings? Or would they be bound by the certificate? It appears that the certificate would be regarded as conclusive.[127] The same question might arise as to whether Congress had in fact proposed an amendment. The Supreme Court has held on at least two occasions that it will accept the enrolled bill as

[126] Fairchild v. Hughes, (1922) 258 U. S. 126, 42 S. Ct. 274; Dillon v. Gloss, (1921) 256 U. S. 368, 41 S. Ct. 510, aff'g Ex parte Dillon, (D. C. Cal. 1920) 262 F. 563; United States ex rel. Widenman v. Colby, (App. D. C. 1920) 265 F. 998, aff'd (1921) 257 U. S. 619, 42 S. Ct. 169. In Ex parte Dillon the court said (p. 565): "Congress might perhaps provide that the Department of State should ascertain and determine the fact of ratification, and that an amendment should not take effect until due promulgation of that determination by proclamation or otherwise; but Congress has not so provided." The constitutional rule laid down in the amendment may become operative at a later date specified in the amendment. This was the case as to the Eighteenth Amendment.

The dictum in Coleman v. Miller, (1939) 307 U. S. 433 at 451, 454, 456, 59 S. Ct. 972, that Congress can implement its decision on political phases of the amending power through its control of the action of the Secretary of State when, in the presence of certified ratifications by three-fourths of the states, the time arrives for promulgation of the adoption of an amendment, appear inconsistent with the earlier view that the date of consummation rather than of promulgation is determinative. (1940) 24 MINN. L. REV. 393 at 401. Professor Noel T. Dowling also suggests that the earlier cases have been overruled. Dowling, "Clarifying the Amending Process," (1940) 1 WASH. & LEE L. REV. 215 at 220.

[127] Leser v. Garnett, (1922) 258 U. S. 130, 42 S. Ct. 217; Chandler v. Wise, (1939) 307 U. S. 474, 59 S. Ct. 992. In Dillon v. Gloss, (1921) 256 U. S. 368, 41 S. Ct. 510, the court took judicial notice of the fact of ratification by three-fourths of the state legislatures. For a good discussion of judicial notice with reference to amendments, see Gottstein v. Lister, (1915) 88 Wash. 462, 153 P. 595. ROTTSCHAEFER, CONSTITUTIONAL LAW (1939) 399, states: "It should be noted that the conclusive effect of the official notice to, and the certification thereof by, the Secretary is based on certain assumptions. How far a court would reach its own independent conclusions on the matters thus assumed cannot be definitely stated." See also Quarles, "Amendments to the Federal Constitution," (1940) 26 A. B. A. J. 617 at 618.

final as to the passage of a statute, and will not examine the legislative journals.[128] The state courts are divided, but the recent tendency has been to adopt the enrolled bill rule.[129]

D.   VALIDATION OF AMENDMENTS THROUGH ACQUIESCENCE

The discussion up to this point has described the procedural requirements for the validity of an amendment. Suppose, however, that a federal amendment has been proclaimed as a part of the Constitution after the apparent ratification by three-fourths of the states and that it has been long regarded as a part of the Constitution. Would it later be open to attack on the ground that there had been some defect in the procedure, or that the amendment was void in substance? Concretely, would the first fifteen amendments, which date back a half a century and more, be subject to being declared null and void by the courts?

In considering the application of the doctrine of acquiescence, it is well to bear in mind that the validity of the original Constitution itself cannot be assailed. This is a political question, so that perhaps the doctrine of acquiescence may be regarded as unnecessary, or as only an added proof of its validity. The validity of an amendment, however is only in part a political question, so that the applicability of the doctrine of acquiescence is likely to be asserted by those who would oppose any attack on amendments long regarded as a part of the Constitution.[130] It should be noted, however, that

[128] Field v. Clark, (1891) 143 U. S. 649, 12 S. Ct. 495; Harwood v. Wentworth, (1896) 162 U. S. 547, 16 S. Ct. 890. Both are cited as controlling in Leser v. Garnett, supra, note 127.

[129] Boyd v. Olcott, (1921) 102 Ore. 327, 202 P. 431. The Montana court took the peculiar view that while an enrolled statute was conclusive, the legislative journals would be resorted to in the case of an amendment. Tax Commission Case, (1923) 68 Mont. 450, 219 P. 817.

[130] Curtis is of the view that although the Thirteenth and Fourteenth Amendments were adopted through compulsion, they have become valid partly through acquiescence. 2 CURTIS, CONSTITUTIONAL HISTORY (1896) 161; see Marbury,

whether the doctrine of the political question or that of acquiescence be applied, the result arrived at amounts to much the
same thing.

Several factors lead to the conclusion that amendments
may not become valid through acquiescence. In the first place,
of the first seventeen amendments only the validity of the
Eleventh has been adjudicated in the courts. It may be alleged that such want of adjudication is an argument to the
effect that any test of their legality is now impossible. In reply
it should be pointed out that the courts have simply assumed
their validity, since the parties have failed to raise the issue.
The Supreme Court has several times stated that it decides
only the points before it.[131] The fact, therefore, that it had
held laws passed under various amendments valid would not
preclude it from inquiring into their validity when the issue
is squarely raised. If, then, some party should expressly argue
that an amendment, either old or recent, is invalid, the courts
would in all probability pass on the matter.[132] The federal
Supreme Court and other courts passing on the validity of
federal amendments have given but little comfort to the
protagonists of the doctrine.[133] However, the doctrine of the

"The Limitations upon the Amending Power," (1919) 33 HARV. L. REV. 223
at 232. See also Platz, "Article Five of the Federal Constitution," (1934) 3
GEO. WASH. L. REV. 17 at 31; (1937) 37 COL. L. REV. 1201; Yawitz, "The
Legal Effect under American Decisions of an Alleged Irregularity in the
Adoption of a Constitution or Constitutional Amendment," (1925) 10 ST.
LOUIS L. REV. 279 at 283; Dodd, "Judicially Non-Enforcible Provisions of
Constitutions," (1931) 80 U. PA. L. REV. 54 at 73; Willis, "The Doctrine of
the Amendability of the United States Constitution, (1932) 7 IND. L. J. 457
at 468; (1929) 23 AM. POL. SCI. REV. 920.

[131] Boyd v. Alabama, (1877) 94 U. S. 645 at 648.

[132] Knight v. Shelton, (C. C. Ark. 1905) 134 F. 423 at 433–437; Machen,
"Is the Fifteenth Amendment Void?" (1910) 23 HARV. L. REV. 169 at 187–
190; Morris, "The Fifteenth Amendment to the Federal Constitution," (1909)
189 No. AM. REV. 82. But in Leser v. Board of Registry, (1921) 139 Md. 46,
114 A. 840, it is asserted that it cannot be assumed that the courts, in passing on
cases arising under amendments, decided on the basis of amendments adopted
in violation of the Constitution.

[133] "The suggestion that the Fifteenth [Amendment] was incorporated in
the Constitution, not in accordance with law, but practically as a war measure,
which has been validated by acquiescence, cannot be entertained." Brandeis, J.,

1939 cases as to political questions might ultimately be applied as to acquiescence.

The strongest support for the doctrine of acquiescence comes from the decisions of the state courts concerning the validity of amendments to the state constitutions. Most of the decisions on the precise point appear to favor the doctrine.[134] The whole number of decisions is so small, however, that their weight may be doubted. Moreover, mere unqualified acquiescence is not sufficient. Two or three limitations seem to have been laid down. The acquiescence must have been for a considerable period. All the branches of the government and the people must have acquiesced in the legality of the amendment. Probably the acquiescence of the people would be implied where the government has acquiesced, and perhaps by the government is meant the legislative and executive, and

in Leser v. Garnett, (1922) 258 U. S. 130, 42 S. Ct. 217. See also State of Ohio ex rel. Erchenbrecher v. Cox, (D. C. Ohio, 1919) 257 F. 334; United States ex. rel. Widenman v. Colby, (App. D. C. 1920) 265 F. 998; Leser v. Board of Registry, (1921) 139 Md. 46, 114 A. 840. *Contra:* Smith v. Good, (C. C. R. I. 1888) 34 F. 204; Appellant's Brief in National Prohibition Cases, (1920) 253 U. S. 350, 40 S. Ct. 486, 588.

On the other hand, Professor Thomas Reed Powell, "Changing Constitutional Phases," (1939) 19 BOST. U. L. REV. 509 at 512, states: "There must be a doctrine of prescription for the acquisition of impeccable constitutionality as there is for the acquisition of title to land."

[134] Niblack, J., dissenting on another point, State v. Swift, (1880) 69 Ind. 512; Prohibitory Amendment Cases, (1881) 24 Kan. 700; Secombe v. Kittelson, (1882) 29 Minn. 555, 12 N. W. 519, Mitchell, J., rendering the opinion; State ex rel. Torreyson v. Grey, (1893) 21 Nev. 378, 32 P. 190; Nesbit v. People, (1894) 19 Colo. 411, 36 P. 221; Weston v. Ryan, (1903) 70 Neb. 211, 97 N. W. 347, but, semble, that could attack if not ratified by the constitutional majority of the popular vote; McCulloch, J., dissenting in Rice v. Palmer, (1906) 78 Ark. 432, 96 S. W. 396; State ex rel. Thompson v. Winnett, (1907) 78 Neb. 379, 110 N. W. 1113; Jones v. McClaughry, (1915) 169 Iowa 281, 151 N. W. 210; O'Neill, J., dissenting in State v. American Sugar Refining Co., (1915) 137 La. 407, 68 So. 742; Armstrong v. King, (1924) 281 Pa. St. 207, 126 A. 263, when the popular vote has been taken, but could attack for insufficient popular vote. Semble, State ex rel. Hay v. Alderson, (1914) 49 Mont. 387, 142 P. 210; Marshall, J., in State ex rel. Postel v. Marcus, (1915) 160 Wis. 354 at 376–379, 407; State ex rel. Twichell v. Hall, (1918) 44 N. D. 459, 171 N. W. 213. *Contra:* semble, People ex rel. Elder v. Sours, (1903) 31 Colo. 369, 74 P. 167, one judge dissenting; McBee v. Brady, (1909) 15 Idaho, 761, 100 P. 97, disaffirming Holmberg v. Jones, (1910) 7 Idaho 752, 65 P. 563.

not necessarily the judiciary. In the third place, the amendment must be fundamental in character, and affect the framework of the government.

E. DESUETUDE OF AMENDMENTS

A final question which suggests itself is whether the Constitution may be indirectly altered through the desuetude of an amendment. It may perhaps be accurately stated that the Fifteenth Amendment has never been enforced according to its true spirit.[135] The status of the Eighteenth Amendment has been asserted to be comparable to it. If an amendment remains a dead letter on the books over a long period of years, may it be contended that it is no longer a part of the Constitution? The idea of enforcement seems to be an essential ingredient in the conception of law. In Rome before the Imperial Era, in Germany, Scotland, and South Africa custom may abrogate statute. In France, Spain, and Italy a contrary view prevails.[136] Similarly under the Anglo-American common law a statute remains in force until it is repealed.[137] The

[135] "It [the Fifteenth Amendment] has been despised, flouted, nullified, evaded. Nevertheless, the Supreme Court of the United States, the lawful guardian of the Constitution, has in no single instance held any state or federal statute or the act of any state or federal officer to be in conflict with the Amendment: and no case in that court can be found in which [it] would have decided differently if the Amendment had never existed. . . .

"Confronted by these remarkable circumstances, the student of constitutional law not unnaturally asks himself: 'Can it be that an enactment which has thus borne the slings and arrows of outrageous fortune for nearly forty years and yet during that time has never affected the result in a single case in the court of the last resort—can it be that such an enactment is indeed part of the fundamental law of the United States?'" This question was raised by Machen, "Is the Fifteenth Amendment Void?" (1910) 23 HARV. L. REV. 169. Since this article the Supreme Court in two cases has held state legislation void as contrary to the amendment. Guinn v. United States, (1915) 238 U. S. 347, 35 S. Ct. 926; Myers v. Anderson, (1915) 238 U. S. 368, 35 S. Ct. 932.

[136] POUND, READINGS IN ROMAN LAW, 2d ed. (1915), Part I, § 2, "Forms," pp. 5–14.

[137] GRAY, THE NATURE AND SOURCES OF THE LAW (1909) § 419 and Appendixes VII and IX.

Constitution of the United States is of course superior to the common law and to statutes. Since statutes do not lose their validity through nonenforcement, it would seem a fortiori that an amendment of the Constitution would not. When an amendment has once become a part of the Constitution, it remains a part until repealed by a later amendment.

CHAPTER IV

The Scope of the Federal Amending Power

ONE of the most recent problems which has arisen with respect to the process of amending the federal Constitution and, next to justiciability, the most important, is the scope of the power to amend.[1] The early case of *Hollingsworth v. Virginia*[2] simply went to the question of procedure. The Supreme Court never considered the matter in its opinions until the validity of the Eighteenth Amendment was assailed, among other grounds, for defects in substance.[3] The briefs in the cases on the Eighteenth and Nineteenth Amendments contained extensive discussions on the subject, and the court rendered decisions disposing of the question. The contention of the opponents of the amendments was that there are certain implied limitations on the power to amend. Before analysis of this contention, it seems proper first to deal with the express limitations, if any, on the power.

A. EXPRESS LIMITATIONS

Article Five contains three express restrictions, two of which have now expired by their own terms. One states "that no Amendment which may be made prior to the year one thousand eight hundred and eight shall in any manner affect the first and fourth clauses in the ninth section of the first article." The former clause provides: "The Migration or Importation of such Persons as any of the States now existing shall think

[1] In 1899 George T. Curtis wrote: "One of the most important subjects that can engage the attention of the statesmen and people of this country is the extent and scope of the power to amend the Constitution of the United States." 2 CURTIS, CONSTITUTIONAL HISTORY (1896) 152.

[2] (1798) 3 Dall. (3 U. S.) 378.

[3] National Prohibition Cases, (1920) 253 U. S. 350, 40 S. Ct. 486, 588.

proper to admit, shall not be prohibited by the Congress prior to the Year one thousand eight hundred and eight, but a Tax or Duty may be imposed on such Importation, not exceeding ten dollars for each Person." The latter provides: "No Capitation, or other direct Tax shall be laid, unless in Proportion to the Census of Enumeration herein before directed to be taken." After 1808 these clauses of course became obsolete as limitations on the power to amend.[4] During the two decades they were in force, however, it seems that there was no constitutional authority reposed in any body whatsoever to change the Constitution contrary to the purport of the clauses, since they are stated as unconditional prohibitions. Even though not only three-fourths of the states, but every one of them, and even though Congress and the then people unanimously desired such changes, it would seem that under the authority and control asserted by the judiciary today over the entire amending process, such changes could have been brought about only by revolution. However, if these limitations had been permanent, perhaps they might have been ignored as making the Constitution unworkable.[5]

At present there is only one express limitation, "that no State, without its Consent, shall be deprived of its equal Suffrage in the Senate." This restriction, it is to be noted, is not absolute, however, inasmuch as if a state consents it may lose its equal suffrage. Thus, this clause is a restriction on the method rather than the scope of amendment. The clause itself

---

[4] The Supreme Court seems to have slipped into error in a dictum in Dodge v. Woolsey, (1855) 18 How. (59 U. S.) 331 at 348, when it refers to the slave trade exception as a "temporary disability to amend, and the other two permanent and unalterable exceptions to the power of amendment." The explanation of this ambiguity seems to be that the slave trade clause in the first clause of section 9 of Article I in itself limits its operation to the year 1808, while the direct tax clause does not. Otherwise the Sixteenth Amendment would be open to attack as void. Strictly speaking, the court is not correct in calling even the equality of the Senate clause unalterable inasmuch as all the states might repeal it. See infra, pp. 84 et seq.; 96 et seq.

[5] ROTTSCHAEFER, CONSTITUTIONAL LAW (1939) 9–10.

could be repealed by an amendment ratified by all the states. Or if every state ratified the amendment, any given state or any number of states could be deprived of their equality. The same result would be reached if the state or states whose representation was reduced, together with enough others to make the necessary three-fourths, adopted such an amendment. On the other hand, if one or more states had their representation *increased*, *all the others* would have to consent since they no longer had equal suffrage. If the states were divided into three groups, the first of which got an increase of two senators, the second of one senator, and the third no increase at all, the second and third groups would have to consent to the increase of the first group. Consent by a state to one reduction in equality would not be consent to a still further reduction. Theoretically, states which got greater representation would not have to consent. It has been suggested that even this express limitation might be disregarded directly, or if not directly, indirectly by first repealing the clause and then depriving a state of its equal representation.[6] Professor Rottschaefer states:

"There has been found no case in which the power to amend has been employed to directly or indirectly modify a constitutional provision expressly excepted from that power. The issues that such an attempt would raise could not be settled by any reasoning derived by logical processes from prevailing conceptions of sovereignty, and those based on considerations of convenience and expediency point to the solution that such attempts to limit the power of amendment should be held

[6] Burgess says that "in dealing with the great questions of public law, we must not, as Mirabeau finely expressed it, lose the *grande morale*, in the *petite morale*." 1 BURGESS, POLITICAL SCIENCE AND COMPARATIVE CONSTITUTIONAL LAW (1891) 154; VON HOLST, THE CONSTITUTIONAL LAW OF THE UNITED STATES (1887) 52, note. See also the suggestion of DODD, THE REVISION AND AMENDMENT OF STATE CONSTITUTIONS (1910) 236; Sandelius, "National Sovereignty versus the Rule of Law," (1931) 25 AM. POL. SCI. REV. 1 at 4. See *contra*: Platz, "Article Five of the Federal Constitution," (1934) 3 GEO. WASH. L. REV. 17 at 26, 40; STIMSON, THE LAW OF THE FEDERAL AND STATE CONSTITUTIONS OF THE UNITED STATES (1908) 357; WOODBURN, AMERICAN POLITICS: THE AMERICAN REPUBLIC AND ITS GOVERNMENT (1903) 209.

futile. The necessities of orderly government do not require that one generation should be permitted to permanently fetter all future generations."[7]

The 1939 decisions of the Supreme Court may ultimately have serious effects on the application of the equality of suffrage in the Senate proviso. The Supreme Court may conclude that this is the type of procedural problem which should be treated as a political question. Or it may decide that this is an issue of substance and a fortiori involves a political question. In either event the proviso would not effectually limit the scope of the federal amending power.

Although there is thus at present only one explicit limitation, attempts have been made at various times to add other express limitations. Comprehensive limitations were proposed at the Constitutional Convention itself, but failed of adoption.[8] Gerry moved to reconsider a proposed draft permitting Congress to call a convention to amend the Constitution on the application of the legislatures of two-thirds of the states. The effect of this provision, he asserted, would make the Constitution paramount to the state constitutions, since a majority of the convention could "bind the Union to innovations that may subvert the state constitutions altogether."[9] Hamilton thought that the latter result was entirely proper. Sherman moved that Congress should be authorized to propose amendments to the states, but that the proposed amendment should not be valid until consented to by all the states. Mr. Wilson favored Sherman's proposal, except that he would allow ratification by two-thirds of the states to be sufficient. On the last day that Article Five was discussed by the convention, Sherman reiterated Gerry's view as to the dangers of an unrestricted power to amend. He favored restricting amending power so "that no state should be affected in its internal police,

[7] CONSTITUTIONAL LAW (1939) 9–10.

[8] See 5 ELLIOT, DEBATES ON THE ADOPTION OF THE FEDERAL CONSTITUTION, (1937 reprint of 1836 2d ed.) 530–532, 551–552.

[9] Ibid. 531.

or deprived of its equality in the Senate."[10] Thus a clear and comprehensive limitation would have been placed on the amending process as relating to interference of any kind with the powers of the states. He again moved to amend Article Five so as to require ratification by all the states. Gerry proposed to limit ratification to the legislature only. Sherman put his proposed limitation in the form of a motion, but Madison objected that if such special provisos were appended every state would demand them for their boundaries, exports, and other matters. After this motion failed, Sherman moved to strike out Article Five altogether. On the motion of Gouverneur Morris the "equal suffrage of the Senate" clause was adopted at the urging of the smaller states. It is significant that the restriction against affecting a state in its internal police proposed together with it by Sherman was not adopted. During the time just preceding the Civil War the Corwin amendment forbidding any amendment abolishing slavery was proposed by Congress, but failed of ratification.[11] While there has since that time been an increasing number of proposals to change the amending process, these have related to the procedure rather than to the nature and substance of amendments.

B. ALLEGED IMPLIED LIMITATIONS

The major controversy as to the scope of the amending power has not been concerned with the meaning of the express limitations, but as to the existence and nature of so-called implied limitations on the power to amend. All sorts of surmises have been offered as to specific things which may not be done.[12] Many of the discussions in legal periodicals have

[10] Ibid. 551.

[11] AMES, THE PROPOSED AMENDMENTS TO THE CONSTITUTION (1897) 286.

[12] Dissolving the federal Union, abolishing the state governments, or lodging all power in Congress, so that it would resemble the British Parliament—Machen, "Is the Fifteenth Amendment Void?" (1910) 23 HARV. L. REV. 169 at 171; repealing the Bill of Rights—JESSUP, THE BILL OF RIGHTS AND ITS

taken the view that there are certain implied limitations, though there has been considerable disagreement as to their underlying bases. The remainder of this chapter will be devoted to an analysis of the *rationale* of these views and a statement and exposition of the arguments in favor of the contrary view that there are no such restrictions whatever on the amending power.

Is there an implied guarantee of continued existence of the states? Perhaps the basic argument advanced in favor of im-

DESTRUCTION BY ALLEGED DUE PROCESS OF LAW (1927); repealing the Ninth and Tenth Amendments—2 CURTIS, CONSTITUTIONAL HISTORY (1896) 160; destroying alleged inalienable rights of personal liberty, or nationalizing women—Abbott, "Inalienable Rights and the Eighteenth Amendment," (1920) 20 COL. L. REV. 183 at 186; departing from the scheme and purpose of the original Constitution—Skinner, "Intrinsic Limitations on the Power of Constitutional Amendment," (1919) 18 MICH. L. REV. 213 at 223; abolition of republican form of government, office of President, the Supreme Court, prohibition of intoxicating liquors, forming several new states within other states, or uniting two existing states, changing Article Five so as to allow ratification by a majority of the state legislatures, or a minority, or none at all—Appellant's Brief in National Prohibition Cases, (1920) 253 U. S. 350, 40 S. Ct. 486, 588; abolition of the Senate or House of Representatives, setting up a hereditary monarchy, abolition of slavery—Representative Pendleton of Ohio, CONG. GLOBE, 38th Cong., 1st sess., pp. 2992–2993; negro suffrage in the states, allowing the Northern states to determine the question of suffrage and not allowing the Southern states to do so—Senator Dixon of Connecticut, CONG. GLOBE, 40th Cong., 3d sess., p. 707; woman suffrage in the states—Appellant's Brief in Leser v. Garnett, (1922) 258 U. S. 130, 42 S. Ct. 217; national income tax—Brown, "The Sixteenth Amendment to the United States Constitution," (1920) 54 AM. L. REV. 843; deprivation of the power of the states to tax—Marbury, "The Limitations upon the Amending Power," (1919) 33 HARV. L. REV. 223 at 226; election of President and the Supreme Court by the people, reenactment of laws by Congress after Supreme Court decision holding them void—Child, "Revolutionary Amendments to the Constitution," (1926) 10 CONST. REV. 27 at 34; national referendum on acts of Congress or on treaties, destruction of Senate's equal legislative power, transfer from the Senate to the House of the power to confirm appointments, make treaties, and try impeachments—Brown, "The Perpetual Covenant in the Constitution," (1924) 219 No. AM. REV. 30 at 33; encroachment on states' police power, prescribing what people wear, eat, or drink—Holding, "Perils to be Apprehended from Amending the Constitution," (1923) 57 AM. L. REV. 481 at 486; the Twelfth Amendment—Senator Tracy of Connecticut, ANNALS OF CONGRESS, 8th Cong., 1st sess. (1803) 163; hereditary monarch, Radin—"The Intermittent Sovereign," (1930) 39 YALE L. J. 514 at 525. For a rather full list, see Bacon, "How the Tenth Amendment Affected the Fifth Article of the Constitution," (1930) 16 VA. L. REV. 771.

plied limitations is the contention that the Constitution guarantees the existence of the states, or, stated less emphatically, that under its aegis the states can not be destroyed, or even deprived of important powers.[13] The inherent sovereignty of the states has been asserted with varying stress ever since the Constitution was adopted. It was the essential doctrine of the Secessionists.[14] Even today it survives in a much mutilated form in the views of those who assert "states' rights." The Civil War seems to have settled by force of arms that secession is unconstitutional. The Supreme Court from earliest times has repeatedly said that the people of the United States are sovereign and that they adopted the Constitution. However much historical strength the view of state sovereignty may have had, the court decisions seem to have been in the opposite direction. It is true that the Court has spoken of an "indestructible Union, composed of indestructible States."[15] But

[13] Marbury's Brief in Myers v. Anderson, (1915) 238 U. S. 368, 35 S. Ct. 932; Brief of Elihu Root, Amicus Curiae, p. 53 ff., National Prohibition Cases, (1920) 253 U. S. 350, 40 S. Ct. 486, 588; Appellant's Brief in Leser v. Garnett, (1922) 258 U. S. 130, 42 S. Ct. 217; Skinner, "Intrinsic Limitations on the Power of Constitutional Amendment," (1920) 18 MICH. L. REV. 213 at 220; Marbury, "The Limitations upon the Amending Power," (1919) 33 HARV. L. REV. 223 at 225; White, "Is there an Eighteenth Amendment?" (1920) 5 CORN. L. Q. 113 at 114. The objection was raised in the Senate and in several of the state legislatures when the Fifteenth Amendment was proposed. CONG. GLOBE, 40th Cong., 3d sess., p. 988 (Hendricks), 995 (Davis), 1639 (Buckalew), Appendix 151 (Doolittle), 158–165 (Saulsbury); MATHEWS, LEGISLATIVE AND JUDICIAL HISTORY OF THE FIFTEENTH AMENDMENT (1909) 57–75.

[14] " . . . if it [an amendment] come fairly within the scope of the amending power, the State is bound to acquiesce, by the solemn obligation which it contracted, in ratifying the constitution. But if it transcends the limits of the amending power,—be inconsistent with the character of the constitution, and the ends for which it was established,—or with the nature of the system,— the result is different. In such case, the State is not bound to acquiesce. It may choose whether it will, or whether it will not secede from the Union." Calhoun, "A Discourse on the Constitution and Government of the United States," WORKS, Cralle ed. (1854) 300. Hayne seems to have taken the same view. 9 DANE, A GENERAL ABRIDGMENT AND DIGEST OF AMERICAN LAW (1829), Appendix 17. See also the arguments in State ex rel. McCready v. Hunt, (1834) 2 Hill L. (S. C.) 1. But see 1 WILLOUGHBY, CONSTITUTIONAL LAW, 2d ed. (1929) 600.

[15] Texas v. White, (1868) 7 Wall. (74 U. S.) 700 at 725; Lane County v. Oregon, (1868) 7 Wall. (74 U. S.) 71.

by this would seem to be meant that such destruction may not be brought about by the simple statutory action of either government, for the court did not mention the amending process.

It may be conceded that perhaps the most fundamental parts of the Constitution are those dividing the powers of sovereignty between the states and the nation. It is undoubtedly true that a substantial redistribution of powers is the most significant change which could be made in our constitutional organization. The Preamble speaks of the Constitution as being ordained and established, among other reasons, "in order to form a more perfect Union." Yet it is remarkable that there is no exception set out in Article Five against amendments which would abolish or greatly diminish the powers of the states. The sole exception is "that no State, without its Consent, shall be deprived of its equal Suffrage in the Senate." This clause merely preserves equality of the states in the Senate, and not the existence of the states themselves. If the preservation of the states were so tremendous a desideratum, it would seem from a logical, if not historical, point of view, that a proviso would have been inserted expressly guaranteeing their continued existence. As a matter of fact, an exception intended effectually to preserve the existence of the states was offered and rejected at the Constitutional Convention. Sherman proposed that "no state shall without its consent, be affected in its internal police." This does not say in so many words that the states may not be abolished, but since the existence of a state is virtually identical with the existence of its police power, the effect was to preserve the states. In fact, Mr. Sherman in making his proposal expressed his fear "that three-fourths of the States might be brought to do things fatal to particular states, as abolishing them altogether. . . ."[16] Since the amending power is placed

---

[16] 5 ELLIOT, DEBATES ON THE ADOPTION OF THE FEDERAL CONSTITUTION (1937 reprint of 1836 2d ed.) 551. See also supra, p. 4 et seq.

in the hands of three-fourths of the states and since they can bind the other one-fourth, it is difficult to see why, if they so choose, they cannot abolish a single state, or a minority of states, or the entire number of states.[17]

To assert that the amending power extends to the destruction of the states is scarcely necessary, however, to meet the arguments generally set forth in favor of implied limitations. Few serious persons propose to abolish the states at present, and there is no popular sentiment desiring such a change. The question is thus largely academic. The proponents of limitations have been prone to assert that every amendment which diminishes the power of the state constitutes an annihilation of the states. In the case of the Nineteenth Amendment, it was argued, for instance, that allowing women to vote in state elections so completely changed the composition of the state as virtually to result in the abolition of the old states and the setting up of new ones. The same criticism has been made of the Fifteenth Amendment. The courts have held, however, that a mere change in the composition of the electorate of the state is not a destruction of the state.[18] A state is not composed simply of the existing electorate, but of the people, territory, and government.[19] A real destruction of a state would seem to consist in abolishing its constitution and the branches of its

[17] "There can be no limitation on the power of the people of the United States. By their authority, the state constitutions were made, and by their authority the Constitution of the United States was established; and they had the power to change or abolish the state constitutions, or to make them yield to the general government, and to treaties made by their authority." Ware v. Hylton, (1796) 3 Dall. (3 U. S.) 198 at 236.

"The people of *all* the States, or the *constitutional* majorities can transfer power from one or more states to the General Government, even against the consent of a *constitutional* minority—as where a state opposes, or even six states oppose eighteen states, and constitutional majorities in Congress, and states can, on the 5th Article, transfer power from the one or six states to the Union, or take back power." 9 DANE, A GENERAL ABRIDGMENT AND DIGEST OF AMERICAN LAW (1829), Appendix 21–22.

[18] "States, like individuals, retain their identity, though changed to some extent in their constituent elements." Texas v. White, (1868) 7 Wall. (74 U. S.) 700 at 728–729. See also Leser v. Garnett, (1922) 258 U. S. 130, 42 S. Ct. 217.

[19] Texas v. White, (1868) 7 Wall. (74 U. S.) 700 at 721.

government, seriously altering its boundaries, or adding it to another state. Not until these facts existed could the court properly be said to be in position to pass on the question whether a state may be destroyed by constitutional amendment.

The view that the states may be destroyed is not a mere corollary of the proposition that the nation is sovereign and indestructible. It would seem that the same three-fourths of the states which could destroy the states could also dissolve the Union.[20] Should the time ever come when the existence of a united nation was thought undesirable, there seems to be no legal objection to the states proceeding by amendment to destroy the nation. It has sometimes been claimed that a nation may not destroy itself. Yet such things have occurred too often in the past to support such a belief. In contemplation of law almost anything is possible. Confederations and federations have existed in the past, and have dissolved. That they could not do so legally would seem to involve an unworkable conception of the law. It is submitted that if an amendment were adopted providing for the annexation of the United States to Great Britain or some other country, such amendment would be constitutional, though the effect

---

[20] Attorney General Lee said in his argument in Hollingsworth v. Virginia, (1798) 3 Dall. (3 U. S.) 378 at 380: "The people limit and restrain the power of the legislature, acting under a delegated authority; but they impose no restraint on themselves. They could have said, by an amendment to the Constitution, that no judicial authority should be exercised, in any case, under the United States; and if they had said so, could a court be held, or a judge proceed on any judicial business, past or future, from the moment of adopting the amendment? On general grounds, then, it was in the power of the people, to annihilate the whole, and the question is, whether they have annihilated a part of the judicial authority of the United States?"

"The people made the Constitution and the people can unmake it. It is the creature of their will, and lives only by their will." Marshall, C. J., in Cohens v. Virginia, (1821) 6 Wheat. (19 U. S.) 264 at 389.

"He [Senator Rowan in Foote's Debates] says the States have *power of right*, that is *constitutional* power, to control and limit the General Government, in all its branches, by amending the Federal Constitution, as provided for in the 5th Article in it. To this I entirely assent." 9 DANE, A GENERAL ABRIDGMENT OF AMERICAN LAW (1829), Appendix 16.

of the amendment would mean the destruction of our national existence.[21] Thus it seems that the amending power is no more favorable to the continued existence of the nation than it is to that of the states.[22] But perhaps the best answer to those who fear the destruction of the states is the fact that the whole power of ratification is left to the states as such. The whole power vested in Congress is to propose, and if the states are to be destroyed, it will be because they acting as states desire their own destruction. It would seem that they may be trusted to perpetuate their own existence.

Is there an implied guarantee of police power of the states? One of the most frequently voiced arguments for implied limitations is the view that the police power and the rights of local self government of the states may not be impaired.[23] This contention may be disposed of at the outset by the reply that since the states themselves may be destroyed, it logically follows that their police power may be taken from them. Moreover, since the Constitution itself was a scheme to shift

[21] Bliss attacks the view that sovereignty may not be ceded, pointing out that it contradicts the facts of history,—the fact that states have voluntarily united with, have become merged or subordinate to other states. BLISS, OF SOVEREIGNTY (1885) 110.

[22] "The Federal and State governments are in fact but different agents and trustees of the people, constituted with different powers and designated for different purposes." Madison, in THE FEDERALIST, No. 46.

Article Five "equally enables the general and the state governments to originate the amendment of errors, as they may be pointed out by the experience on the one side, or the other." Madison in THE FEDERALIST, No. 43.

[23] Root's Brief, p. 53 ff., in National Prohibition Cases, (1920) 253 U. S. 350, 40 S. Ct. 486, 588; STEVENSON, STATES' RIGHTS AND NATIONAL PROHIBITION (1927) 79–96; Skinner, "Intrinsic Limitations on the Power of Constitutional Amendment," (1920) 18 MICH. L. REV. 213 at 220. It is sometimes broadly asserted that only the states have police power and that such power is unlimited. But the federal government itself exercises a considerable degree of it indirectly through the taxing, commerce, and postal powers. A list of such powers is set out in Shawnee Milling Company v. Temple, (C. C. Iowa, 1910) 179 F. 517 at 524. Even apart from amendments to that end, the police power of the states is limited by the Constitution itself in the view of Holmes, J., in Noble State Bank v. Haskell, (1910) 219 U. S. 104, 31 S. Ct. 186.

some of the powers formerly held by the states to the federal government, there seems no convincing reason why subsequent transfers of power may not occur.[24] An express proviso safeguarding the police power of the states was rejected by the Constitutional Convention.[25] The equal suffrage in the Senate proviso indicated that the framers of the Constitution contemplated other deprivations of states' powers as valid. The police power when broadly defined means all the powers of the state.[26] To say that this power may not be infringed is thus equivalent to asserting that no change affecting the powers of a state may be made by amendment. Such a view would confine amendments to changes in the federal government, changes moreover which would take away powers from that government. This is true because all powers not prohibited to the states are reserved to the states and to the people. Hence all powers conferred on the federal government are conferred at the expense of the states, except in the case of those reserved to the people, whose consent is implicit in the amending process.

The critics of the Eighteenth Amendment asserted, rightly it appears, that it impaired the police power of the states. From this they concluded that it was invalid. They pointed

[24] "The extent of the encroachment upon the police powers of the states is a political matter, to be determined by the people. That the exercise of the amending power granted by article V may encroach upon some of the state rights is true; but that is inevitable, and was necessarily contemplated when the power to amend was granted." Feigenspan v. Bodine, (D. C. N. J. 1920) 264 F. 186 at 192.

"Nor however difficult it may be supposed to unite two thirds, or three fourths of the state legislatures, in amendments which may affect local interests, can there be any room to apprehend any such difficulty in a union on points which are merely relative to the general liberty or security of the people. We may safely rely on the disposition of the state legislatures to erect barriers against the encroachments of the national authority." Hamilton, in THE FEDERALIST, No. 85.

[25] Supra, p. 4 et seq. That such provision was thought unnecessary, just as was the Bill of Rights, see Bacon, "How the Tenth Amendment Affected the Fifth Article of the Constitution," (1930) 16 VA. L. REV. 771 at 773.

[26] In Feigenspan v. Bodine, (D. C. N. J. 1920) 264 F. 186 at 191, the court concedes that "the police power in a very large sense is the state itself."

out that the previous amendments had not encroached on
the police power, or if reminded of the Civil War Amendments, asserted either that they do not affect the police power
or that the question of their validity is a political question
on the ground that they were adopted as war measures. The
first ten amendments, it is true, are limitations on the powers
of the federal government only.[27] The Eleventh Amendment
protects the states from suit by individuals in the federal
courts. The Twelfth Amendment merely changed the mode
of electing the President and Vice-President of the United
States. Thus until 1865, when the Thirteenth Amendment
was ratified, no amendment had been adopted interfering
with the powers of the states. This is perhaps the explanation
of the belief that the states' police power was exempt from
constitutional diminution. The three Civil War Amendments, however, clearly infringed upon the powers of the
states.[28] Slavery had formerly been a purely domestic institution which only the state itself could regulate. The effect
of the Fourteenth Amendment was to bring into the federal
courts a tremendous number of cases arising out of the due
process clause, and to vest the Supreme Court with a wide

[27] But it is a significant fact, noted in the early case of Jackson ex dem.
Wood v. Wood, (1824) 2 Cow. (N. Y.) 819 at 820, that the House of Representatives at the first session of Congress adopted an amendment providing
"that no state should infringe the right of trial by jury, in criminal cases, nor
the right of conscience, nor the freedom of speech or of the press." Cf. ANNALS
OF CONG., 1st Cong. 1st sess. (1789) 435.

[28] In a dissenting opinion in the Slaughter House Cases, (1872) 16 Wall.
(83 U. S.) 125, Swayne, J., said: "These [reconstruction] amendments are a
new departure, and mark an important epoch in the constitutional history of
the country. They trench directly upon the power of the States, and deeply affect
those bodies. They are, in this respect, at the opposite pole from the first eleven."
In referring to the Thirteenth and Fourteenth Amendments, Strong, J., said in Ex
parte Virginia, (1880) 100 U. S. 339 at 345, that "They were intended to be,
what they really are, limitations of the powers of the States and enlargements
of the powers of Congress." The Fifteenth Amendment was held to be such a
limitation in Guinn v. United States, (1915) 238 U. S. 347, 35 S. Ct. 926.
See also the Solicitor General's argument in the National Prohibition Cases,
(1920) 253 U. S. 350, 40 S. Ct. 486, 588; United States v. Sprague, (1931)
282 U. S. 716, 51 S. Ct. 220.

supervisory power over state legislation. The Fifteenth Amendment forbade the states to deny the right to vote on account of race or color. Inasmuch as the power to determine their electorate is fundamental, this clearly was a limitation on the states. Since these amendments have never been held invalid, it would seem to follow that the Eighteenth Amendment is valid though the states' police power is impaired. The briefs against the Eighteenth Amendment fully set out the argument as to police power, and the Supreme Court, nevertheless, held it valid.[29] In view of the nature of the Civil War Amendments, and of the holding of the Supreme Court as to the Eighteenth Amendment, it would seem conclusive that the amending power may alter the police power of the states at will. A final query for the proponents of implied limitation is: if the powers of the nation may be limited as they were by the earlier amendments, why cannot the powers of the states be similarly cut down? Unless the powers of both may be altered, the utility of the amending process is greatly weakened.

Does the proviso for equality of suffrage in the Senate imply other restrictions? Resort is sometimes had to the clause guaranteeing equality of suffrage in the Senate as an express limitation, or as a basis for deducing implied limitations.[30] The true character of the clause as simply a limitation on the procedure of amendment has already been pointed out.[31] This

[29] National Prohibition Cases, (1920) 253 U. S. 350, 40 S. Ct. 486, 588.

[30] Machen, "Is the Fifteenth Amendment Void?" (1910) 23 HARV. L. REV. 169 at 172–176, contends that the Senate cannot be abolished, or made an advisory body; nor may the states be abolished, nor altered in their composition as by adding negroes to the electorate, or by changing their boundaries. He also asserts that by "state" is meant the people of the state, not the physical territory thereof. See also Appellant's Brief in Leser v. Garnett, (1922) 258 U. S. 130, 42 S. Ct. 217; Appellant's Brief in Myers v. Anderson, (1915) 238 U. S. 368, 35 S. Ct. 932; Marbury, "The Limitations Upon the Amending Power," (1919) 33 HARV. L. REV. 223 at 228; White, "Is There an Eighteenth Amendment?" (1920) 5 CORN. L. Q. 113 at 116.

[31] See supra, p. 84 et seq.

clause provides simply for the equal representation of each state in the Senate. It should be limited to its proper scope. It says nothing about the continued existence of the state itself, nor of the freedom of the state from a whole or partial loss of its powers through amendment. That it was not intended to cover more than the single matter of equality in the Senate is evident from the history of its adoption by the Constitutional Convention. Sherman there expressed his fear that the amending power might do two things: destroy the states and deprive them of their equality in the Senate. He therefore moved the adoption of a proviso that no state without its consent should "be affected in its internal police, or deprived of its equal suffrage in the Senate."[32] Thus the first part of the proviso would protect the existence of the states, and the latter their equality in the Senate. His motion failed, but immediately thereafter Gouverneur Morris' proposal of the present equality clause was adopted. It would therefore seem reasonable that historically at least the clause is confined to protecting the equality of the states in the Senate.[33]

Historical considerations aside, it seems that a logical analysis of the words of the clause leads to a similar result.[34] The clause purports to deal with the equal suffrage of a state. It makes no provision for the perpetual existence of the states, or of the police power of the states, or of the Senate. Seemingly all three of these could be abolished. Theoretically,

[32] Supra, pp. 4 et seq.; 86 et seq.

[33] "The exception in favour of the equality of suffrage in the senate, was probably meant as a palladium to the residuary sovereignty of the states, implied and secured by that principle of representation in one branch of the legislature; and was probably insisted upon by the states particularly attached to that equality." Madison, in THE FEDERALIST, No. 43. Iredell, however, asserts that it was adopted "in order that no consolidation should take place." 4 ELLIOT, DEBATES ON THE ADOPTION OF THE FEDERAL CONSTITUTION (1937 reprint of 1836 2d ed.) 177.

[34] Dodd, "Amending the Federal Constitution," (1921) 30 YALE L. J. 321 at 330.

even though the states or the Senate or both were abolished, a state would not be deprived of its equality as to suffrage in the Senate. If all the states were abolished, the relation of equality would be undisturbed, although the states themselves no longer existed. If simply a part of the states were abolished, it would scarcely be appropriate to speak of them as losing their equality in the Senate for they would lose their very existence. The possibility of equality of a state would seem to flow from the existence of the state, and not the existence of the state from the characteristic of equality in the Senate. In other words, the existence of the state seems to be the primary matter, and equality only a secondary possibility.

Similarly, if the Senate were abolished, the equality of suffrage would not be disturbed, as each state would have no senators at all.[35] If the next step were to abolish the states themselves, it would seem absurd that reliance could be placed on the equality clause to prevent their abolition. Inasmuch as the equality clause had lost any subject-matter on which to operate with respect to its chief purpose, namely, the preservation of equality in the Senate, it would appear far-fetched to maintain that it continued to operate in such a way as to preserve the states themselves.

The chief objection to a broad interpretation of the clause is that so much is made to hinge on so little. Not only are the states to continue to be equally represented in the Senate, but they themselves are to continue in perpetuity, and, on the same logic, the Senate is also to go on forever. It seems only reasonable that had the framers intended to guarantee the existence of the states and to impose similar implied limitations deduced from the clause, they would not have left such weighty matters to implication. The conclusion seems inevitable that the implied limits deduced from the equality

[35] Lee, "Abolishing the Senate by Amendment," (1930) 16 VA. L. REV. 364.

clause are hung on too small a peg. The stretching of this seemingly innocent and insignificant exception offends the intuitive sense of the limits of legal casuistry.

Do the Bill of Rights and the Fourteenth Amendment limit other amendments? To the layman, the Bill of Rights and the Fourteenth Amendment may be thought so fundamental in their nature as to be limitations on the amending power.[36] But however significant they may be, they were not parts of the original Constitution. They may be repealed just as any other amendment and are no more sacred from a legal standpoint than any other part of the Constitution. As one authority has said:

"Even these constitutional limitations, however, do not deny the group's right to revise the scale of values handed down to it from the past; they merely restrict the legal methods of their revision. The argument sometimes advanced that there are implied limits on the power to amend the federal Constitution is clearly untenable. There is, perhaps, no politically organized society whose legal system does not assume a right of such revision vested in some one or more of its organs. The only method which it would be at all logical for the law to deny is that by revolution."[37]

It is sometimes argued that the Bill of Rights was in reality a part of the original Constitution and was intended to constitute a limitation on Article Five.[38] But the states adopted the Constitution unconditionally, and the obligation to incorporate the Bill of Rights was entirely moral, not legal. Even if it had been a part of the original Constitution, it would not necessarily limit the amending power. It contains

[36] JESSUP, THE BILL OF RIGHTS AND ITS DESTRUCTION BY ALLEGED DUE PROCESS OF LAW (1927).

[37] Rottschaefer, "Legal Theory and the Practice of Law," (1926) 10 MINN. L. REV. 382 at 393.

[38] Skinner, "Intrinsic Limitations on the Power of Constitutional Amendment," (1920) 18 MICH. L. REV. 213 at 221; JESSUP, THE BILL OF RIGHTS AND ITS DESTRUCTION BY ALLEGED DUE PROCESS OF LAW (1927).

no express, nor even any reasonably implied, reference to Article Five. No other clauses of the original Constitution have ever been construed to limit the power. In the state decisions no attempts have been made to construe a state bill of rights as a limit on the state's power to amend its constitution, except in a single Arkansas case, and this case simply holds that the legislature, which was vested with the amending power, could not so amend.[39] In dictum it declared that the people in Convention might do so. An Oregon decision expressly held that the bill of rights might be altered.[40] In a recent decision of a federal circuit court it was argued that the effect of the Fourteenth Amendment was to require the submission of all future amendments to the people, but the court rejected the contention.[41]

Does the Tenth Amendment limit other amendments? In the opinion of many,[42] a conclusive argument in favor of implied limitations is the Tenth Amendment: "The powers not

[39] Eason v. State, (1851) 11 Ark. 481, overruling State v. Cox, (1848) 8 Ark. 436, which had held the bill of rights subject to the ordinary amending process. The case is explicable by the peculiar wording of the Arkansas Constitution and the nature of the amending process.

[40] Ex parte Kerby, (1922) 103 Ore. 612, 205 P. 279. See also Woods' Appeal, (1874) 75 Pa. 59, holding that a constitutional convention could propose a constitution repealing the state bill of rights. Jameson sees no reason "why, in the absence of constitutional restriction, the legislature should not be at liberty to propose amendments to either part of the Constitution, the frame of government, or the Bill of Rights." JAMESON, CONSTITUTIONAL CONVENTIONS, 4th ed. (1887) 580.

[41] Peter Hand Co. v. United States, (C. C. A. 7th, 1924) 2 F. (2d) 449. In Root's argument in the National Prohibition Cases, (1920) 253 U. S. 350, 40 S. Ct. 486, 588, it is suggested that the due process clause is unalterable.

[42] 2 CURTIS, CONSTITUTIONAL HISTORY (1896) 154, 160–162; STEVENSON, STATES' RIGHTS AND NATIONAL PROHIBITION (1927) 37–57; Skinner, "Intrinsic Limitations on the Power of Constitutional Amendment," (1919) 18 MICH. L. REV. 213 at 219; Appellant's Brief in National Prohibition Cases, (1920) 253 U. S. 350, 40 S. Ct. 486, 588; Bacon, "How the Tenth Amendment Affected the Fifth Article of the Constitution," (1930) 16 VA. L. REV. 771. *Contra:* Taft, "Amendment of the Federal Constitution," (1930) 16 VA. L. REV. 647. Governor Haight of California recommended rejection of the Fifteenth Amendment, asserting that "It was clearly understood that a 'reserved power' was one withdrawn and excluded entirely from the operation of any and every

delegated to the United States by the Constitution, nor prohibited by it to the States, are reserved to the States respectively, or to the people."

First of all, it should be noted that the provision is not a
part of the original Constitution. It is one out of several
amendments and is itself subject to repeal. It is not a part of
Article Five and makes no reference to that article. It did
not reserve the amending power, it reserved only the nondelegated powers, whereas the amending power had been
previously delegated.[43] The first ten amendments have invariably been interpreted as limitations on the federal government. The federal government is to be distinguished from
the amending body, which is made up not only of Congress
but of the state legislatures or state conventions. The distinc

clause of the Federal Constitution, including the clause in reference to amendments." CALIFORNIA SENATE JOURNAL, 1869–70, p. 144 at 149, cited in
MATHEWS, LEGISLATIVE AND JUDICIAL HISTORY OF THE FIFTEENTH AMEND
MENT (1909) 73. But see Feller, "The Tenth Amendment Retires," (1941)
27 A. B. A. J. 223.

[43] "The Tenth Amendment "disclosed the widespread fear that the National
Government might, under the pressure of a supposed general welfare, attempt to
exercise powers which had not been granted. With equal determination the
framers intended that no such assumption should ever find justification in the
organic act, and that if in the future further powers seemed necessary they
should be granted by the people in the manner they had provided for amending
that act." Brewer, J., in Kansas v. Colorado, (1907) 206 U. S. 46 at 90, 27
S. Ct. 655.

"Reserved powers are so called because they have never been surrendered.
When the requisite number of states concur, the people surrender to the United
States additional power." State of Ohio ex rel. Erchenbrecher v. Cox, (D. C.
Ohio, 1919) 257 F. 334 at 342.

"The tenth article of amendment, if not merely declaratory of what was
necessarily implied in the Constitution as originally adopted, established that
the undelegated powers were reserved to the several states or to the people.
However, this residuum was not a fixed quantity, but would change, becoming
less or greater, as an amendment increased or diminished the powers of the
United States government." Feigenspan v. Bodine, (D. C. N. J. 1920) 264 F.
186 at 192.

"It is evident that among the rights which are neither given to the federal
government nor reserved to the separate states is the weightiest of all, yes, the
one which embraces all the others, i. e., the right to change the Constitution
and to partition power in whatever way is desired, between the federal government and the states." VON HOLST, THE CONSTITUTIONAL LAW OF THE UNITED
STATES, Mason ed., (1887) 51.

tion is fundamental. The federal government is limited, while the amending body, which is the highest agent of the people and exercises sovereignty,[44] is unlimited,[45] except by the equality in the Senate clause. If the Tenth Amendment were to be construed as affecting the amending body, it would be a limitation on the states, which perform the most important part of the amending process, namely, ratification.

A very practical argument against construing the amendment as a limitation on the amending body is the fact that such a construction would operate to nullify the grant of the amending capacity or to seriously impair its usefulness. No change could be made in the national government except such as left it with its previous powers, or with less powers than it had before. That is, no new powers could ever be conferred on the national government, since any such powers would have to come from the residuum reserved to the states. New powers could be conferred on the states alone, and no powers could be taken from them. In view of the apparently natural growth of the activities of the national government not only in recent years but from the very beginning, a serious crisis might be developed if no new powers could be given it. The fact that since the Civil War the amendments have limited the states and given new powers to the national government clearly indicates the trend of the growth of the living Constitution. Even if the Tenth Amendment were interpreted as an "invisible radiation" limiting the amending power, it should be noted that the powers not delegated or prohibited by the Constitution are reserved to the states, "or to the peo-

[44] See infra, chap. VI.

[45] "A fundamental error running through all these provoking essays is the confounding of government with sovereignty, a failure to distinguish between a political society or state and the active agencies or governmental organs which that society creates and endows with power." McGovney, "Is the Eighteenth Amendment Void Because of its Contents?" (1920) 20 COL. L. REV. 499 at 500.

ple." By the people is meant the people of the United States.[46] Since the people when acting in their highest capacity do so through the amending process, it would seem that their agent, the amending body, can redistribute the powers of the states and the nation at will.

Is there a restriction that an amendment may not be legislative in character? The amending process is not the regular legislative process of the federal government. Ordinarily it is the business of Congress to legislate for the nation, and of the state legislatures for the respective states. The Constitution confers all legislative powers on Congress. From this it has sometimes been deduced that an amendment may not be legislative in character.[47] In political science a distinction is made between constitutional content of an organic character and that of a legislative character. The distinction, however, is one of policy, not of law.[48] It would indeed be peculiar if the

[46] "The preamble of the Constitution declares who framed it, 'We the people of the United States,' not the people of one State, but the people of all the States; and Article X reserved to the people of all the States the powers not delegated to the United States. The powers affecting the internal affairs of the States not granted to the United States by the Constitution, nor prohibited by it to the States, are reserved to the States respectively, and all powers of a national character which are not delegated to the National Government by the Constitution are reserved to the people of the United States." Brewer, J., in Kansas v. Colorado, (1907) 206 U. S. 46 at 90, 27 S. Ct. 655.

von Holst says that if the phrase were intended to mean the people of the individual states the word "thereof" would have to be added. VON HOLST, THE CONSTITUTIONAL LAW OF THE UNITED STATES, Mason ed. (1887) 51, note; see also JAMESON, CONSTITUTIONAL CONVENTIONS, 4th ed. (1887) 87, note 1. *Contra:* COOLEY, GENERAL PRINCIPLES OF CONSTITUTIONAL LAW, 3d ed., (1898) 29; and 2 CURTIS, CONSTITUTIONAL HISTORY (1896) 160, note. The latter two say the phrase means the people of the individual states.

[47] State ex rel. Halliburton v. Roach, (1910) 230 Mo. 408, 130 S. W. 689, Root's Brief, p. 3 ff., in the National Prohibition Cases, (1920) 253 U. S. 350, 40 S. Ct. 486, 588; Marbury, "The Limitations upon the Amending Power," (1919) 33 HARV. L. REV. 223 at 230; Holding, "Perils to be Apprehended from Amending the Constitution," (1923) 57 AM. L. REV. 481 at 488; State ex rel. Mullen v. Howell, (1919) 107 Wash. 167, 181 P. 920.

[48] As between the three departments of government "the power to legislate is exclusive in the Congress; but there is no warrant here for the assumption

authority which can delegate to Congress the authority to legislate, could not itself legislate. The framers of the Constitution seem to have contemplated amendments of a legislative nature when they wrote in the twenty-year limitations as to the slave trade and the imposition of direct taxes without apportionment. It may be impolitic to write clauses which are legislative in their nature into the Constitution, but the legality of so doing apparently is not open to question. The wisdom of the Fifteenth and the Eighteenth Amendments may well be open to serious criticism, but their legality seems unassailable.

Moreover, if the Eighteenth Amendment be invalid as being legislative in nature, it would seem that a number of earlier amendments must fall on the same ground. The Thirteenth Amendment legislated slavery out of existence, the Fourteenth Amendment legislated on several subjects, such as citizenship, the exclusion of rebels from office, and the repudiation of debts of rebelling states. Yet it has not been seriously pretended that these amendments are void because of their legislative content.

A practical argument against differentiating between legislative and non-legislative amendments is the fact that there is no satisfactory and clean-cut distinction between the two. Until the Supreme Court had put the stamp of approval on each proposed amendment, there would be no way of ascertaining its legislative character. Power of a despotic nature would be vested in the Supreme Court, and the court might

that, as between Congress and the people, in whom the ultimate right of sovereignty resides, only Congress could legislate.

"The limitations upon the people's power to change their Constitution are no more than they have chosen to make them. In so far as article I of the Constitution is concerned, there is no limitation upon the sovereign right of the people to legislate a rule, act, or principle into their organic law." Feigenspan v. Bodine, (D. C. N. J. 1920) 264 F. 186 at 191. See also Appellant's Brief in State ex rel. Halliburton v. Roach, (1910) 230 Mo. 408, 130 S. W. 689. But see JAMESON, CONSTITUTIONAL CONVENTIONS, 4th ed. (1887) 429.

be drawn into partisan controversy. It may perhaps be alleged that by a true amendment is meant a change in the structure of the government, or a change of extraordinary importance in the life of the nation. Perhaps the former test would not be impossible of application. Under it the first twelve amendments, the Fifteenth, the Sixteenth, which permits Congress to impose taxes on incomes without apportionment, the Seventeenth, providing for the popular election of Senators, and the Nineteenth, providing for woman suffrage, would all be valid. But the Thirteenth, parts of the Fourteenth, and Eighteenth Amendments would all be invalid. Moreover, the difficulties of applying this test are greater than at first appears. Almost every change in the structure of government involves some redistribution of power and is partially legislative in nature. On the other hand, almost every change of a legislative character directly or indirectly involves a change in the structure of the government.

The difficulties of the second test are even more manifest. When the inertia of the amending process has been overcome, it is scarcely possible to say that the proposed amendment is not of constituent importance.[49] When the Prohibition Amendment was adopted, despite some contrary beliefs, there seems to have been a tremendous public sentiment which had long favored it. The same may be said of the Civil War Amendments. In the United States, where the dogma of popular sovereignty is so firmly rooted, there would seem to be no valid legal objection to the people's writing their convictions into the Constitution on any subject they choose

[49] "There being no express inhibition in the Constitution of the United States against ordaining a final permanent law, what authority is there for implying one? . . . I fail to perceive anything in any part of the organic law that would justify a judicial interpretation forbidding the people to do so when they are convinced that on a given subject the time has come to prevent perennial changes in respect thereto." Feigenspan v. Bodine, (D. C. N. J. 1920) 264 F. 186 at 193.

in the absence of express constitutional prohibition. Many of the state constitutions are a standing witness of this fact, and the decisions seem to uphold amendments of every nature.

Is there a restriction that an amendment must be germane? It has sometimes been suggested that an amendment must be germane.[50] That is, a proposed amendment must relate immediately to some specific clause in the Constitution, or must be in harmony with the "spirit" of the Constitution. Article Five gives no hint of such a limitation. The first twelve amendments and the Sixteenth and Seventeenth doubtless meet the test. But the Civil War Amendments and the Eighteenth and Nineteenth Amendments are not necessarily germane as respects any previous articles in the Constitution. As long as they are permitted to remain on the books it seems that little attention can be paid to any such objection.

But assuming for the sake of argument that germaneness is a test of validity, it is difficult to see what would not be germane to the Constitution. The Constitution assumes to deal with all political power whatsoever, giving specific powers to the federal government, providing for changes by an amending power, and reserving all other power to the states or to the people. The general spirit and purpose of the Constitution, whatever they may be, cannot be isolated with scientific accuracy. Perhaps the best statement of the purpose, though having no legal force, is that to be found in the Preamble:

"We the People of the United States, in order to form a more perfect Union, establish Justice, insure domestic Tranquility, provide for the common defence, promote the general Welfare, and secure the Blessings of Liberty to ourselves and our

---

[50] Root's Brief in the National Prohibition Cases, (1920) 253 U. S. 350, 40 S. Ct. 486, 588; Campbell, C. J., dissenting in People ex rel. Elder v. Sours, (1903) 31 Colo. 369, 74 P. 167; speech of Uriah Tracy in the Senate on the Twelfth Amendment, ANNALS OF CONGRESS, 8th Cong., 1st sess. (1803) 163; Morris, "The Fifteenth Amendment to the Federal Constitution," (1909) 189 No. AM. REV. 82; Emery, "The 18th Amendment of the Constitution of the United States," (April, 1920) 13 ME. L. REV. 121 at 122.

Posterity, do ordain and establish this Constitution for the United States of America."

The statement of purposes is thus very broad. Among them is the promotion of the general welfare. If an amendment is conducive to the general welfare, it is then germane.[51] It would seem that a court could not set up its own notion of what the general welfare was, and would have to assume that what Congress and three-fourths of the states have approved promotes the general welfare whether or not in reality it actually does. With such a broad test it would seem that no amendment can be annulled for not being germane.[52] That its makers entertained broad views of the purposes of the Constitution there can seem little doubt.[53] Realizing the imperfections of their work, it is not reasonable to surmise that they intended that future generations should not make such alterations as they thought best. Today, at a time when absolutes are discredited, it must not be too readily assumed that there are fundamental purposes in the Constitution which shackle the amending power and which take precedence over the general welfare and needs of the people of today and of the future.

[51] State of Ohio ex rel. Erchenbrecher v. Cox, (D. C. Ohio, 1919) 257 F. 334.

[52] "When the people place limitations upon their power to modify the Constitution, these limitations cannot be extended by what others may think or believe to be a purpose. Purpose or no purpose, the way to amend is pointed out; that way must be followed, and, when followed is sufficient. Whatever may be the result, or however confusing or perplexing, or even useless may be the consequences, the Constitution becomes the will of the people when it is adopted by their vote in the method provided." Crane, J., concurring in Browne v. City of New York, (1925) 241 N. Y. 96 at 126, 149 N. E. 211. See also, Miller, "Amendment of the Federal Constitution: Should It Be Made More Difficult?" (1926) 10 MINN. L. REV. 185 at 199.

[53] ". . . the public good, the real welfare of the great body of the people, is the supreme object to be pursued . . . no form of government whatever has any other value, than as it may be fitted for the attainment of this object. Were the plan of the convention adverse to the public happiness, my voice would be, Reject the plan. Were the union itself inconsistent with the public happiness, it would be, Abolish the union. In like manner, as far as the sovereignty of the state cannot be reconciled to the happiness of the people, the voice of every good citizen must be, Let the former be sacrificed to the latter." Madison, in THE FEDERALIST, No. 45.

Is there a restriction that an amendment cannot add but only alter? An argument very much like the foregoing is that an amendment may alter, but may not add. This contention is largely a quibble on the definition of the word "amendment." It is asserted that by amending the Constitution is meant the changing of something that is already in the Constitution, and not the addition of something new and unrelated. Cases prescribing the very limited meaning of amendment in the law of pleading are cited as authoritative.[54] It would seem improper, however, to accept such a definition, as amendments to constitutions have always been construed more liberally and on altogether different principles from those applied to amendments of pleadings. A mere glance at the Civil War and the Eighteenth and Nineteenth Amendments, as well as at many amendments made to state constitutions, is enough to show that by an amendment is meant an addition as well as an alteration.[55] The United States Senate

[54] For example, Machen, "Is the Fifteenth Amendment Void?" (1910) 23 HARV. L. REV. 169 at 170, note, cites the following cases holding that an amendment to a pleading cannot substitute a new case: Shields v. Barrow, (1854) 17 How. (58 U. S.) 130 at 144; Goodyear v. Bourn, (D. C. N. Y. 1855) 3 Blatchf. 266, F. Cas. No. 5561; Givens v. Wheeler, (1882) 6 Colo. 149. He also cites 2 MORAWETZ, PRIVATE CORPORATIONS, 2d ed. (1886) § 1096, which merely states that a reserved power to amend a charter of incorporation does not extend to the substitution of a new charter. In Livermore v. Waite, (1894) 102 Cal. 113, 36 P. 424, the court says that an amendment must not fundamentally alter the Constitution, and must improve, or better carry out its purpose. See also Morris, "The Fifteenth Amendment to the Federal Constitution," (1909) 189 No. AM. REV. 82; Appellant's Brief in National Prohibition Cases, (1920) 253 U. S. 350, 40 S. Ct. 486, 588.

[55] McKenna, J., dissenting on other issues in the National Prohibition Cases, supra, 253 U. S. at 401, states that the references in Article Five and in Article Six, sec. 2, to "this Constitution" do not forbid an amendment inconsistent with a clause in the Constitution before amended, and are not a limitation on the amending power. "What other purpose could an amendment have?"
"The Constitution is the organic and fundamental law, but that law may be changed, added to, or repealed, if that is done by the states and the people themselves in the way provided. Their power to better it, as they think, is not to be hamstrung by mere rigidity of definition of words. Adding something new to the organic law is an amendment of the organic law, in the judgment of this court." State of Ohio ex rel. Erchenbrecher v. Cox, (D. C. Ohio, 1919) 257 F. 334 at 343.

under its power to amend revenue bills may substitute entirely new bills. In fact, the amending process would be largely futile if no additions could be incorporated. The fathers of the Constitution neither expressly nor by reasonable implication gave ground for any such understanding of the process. Perhaps the best evidence of contemporary construction is to be found in the heading of the joint resolution of Congress submitting the first ten amendments commencing, "Articles in addition to and Amendment of the Constitution."[56]

Is there a law above amending power and the Constitution? In surveying the arguments as to implied limitations, it seems necessary to consider a doctrine which has proved peculiarly attractive to some, namely, that there is a law higher than the written Constitution which is inviolable and constitutes a limitation on the power to amend. Strange bedfellows are to be found adhering to this view. It is likely to be urged by the most naive man in the street and also by learned lawyers and philosophers. Large masses of the people of the United

"The Constitution is a mere grant of power to the federal government by the several states and any amendment which adds to or in any manner changes the powers thus granted comes within the legal and even within the technical definition of that term." Ex parte Dillon, (D. C. Cal. 1920) 262 F. 563 at 567 aff'd Dillon v. Gloss, (1921) 256 U. S. 368, 41 S. Ct. 510.

" 'Words in the Constitution of the United States do not ordinarily receive a narrow and contracted meaning, but are presumed to have been used in a broad sense with a view to covering all emergencies.' . . . The definitions of the word 'amendment' include additions to, as well as correction of, matters already treated; and there is nothing in its immediate context (article V) which suggests that it was used in a restricted sense." Feigenspan v. Bodine, (D. C. N. J. 1920) 264 F. 186 at 190, quoting from In re Strauss, (1905) 197 U. S. 324 at 330, 25 S. Ct. 535.

"A Constitution has an organic life in such a sense, and to such a degree that changes here and there do not sever its identity." Cardozo, J., in Browne v. City of New York, (1925) 241 N. Y. 96 at 111, 149 N. E. 211.

[56] "An amendment to the Constitution, which is made by the addition of a provision on a new and independent subject, is a complete thing in itself, and may be wholly disconnected with other provisions of the Constitution; such amendments for instance as the first ten amendments to the Constitution of the United States. These were therein referred to as articles in addition to and amendment of the Constitution." State ex rel. Greenlund v. Fulton, (1919) 99 Ohio St. 168, 124 N. E. 172.

States view the Constitution as something sacrosanct and protected from serious alteration. The language of the Declaration of Independence as to inherent and inalienable rights is unhesitatingly accepted by many as having a legal as well as a political and ethical significance.[57] Seward, Secretary of State under Lincoln, once said that "there is a higher law than the Constitution which regulates our authority," but he was careful to add that he would "adopt none but lawful, constitutional and peaceful means to secure even that end."

The view of unlimited internal sovereignty of the state has undergone serious criticism during the last century at the hands of the political pluralists, who deny the absolute and indivisible sovereignty of the state, as viewed internally and apart from international law. Since the state is not supreme, neither is the amending body, for the amending body is virtually the state, or at least its most powerful agent. The theories of pluralism of the last century were mainly developed by Gierke in Germany, and by Maitland, Figgis, and Laski in England, by Duguit in France, and by Krabbe in the Netherlands. Krabbe, like many of the other pluralists, views the state as the creature of law, and law alone is sovereign. Perhaps their whole position is best summed up in the words of Duguit:

"The more I advance in age and seek to penetrate the problem of law, the more I am convinced that law is not a creation of the state, that it exists without the state, that the notion of law is altogether independent of the state, and that the rule

[57] Abbott, "Inalienable Rights and the Eighteenth Amendment," (1920) 20 COL. L. REV. 183 at 184, says that "the question is not whether we can take a drink now and again, but whether in this federal Union of ours there resides any power which is literally absolute, that is, without even those ultimate limitations which we are accustomed to speak of as the constitutional guarantees of our liberties. . . . For the first time in the history of the American Union an amendment to the Constitution has been adopted, or claimed to have been adopted, which attempts to limit the personal liberties of the people. . . . There are a number of constitutive principles of private rights which have been so wrought into the fabric of our institutions that they cannot be abrogated."

of law imposes itself on the state as it does upon individuals."[58]

The theories of pluralism have found little support in the United States among the political scientists and scarcely any among the lawyers.[59] Professor McIlwain states that pluralism is "equivalent to a repudiation of all control over the individual citizen except that which he voluntarily imposes upon himself."[60] Many pluralists concede the *legal* sovereignty of the state. Our legal views are of course traceable to those of the English common law. The analytical view of the law as a body of rules laid down by the sovereign or recognized and enforced by the courts runs back to Hobbes, Blackstone, Bentham, and Austin. Their views and those of Holland and Salmond, and of John Chipman Gray in the United States, are representative of the prevalent view of the law held by lawyers in this country. It is true that in the United States the strictly analytical view is considerably modified by the large proportion of the law to be found in the cases rather than in statutes, and also by the doctrine of judicial review. The Supreme Court of the United States has the last word in the construction not only of treaties and statutes, but of the Constitution itself, and if it laid down implied limitations on the amending power, such limitations would doubtless be accepted as constitutional. Theoretically, however, the Constitution is supreme over all, including the Supreme Court, whose members take an oath to support it. In looking for limitations on the power to amend, it is therefore the duty

---

[58] 1 Ducuit, Traité de Droit Constitutionnel, 2d ed. (1921) 33.

[59] "The very meaning of sovereignty is that the decree of the sovereign makes law." Holmes, J., in American Banana Co. v. United Fruit Co., (1909) 213 U. S. 347 at 358, 29 S. Ct. 511.

"Sovereignty itself is, of course, not subject to law, for it is the author and source of law; but in our system, while sovereign powers are delegated to the agencies of government, sovereignty itself remains with the people, by whom and for whom all government exists and acts." Yick Wo v. Hopkins, (1886) 118 U. S. 356 at 370, 6 S. Ct. 1064.

[60] "A Fragment on Sovereignty," (1933) 48 POL. SCI. Q. 94 at 105.

of the Court to look to the Constitution itself. The Constitution does not recognize any such type of law as Natural Law, or the Law of God, or the Law of Reason.[61] The medieval sovereigns were regarded as being subject to Natural Law and the Law of God. The Law of God has since been relegated to theology. The growth of the modern independent nations of Europe meant the emergence of a national law governing each nation, and the disappearance of natural law. In England some isolated cases decided or intimated that an act of Parliament "contrary to common right and reason" was void.[62] Blackstone at times suggests that all laws are subject to natural law and at other times maintains that there is nothing superior to an act of Parliament. Since his time Austin and Bentham quite definitely gave the bent to Anglo-American legal theory, so that today natural law is regarded as non-

[61] "The theory that laws may be declared void when deemed to be opposed to natural justice and equity, although they do not violate any constitutional provision, has some support in the dicta of learned judges, but has not been approved, so far as we know, by any authoritative adjudication, and is repudiated by numerous authorities. . . . no law can be pronounced invalid, for the reason simply that it violates our notions of justice, is oppressive and unfair in its operation, or because, in the opinion of some or all of the citizens of the State, it is not justified by public necessity, or designed to promote the public welfare." Bertholf v. O'Reilly, (1878) 74 N. Y. 509 at 514–516.

In Buckner v. Street, (C. C. Ark. 1871) 1 Dill. 248 at 251, F. Cas. No. 2098, it is said, however, that there are no limitations on the sovereign people of the United States, "if we except those imposed by the Deity." To the same effect, see 9 DANE, A GENERAL ABRIDGMENT AND DIGEST OF AMERICAN LAW (1829), Appendix 64. In Booth v. Town of Woodbury, (1864) 32 Conn. 118 at 127, it is asserted that the people are "under no restraint except that imposed by the principles of natural justice."

[62] "Is the right of the people of the United States to do this thing questioned? It could be questioned only on the grounds advanced by Lord Coke, in Bonham's case, that the common law controlled acts of parliament, and adjudged them void when against common right and reason. But all the judges since his time have said that it was for parliament and the king to judge what common right and reason was; and Lord Campbell styles what was said by Lord Coke in this case, 'nonsense still quoted by silly people. . . .' A stronger epithet than that applied by the Lord Chancellor to those who quote Lord Coke's dictum in Bonham's case as authority, might justly be applied to those who question the power and authority of the people of the United States, by amendment of their constitution of government, to abolish slavery. . . ." Buckner v. Street, (C. C. Ark. 1871) 1 Dill. 248 at 255, F. Cas. No. 2098. But cf. Plucknett, "Bonham's Case and Judicial Review," (1926) 40 HARV. L. REV. 30.

existent or as ideal law and is relegated to ethics and political philosophy. While there are ever-recurring revivals of a belief in natural law, and while sound philosophic reasons may perhaps be offered in its behalf, it seems that such a view of the law has little chance in the interpretation of American constitutional law. In the words of one, both judge and philosopher:

"If there is any law which is back of the sovereignty of the state, and superior thereto, it is not law in such a sense as to concern the judge or the lawyer, however much it concerns the statesman or the moralist. The courts are creatures of the state and of its power, and while their life as courts continues, they must obey the law of their creator."[63]

Is there an implied limitation that amendments taking away individual liberties must be ratified by state conventions? In the decade of the thirties there were some interesting developments with respect to the scope of the amending power. The first of these was in 1931 in the case of *United States v. Sprague.*[64] There the assailants of the Eighteenth Amendment, instead of asserting that such amendment was beyond the scope of the amending power, took the narrower ground that there were limitations on the scope of amendments which could be ratified by state legislatures. That is to say, while

---

[63] CARDOZO, THE GROWTH OF THE LAW (1924) 49. McGovney says: "Against a sovereign organized political society an individual member of it has no *legal* rights. That, at least, is the situation under the present state of organization or unorganization of the human race into separate, independent, sovereign societies. There is no law superior to their wills governing their relations with their own members. On the other hand, as against government, in the United States, our political society has secured to the individual many privileges and immunities. What society has thus created, cannot society take away or alter? *Legally* certainly society may do so." McGovney "Is the Eighteenth Amendment Void Because of its Contents?" (1920) 20 COL. L. REV. 499 at 501.

"Certainly no successful attempt has been made to indicate why a constitution might not originally command or prohibit anything physically possible." Radin, "The Intermittent Sovereign," (1930) 39 YALE L. J. 514 at 521.

[64] (1931) 282 U. S. 716, 51 S. Ct. 220, noted (1932) 27 ILL. L. REV. 72; (1931) 29 MICH. L. REV. 777; (1931) 79 U. PA. L. REV. 807; Creekmore "The Sprague Case," (1931) 3 MISS. L. J. 282.

there were no limitations as to what might be ratified by state conventions, there were such limitations as to state legislatures. The legislative ratifying power could not deal with an amendment conferring upon the federal government new direct powers over individuals. It could deal only with such proposals as involved a change in the machinery of the federal government. It was argued that the original Constitution had been ratified by state conventions because the legislatures were deemed incompetent to surrender the liberties of the people to the new government to be established by the Constitution. The Tenth Amendment, reserving to the states or to the people the powers not delegated to the federal government, was alleged to have removed whatever doubt there formerly existed under the original Constitution.[65] The trial court rejected these theories, yet on the basis of a strange mixture of "political science" and "a scientific approach to the problem of government," it held the amendment void because not ratified by conventions.[66] But the Supreme Court gave no weight to either of these theories and held unequivocally that the choice of the method of ratification rested "in the sole discretion of Congress."[67] Thus the scope of the amending process seems to be the same no matter what the method of ratification. And though there are no cases on it, probably the scope is the same no matter what the method of proposal, whether by national convention or by Congress. In fact, reasoning backwards, since as seen in Chapter III, on the procedure of amendment, a national convention has very broad powers of proposal, it follows that Congress also has.[68]

[65] Bacon, "How the Tenth Amendment Affected the Fifth Article of the Constitution," (1930) 16 VA. L. REV. 771. *Contra:* Taft, "Amendment of the Federal Constitution," (1930) 16 VA. L. REV. 647.

[66] United States v. Sprague, (D. C. N. J. 1930) 44 F. (2d) 967 at 982, 984.

[67] 282 U. S. at 730.

[68] See chap. III, p. 44 et seq. To carry out the reasoning still further, since the Sprague case holds that a state legislature has the same power as a state convention in ratifying amendments, Congress has the same powers as a national convention in proposing amendments.

C. GENERAL ARGUMENTS AGAINST IMPLIED LIMITATIONS

In addition to the arguments against specific alleged limitations, there are a number of general arguments refuting the existence of implied limitations altogether.

Expressio unius est exclusio alterius. Perhaps the most obvious and at the same time the most powerful argument against the existence of any implied limitations is the presence within the amending clause itself of the explicit limitations which have previously been described. The existence of these limitations shows that the makers of the Constitution evidently gave some thought and consideration to limitations on the power to amend. The slave trade, direct taxes, and equality of representation in the Senate were all matters of great controversy in the Constitutional Convention, and each was settled by compromise. Three limitations were plainly set forth in the same clause of the Constitution that granted the amending power. Several proposed limitations offered at the Constitutional Convention, one of them of vital importance, in that it proposed to exempt the police power of the states from interference, were rejected.[69] The makers of the Constitution seemingly intended to provide for a broad power of amendment.[70] As Madison suggested, if limitations of one kind were adopted, limitations of another kind would also be demanded.[71] Certainly no power conferred in the Constitution is ultimately of more importance than the amending power. If the fathers were careful in the drafting of any clause

[69] Supra, p. 4 et seq.

[70] "The rejection of most of the proposed limitations on this power and the inclusion of but one permanent disability or restriction is strong evidence that, save as to the included exception, it was intended that the legislative departments of the governments of both the United States and the several states, acting in a special capacity for such purpose, should be practically unlimited in their power to propose and adopt amendments." Feigenspan v. Bodine, (D. C. N. J. 1920) 264 F. 186 at 195. See also, Pillsbury, "The Fifteenth Amendment," (1909) 16 ME. ST. B. A. PROC. 17.

[71] 5 ELLIOT, DEBATES ON THE ADOPTION OF THE FEDERAL CONSTITUTION (1937 reprint of 1836 2d ed.) 552. See supra, p. 4 et seq.

of the Constitution, it would seem that certainly nothing would be left to implication concerning the bounds of the amending power. The issue would seem to be a proper case for the application of the maxim, *Expressio unius est exclusio alterius.*[72] This maxim admittedly is not of universal application. Instances may well be cited where it would be improper to apply it. As Chief Justice Taft said in a recent case: "This maxim properly applies only when in the natural association of ideas in the mind of the reader that which is expressed is so set over by way of strong contrast to that which is omitted that the contrast enforces the affirmative inference that that which is omitted must be intended to have opposite and contrary treatment."[73] The application varies with the circumstances. The maxim is not limited to the law of property, or to contracts, or to statutory law. It may be and has been applied in the construction of a constitution.[74] The setting out of the express limitations in Article Five with no suggestion or implication of any other limitations, and the grant of the power to amend in broad and general terms would fairly seem to be a case where the maxim may appropriately be applied.

View of framers of Constitution as to its imperfect nature.

Additional support for the broad view of the power to amend

[72] In Gibbons v. Ogden, (1824) 9 Wheat. (22 U. S.) 1 at 191, Marshall, C. J., said: "It is a rule of construction, acknowledged by all, that the exceptions from a power mark its extent; for it would be absurd, as well as useless, to except from a granted power, that which was not granted. . . ."

[73] Ford v. United States, (1927) 273 U. S. 593 at 611, 47 S. Ct. 531.

[74] It was applied to amendments of state constitutions in In re Constitutional Convention, (1883) 14 R. I. 649 at 651; Carton v. Secretary of State, (1908) 151 Mich. 337, 115 N. W. 429; Tax Commission Case, (1923) 68 Mont. 450, 219 P. 817. Applied to other parts of state constitutions: Head v. Head, (1847) 2 Ga. 191; People v. Angle, (1888) 109 N. Y. 564, 17 N. E. 413; State ex rel. Banker v. Clausen, (1927) 142 Wash. 450, 253 P. 805. It has also been applied to construction of a treaty: Matter of Washburn, (1819) 4 Johns. Ch. (N. Y.) 106 at 114. Jameson advocates its use with caution. JAMESON, CONSTITUTIONAL CONVENTIONS, 4th ed. (1887) 602–610. See also Barto v. Himrod, (1853) 4 Seld. (N. Y.) 483 at 493; Woods' Appeal, (1874) 75 Pa. 59; BROOM, LEGAL MAXIMS, 7th Am. ed. (1874) 653.

is found in the fact that the framers of the Constitution regarded their work as far from perfect and consequently anticipated a wide use of the power to amend.[75] The Constitution is the product of several great compromises. A considerable group in the Constitutional Convention and a large minority of the people were opposed to the adoption of the Constitution as submitted. Even those members of the Convention who favored it were lukewarm in their support, and defended it solely on the ground of expediency. Such members as Benjamin Franklin expressed their unenthusiastic opinion

[75] Mason said at the Convention: "The plan now to be formed will certainly be defective, as the Confederation has been found on trial to be. Amendments, therefore, will be necessary; and it will be better to provide for them in an easy, regular, and constitutional way, than to trust to chance and violence." 5 ELLIOT, DEBATES ON THE ADOPTION OF THE FEDERAL CONSTITUTION (1937 reprint of 1836 2d ed.) 182.

Iredell, later a Supreme Court justice, declared before the North Carolina ratifying convention: "Mr. Chairman, this is a very important clause. . . . The misfortune attending most constitutions which have been deliberately formed, has been, that those who formed them thought their wisdom equal to all possible contingencies, and that there could be no error in what they did. The gentlemen who framed this Constitution thought with much more diffidence of their capacities, and undoubtedly, without a provision for amendment it would have been more justly liable to objection, and the characters of its framers would have appeared much less meritorious. This, indeed, is one of the greatest beauties of the system, and should strongly recommend it to every candid mind." 4 ibid. 176.

"In regard to the Constitution of the United States, it is confessedly a new experiment in the history of the nations. Its framers were not bold or rash enough to believe, or to pronounce it to be perfect. . . . They believed, that the power of amendment was, if one may so say, the safety-valve to let off all temporary effervescences and excitements; and the real effective instrument to control and adjust the movements of the machinery, when out of order, or in danger of self-destruction." 2 STORY, COMMENTARIES ON THE CONSTITUTION OF THE UNITED STATES, 3d ed. (1857), § 1828.

"As to individual states and the United States, the Constitution marks the boundary of powers. . . . If the Constitution is found inconvenient in practice in this or any other particular, it is well that a regular mode is pointed out for amendment." Cushing, J., in Chisholm v. Georgia, (1793) 2 Dall. (2 U. S.) 419 at 468.

"The people who adopted the Constitution knew that in the nature of things they could not foresee all the questions which might arise in the future, all the circumstances which might call for the exercise of further national powers than those granted to the United States, and after making provision for an amendment to the Constitution, by which any needed additional powers would be granted, they reserved to themselves all powers not so delegated." Brewer, J., in Kansas v. Colorado, (1907) 206 U. S. 46 at 90, 27 S. Ct. 655.

of it. One of the arguments asserted in its favor was that it was capable of alteration. In fact, many state conventions adopted it on the tacit understanding that a Bill of Rights would be immediately incorporated. Altogether it seems unreasonable that its framers regarded the Constitution as exempt from alteration except when expressly so provided. As Mr. Justice Holmes has said, the Constitution "is an experiment."[76] It is only in the generations since the Constitution was adopted that a sort of halo of sanctity has been attached to it. People have sought certainty in political affairs only in a somewhat lesser degree than they have in religion. The Constitution has come to have a significance to the people of the United States such as has never become attached to the written constitution of any other state. Gladstone's dictum that "the American Constitution is the most wonderful work ever struck off at a given time by the brain and purpose of man" is a shibboleth of American politics. Many appear to have forgotten

"that the Constitution is not an end in itself, but rather a means, or an instrument, if you please, adopted for the specific purpose of regulating the public affairs and preserving the individual rights of the nation. . . . But it would be asking the impossible to expect one generation to plan a government that should endure through all time and through revolutionary changes in every aspect of life."[77]

Article Five as sui generis. A third important consideration in favor of the view that the power to amend is unlimited except as to the equal suffrage in the Senate clause is the peculiar status of Article Five. The article seems to be *sui generis.*[78]

[76] Abrams v. United States, (1919) 250 U. S. 616 at 630, 40 S. Ct. 17, dissenting opinion.

[77] Bates, "How Shall We Preserve the Constitution?" (1926) 44 KAN. S. B. A. PROC. 128 at 143.

[78] The view of Skinner, "Intrinsic Limitations on the Power of Constitutional Amendment," (1920) 18 MICH. L. REV. 213 at 221, that Article Five is limited by the provisions of the original Constitution, including in this the Bill of Rights, seems to have found little support.

No other articles of the Constitution are to be looked to when the legal status of an amendment is in question. This seems to be true in the procedure of amendment. Congress when proposing and the states when ratifying are not bound by the rules of legislative action.[79] A simple compliance with Article Five is enough and no limitations are read in from other clauses of the federal Constitution. The proponents of implied limitations forget that Article Five is as much a part of the Constitution as any other part of it. Admittedly, limitations on the scope of an amendment are more fundamental than those on the procedure. Since limitations gathered from other clauses and from the general character and "spirit" of the Constitution have not been generally implied as to procedure, it would seem illogical and a serious matter to imply limitations as to substance. Article Five, the sole fountain head of the power to amend, is silent and appears to confer the power in broad and sweeping terms. Suggested limitations must be critically viewed, and compared with its provisions, and not the provisions of the remainder of the Constitution.

Danger of limiting the scope. An argument of tremendous practical importance is the fact that it would be exceedingly dangerous to lay down any limitations beyond those expressed.[80] The critics of an unlimited power to amend have too often neglected to give due consideration to the fact that

[79] Supra, pp. 48, 62–63. But Congress may derive additional power from the power under Article One to pass all necessary and proper laws. ROTTSCHAEFER, CONSTITUTIONAL LAW (1939) 387.

[80] "The Constitution of any government which cannot be regularly amended when its defects are experienced, reduces the people to this dilemma—they must either submit to its oppressions, or bring about amendments, more or less, by civil war." Iredell before the North Carolina Ratifying Convention, 4 ELLIOT, DEBATES ON THE ADOPTION OF THE FEDERAL CONSTITUTION (1937 reprint of 1836 2d ed.) 176–177.

"If the plaintiff is right in its contention of lack of power to insert the Eighteenth Amendment into the United States Constitution because of its subject-matter, it follows that there is no way to incorporate it and others of like character into the national organic law, except through revolution. This, the plaintiff concedes, is the inevitable conclusion of its contention. This is so startling a proposition that the judicial mind may be pardoned for not readily acceding

alteration of the federal Constitution is not by a simple majority or by a somewhat preponderate majority, but by a three-fourths majority of all the states.[81] Undoubtedly, where a simple majority is required, it is not an especially serious matter for the courts to supervise closely the amending process both as to procedure and as to substance. But when so large a majority as three-fourths has finally expressed its will in the highest possible form outside of revolution, it becomes perilous for the judiciary to intervene. This may account for the resort to the doctrine of political questions in the child labor amendment cases of 1939.[82] In fact, the amending process in the past has been so difficult that it may perhaps be said that amendment in effect has been brought about by judicial interpretation.[83] It is of course the business of the judiciary to enforce the law. But it is, and probably always has been, an unformulated ground of action in the judicial mind never so to act as to come squarely in conflict with the executive and legislature and a large group of the people. In the last analysis, self-preservation is perhaps as basic a motive in judicial action as in any other type of human activity.

It would seem, however, that there is no necessity to resort to the ground of self-preservation as a reason for the

to it, and for insisting that only the most convincing reasons will justify its acceptance." Feigenspan v. Bodine, (D. C. N. J. 1920) 264 F. 186 at 189–190.

When passing on the validity of amendments, "The court may, and should, and must, on such great occasions, look to effects and consequences." Marshall, J., in State ex rel. Postel v. Marcus, (1915) 160 Wis. 354 at 357, 152 N. W. 419. In the National Prohibition Cases, (1920) 253 U. S. 350, 40 S. Ct. 486, 588, Hughes points out in his brief that judicial construction has always been open to change through amendment, but if the court itself limits the amending power, the subject is taken beyond the reach of popular control.

[81] Such critics assume "that the ultimately sovereign people have inferentially deprived themselves of that portion of their sovereign power, once possessed by them, of determining the content of their own fundamental law." ROTTSCHAEFER, CONSTITUTIONAL LAW (1939) 9. See also ibid. 398.

[82] Chandler v. Wise, (1939) 307 U. S. 474, 59 S. Ct. 992; Coleman v. Miller, (1939) 307 U. S. 433, 59 S. Ct. 972. See supra, p. 18 et seq.

[83] See Coudert, "Judicial Constitutional Amendment," (1904) 13 YALE L. J. 331.

courts refraining from limiting the power to amend. As has been iterated and reiterated, the court is bound by no express limitations except the equal suffrage clause, which limits only the method of amendment. If the judiciary in the absence of such limitations go ahead and deliberately lay them down, it would seem that they are positively courting disaster.[84] In refusing to lay down restrictions, the court is not affirmatively violating any express clause of the Constitution. It is not violating any broad general provision, nor the "spirit" of the Constitution. In the absence of any other express limitations and in view of the reasonable conclusion that there are no other limitations, it seems that the court is merely doing its plain duty in refusing to discover any new restrictions. Considering the danger of implying such restrictions, and the unreasonableness of any such implications, it would seem that the onus is on the protagonists of the view of limited power to demonstrate clearly the legal basis of their view.

Rejection of implied limitation by the courts. It is a fact of no little importance that the Supreme Court of the United States and the inferior federal courts have given no encouragement to the view that there are implied limitations. To be sure, the Supreme Court has not categorically declared that

[84] "Impressive words of counsel remind us of our duty to maintain the integrity of constitutional government by adhering to the limitations laid by the sovereign people upon the expression of its will. . . . Not less imperative, however, is our duty to refuse to magnify their scope by resort to subtle implication. . . . Repeated decisions have informed us that only when conflict with the Constitution is clear and indisputable will a statute be condemned as void. Still more obvious is the duty of caution and moderation when the act to be reviewed is not an act of ordinary legislation, but an act of the great constituent power which has made Constitutions and hereafter may unmake them. Narrow at such times are the bounds of legitimate implications." Cardozo, J., in Browne v. City of New York, (1925) 241 N. Y. 96 at 112, 149 N. E. 211.

"Constitutions are not designed for metaphysical or logical subtleties, for niceties of expression, for critical propriety, for elaborate shades of meaning or for the exercise of philosophical acuteness or judicial research. . . . The people make them; the people adopt them, the people must be supposed to read them, with the help of common sense; and cannot be presumed to admit in them any recondite meaning or any extraordinary gloss." 1 STORY, COMMENTARIES ON THE CONSTITUTION OF THE UNITED STATES, 3d ed. (1858) § 451.

there are no such limits.[85] But it has either expressly or tacitly rejected every limitation urged upon it. The court did not pass on the question of restrictions in an opinion until the validity of the Eighteenth Amendment was adjudicated. The Fifteenth Amendment seems to have been the first that was ever attacked on that ground as exceeding the scope of the amending power. Even that attack was made only in comparatively recent years. But though the briefs of the appellant asserted the existence of limitations, the court completely ignored the contention in its decision.[86] When the legality of the Eighteenth Amendment was tested, the opinion was a mere syllabus statement that the amendment was "within the power to amend." Chief Justice White criticized the absence of any reasoning, and Justice McReynolds expressed himself as unable to come to any conclusion.[87] The scope of the power of amendment was first discussed by the court at any length in *Leser v. Garnett*[88] when the Nineteenth Amendment was attacked. In that case, too, the court upheld the amendment as against any implied restrictions. Manifestly the doctrine of implied limitations will have to rear its structure on something else than court decisions.

"Abuse" of the amending power an anomalous term. The proponents of implied limitations resort to the method of

[85] The Supreme Court "has not . . . ever decided or stated that there are no implied limits on the amending power. It is a practical certainty, that, if it ever passes on that question, it will hold that there are no such implied limits upon that power." ROTTSCHAEFER, CONSTITUTIONAL LAW (1939) 398.

[86] Myers v. Anderson, (1915) 238 U. S. 368, 35 S. Ct. 932. The lower court, Anderson v. Myers, (C. C. Md. 1910) 182 F. 223, expressly rejected the argument in favor of implied limitations.

[87] National Prohibition Cases, (1920) 253 U. S. 350, 40 S. Ct. 486, 588. Other cases passing on the scope are Buckner v. Street, (C. C. Ark. 1871) 1 Dill. 248, Fed. Cas. No. 2098; State of Ohio ex rel. Erchenbrecher v. Cox, (D. C. Ohio, 1919) 257 F. 334; Feigenspan v. Bodine, (D. C. N. J. 1920) 264 F. 186; Carson v. Sullivan, (1920) 284 Mo. 253, 223 S. W. 571.

[88] (1922) 258 U. S. 130, 42 S. Ct. 217.

reductio ad absurdum in pointing out the abuses which might occur if there were no limitations on the power to amend. The Supreme Court might be abolished. A monarchy might be set up. The women of the nation might be nationalized. In reply it should be pointed out in the first place that the fact that a power may be abused does not necessarily militate against the existence of the power.[89] The Supreme Court has declared over and over again that the possibility of abuse is not to be used as a test of the existence or extent of a power.[90] Thus the postal and taxing powers of the federal government may be abused, but that does not affect their existence or their scope. The possibility of abuse of intergovernmental taxation has not prevented the Supreme Court from recently permitting it.[91] Moreover, there seems to be no consensus as to what is and what is not an abuse of the amending power.

In the second place the amending power is a power of an altogether different kind from the ordinary governmental powers. If abuse occurs, it occurs at the hands of a special organization of the nation and of the states representing an extraordinary majority of the people, so that for all practical

[89] "The fear that sustaining the right of the people to extinguish the traffic in intoxicating liquors opens the door to a like prohibition of other business, therefore, is not well founded. But, if it were, it would be of little force in dealing with the question of power. The right to exercise power inevitably carries with it the possibility of abuse, but abuse in the exercise of power is no argument against its existence. The line between a proper use and abuse of power cannot be settled in advance; but it may be said, and that is as far as the present inquiry warrants, that whenever any other business produces like evils it may be disposed of in the same way." Feigenspan v. Bodine, (D. C. N. J. 1920) 264 F. 186 at 192.

[90] In re Rapier, (1892) 143 U. S. 110, 12 S. Ct. 374; McCray v. United States, (1904) 195 U. S. 27, 24 S. Ct. 769.

[91] James v. Dravo Contracting Co., (1937) 302 U. S. 134, 58 S. Ct. 208; Silas Mason Co. v. Tax Commission of Washington, (1937) 302 U. S. 186, 58 S. Ct. 233; Allen v. Regents of the University System of Georgia, (1938) 304 U. S. 439, 58 S. Ct. 980; Helvering v. Mountain Producers Corp., (1938) 303 U. S. 376, 58 S. Ct. 623; Helvering v. Gerhardt, (1938) 304 U. S. 405, 58 S. Ct. 969; Graves v. People ex rel. O'Keefe, (1939) 306 U. S. 466, 59 S. Ct. 595.

purposes it may be said to be the people, or at least the highest
agent of the people, and one exercising sovereign powers.[92]
Thus the people merely take the consequences of their own
acts, whereas where the abuse of a governmental authority
occurs, there is abuse by a mere governmental agent of the
people, and the people suffer the consequences of the arbi-
trary acts of individuals. It seems natural that somewhere
there resides within the nation the power to do anything, and
logically this authority resides in the amending body. It
seems anomalous to speak of "abuse" by such a body. Unless
the view be adopted that the people of the United States are
not sovereign and that they are not to be trusted to alter their
fundamental institutions but are to be carefully safeguarded
by a small group of men who know or think they know what
is best for the people, it seems necessary to conclude that they
have a full capacity to amend, free from any implicit limits,
no matter what abuses may result.

The consequences of the view just stated are not as ominous
as they may appear at first blush. No abusive assaults on our
constitutional system have as yet been made by amendment.

[92] "In this connection it should not be overlooked that the ultimate power to
amend the United States Constitution is not given to the federal government,
but to the people of the several states. The power of Congress in that respect
ends with its proposing the amendment to the states. The ultimate and controlling act is by the people themselves, acting through their chosen representatives."
Feigenspan v. Bodine, (D. C. N. J. 1920) 264 F. 186 at 195.

"Has it ever been pretended that the limitations of the power of the states
were also limitations on the whole people of the United States, when acting in
their aggregate, sovereign capacity in amending or altering their constitution
or government?" Buckner v. Street, (C. C. Ark. 1871) 1 Dill. 248 at 249, Fed.
Cas. No. 2098.

"An amendment, which has the deliberate judgment of two thirds of
Congress, and of three fourths of the states, can scarcely be deemed unsuited to
the prosperity or security of the republic. It must combine as much wisdom
and experience in its favor, as ordinarily can belong to the management of
any human concerns." 2 STORY, COMMENTARIES ON THE CONSTITUTION OF THE
UNITED STATES, 3d ed. (1858) § 1830.

"I grant that if three-fourths should make the chief magistrate hereditary,
it would be a gross abuse of power. Against this, and other abuses, we have
provided, by requiring so large a majority as three-fourths, and this is the
only guard we have thought necessary. The right in the one-fourth to correct
the abuse, is revolutionary, not sovereign." Argument of Blanding in State ex
rel. McCready v. Hunt, (1834) 2 Hill L. (S. C.) 1 at 172.

The language used in attacking the Fifteenth, Eighteenth, and Nineteenth Amendments has been much stronger and more suggestive of violence than the occasion warranted. However inexpedient negro suffrage and prohibition may be, it cannot be seriously pretended that they have weakened or seriously altered the general tenor of the Constitution. It may be that serious abuses may occur in the future; it can scarcely be said that they have occurred up to this time. It may be objected that the possibility of abuses in the future should be provided for. In reply, it may be said that the nation has not been threatened by the absence of such implied limitations thus far, and that there have been no wanton abuses. The generation of today cannot know the needs of the generation of tomorrow. Any restrictions which might be laid down now might easily turn out to be futile, while such as might prove beneficial may not be known or suggested by the leaders of the present era.[93] It seems best in this matter to permit each generation to take care of itself. In the last analysis, political machinery and artificial limitations will not protect the American people from themselves. "The perpetuity of American institutions will depend not upon special mechanisms or devices, nor even upon any particular legislation, but rather upon the good conscience and intelligence and the attitude of the American people themselves."[94]

Political questions. A recent development, though not directly dealing with the scope of the amending power, is the doctrine of "political questions" developed in the cases deal-

---

[93] "The framers of the Constitution could not foresee the form or character of amendments which might become necessary in the future and wisely left all such questions in the hands of those who might be charged with official duty when the necessity for the change and the character of the change to be made became apparent." Ex parte Dillon, (D. C. Cal. 1920) 262 F. 563 at 567–568.

[94] Bates, "How Shall We Preserve the Constitution?" (1926) 44 KAN. S. B. A. PROC. 128 at 147: "Now and then an extraordinary case may turn up, but constitutional law like other mortal contrivances has to take some chances, and in the great majority of instances no doubt justice will be done." See also Holmes, J., in Blinn v. Nelson, (1911) 222 U. S. 1 at 7, 32 S. Ct. 1.

ing with the child labor amendment.[95] If the time limit for ratification and the effect of prior rejections by states and possibly the right of the lieutenant governor of a state to cast a deciding vote when the state senate was equally divided, were political questions, why would not the scope of the amending power be a political question? The practical dangers of limiting the scope and the difficulties in laying down implied limitations might well justify the Supreme Court in disposing of the problem by calling it a political question. In the opinion of the writer, however, it would be more straightforward and courageous and less confusing to rule that there are no implied limitations.

[95] Coleman v. Miller, (1939) 307 U. S. 433, 59 S. Ct. 972; Chandler v. Wise, (1939) 307 U. S. 474, 59 S. Ct. 992.

CHAPTER V

Sovereignty and the Federal
Amending Clause

A. DEFINITION AND CHARACTERISTICS OF SOVEREIGNTY

IT has frequently been asserted that the most important and at the same time the most controverted topic of political science is that of sovereignty. It is significant in constitutional law and in international law only in a somewhat lesser degree. In fact, in its first development it seems to have been a juristic conception.[1] Its first modern exponent, Jean Bodin, was a French lawyer.[2] Its chief theorist of the common law was John Austin, another jurist.[3] The problem is of peculiar importance in a federal state such as the United States, since its location is not an obvious fact as it is in a unitary state. The Civil War was fought largely over conflicting conceptions of sovereignty and its location.[4] Even today the question of states' rights is not a merely speculative matter. The in-

[1] For the history of the concept of sovereignty, see EMERSON, STATE AND SOVEREIGNTY IN MODERN GERMANY (1928); HOLDSWORTH, SOME LESSONS FROM OUR LEGAL HISTORY (1928) 112–141; WARD, SOVEREIGNTY (1928) 1–48; EASTWOOD AND KEETON, THE AUSTINIAN THEORIES OF LAW AND SOVEREIGNTY (1929) 38–61; COHEN, RECENT THEORIES OF SOVEREIGNTY (1937) 7–128; McIlwain, "A Fragment on Sovereignty," (1933) 48 POL. SCI. Q. 94.

[2] For the view that Bodin was not such an absolutist after all, but that he supposed the sovereign to be subject to natural law, international law, and the constitutional laws of monarchy, see Shepard, "Sovereignty at the Cross Roads: A Study of Bodin," (1930) 45 POL. SCI. Q. 580. Accord: McIlwain, "A Fragment on Sovereignty," (1933) 48 POL. SCI. Q. 94. For the more usual view of Bodin, see Hearnshaw, "Bodin and the Genesis of the Doctrine of Sovereignty," TUDOR STUDIES (1924) 109 at 124–125.

[3] For a short summary of Austin's theories, see Smith, "The English Analytical Jurists," (1887) 21 AM. L. REV. 270.

[4] "For this question of loyalty to a sovereign is one which, more than any other, has divided men in their political, social, and even domestic relations." HURD, THE THEORY OF OUR NATIONAL EXISTENCE (1881) 537.

creased activities of the federal government have revived the controversy over sovereignty, if in truth it may be assumed that the issue had ever become obsolete. The 1939 cases treating certain phases of the amending process as political questions may further revive the question.[5] The problem in the United States seemingly may be regarded as perennial. Hence efforts at its reanalysis can never be regarded as superfluous or futile.

The problem of sovereignty may be approached from the viewpoints of law, of political science, and of philosophy. It is one of the chief technical terms of each of these fields of knowledge. Each has given the term a meaning with a content different from that of the other sciences. In fact, the same science has at different periods of time defined the word in a varying manner. In the words of Bryce:

"As the borderland between two kingdoms used in unsettled states of society to be the region where disorder and confusion most prevailed, and in which turbulent men found refuge from justice, so fallacies and confusions of thought and language have most frequently survived and longest escaped detection in those territories where the limits of conterminous sciences or branches of learning have not been exactly drawn. The frontier districts, if one may call them so, of Ethics, of Law, and of Political Science have been thus infested by a number of vague or ambiguous terms which have produced many barren discussions and caused much needless trouble to students. . . .

"No offender of this kind has given more trouble than the so-called 'Doctrine of Sovereignty.' "[6]

Before plunging into one of the most fiercely controverted subjects of both legal and political theory, it becomes necessary to make clear the purpose of this discussion and the attitude of the writer towards the concept of sovereignty. The writer has no new definition of the term to offer. Nor does

---

[5] See Chapter II, supra.
[6] BRYCE, STUDIES IN HISTORY AND JURISPRUDENCE (1901) 503–504.

he subscribe to the views of any particular publicist or school of legal philosophy. He does not believe that there is any one specific, precise conception which undebatably deserves the appellation of sovereignty. This discussion will accept as the definition of sovereignty and as the list of its chief characteristics those which most authorities at the present time appear to adopt. The writer thoroughly agrees with Dean Edwin D. Dickinson, who says: "Probably nowhere in law, private or public, is there to be found a more tyrannical phrase than 'the sovereignty of the state.' "[7] This discussion is not intended to give new emphasis to the importance of sovereignty. But the subject has been so constantly discussed that a treatment of the federal amending process would be incomplete without it. In the words of Professor McIlwain:

"It requires considerable courage, or presumption, as some might prefer to style it, to ask a reader's attention once more to so well-worn a topic as sovereignty. Few political conceptions have been the subject of so much discussion amongst us in the last hundred years. But this very fact is proof of its vital importance in our modern world; and the wide variety of the views held concerning its essence, as well as the conflicting conclusions to which these views still lead, may furnish sufficient excuse for another attempt to clarify some of our ideas touching this central formula under which we try to rationalize the complicated facts of our modern political life."[8]

One is confronted also with Professor McIlwain's challenge: "Our theory, such as it is, has been mainly a theory of lawyers who were usually content to accept their explanation of government as secondhand from later English legal sources such as the Commentaries of Sir William Blackstone. . . ."[9]

---

[7] Dickinson, "New Avenues to Freedom," (1931) 25 MICH. L. REV. 622 at 623. Carl J. Friedrich is "inclined to discard for political science the concept of sovereignty (as well as that of the state) as of no scientific value for a realistic approach. . . ." Book Review, (1937) 7 BROOKLYN L. REV. 266.

[8] McIlwain, "A Fragment on Sovereignty," (1933) 48 POL. SCI. Q. 94.

[9] Ibid. at 105.

It is the purpose of this discussion to deal with sovereignty from the point of view of law. It therefore becomes necessary to distinguish between what have been respectively called legal sovereignty and political sovereignty. A person or body is said to have legal sovereignty when he or it has unlimited law-making power, and when there is no person or body legally superior to him or it.[10] Perhaps it would be correct to say that the possession of unlimited law-making power is enough, for it is difficult to see how there can be any superior to a group which can make laws on all subjects since that group could pass a law abolishing the powers of the supposed superior. In other words, sovereignty is legal absolutism. By the political sovereign, on the other hand, is meant the group within a state which in actual fact determines the bent of governmental action. Legal sovereignty is consciously exercised; political sovereignty generally is not. In a normally peaceful state the legal sovereign and the political sovereign will generally be coincident. But in time of disturbance political sovereignty may rest in the army, or in the Church, or in labor unions, or in other groups. The proper relation of the

[10] "It should, however, be carefully noted that the term 'sovereignty,' as long as it is accurately employed in the sense in which Austin sometimes uses it, is a merely legal conception, and means simply the power of law-making unrestricted by any legal limit." DICEY, LAW OF THE CONSTITUTION, 8th ed. (1915) 70. See also, 1 AUSTIN, JURISPRUDENCE, 4th ed. (1873) 226; BROWN, THE AUSTINIAN THEORY OF LAW (1906) §§ 539, 545; BRYCE, STUDIES IN HISTORY AND JURISPRUDENCE (1901) 505, 509; Dickinson, "A Working Theory of Sovereignty: I," (1927) 42 POL. SCI. Q. 524 at 532; Harrison, "The English School of Jurisprudence," (1878) 30 FORTNIGHTLY REV. 475 at 492; LEWIS, REMARKS ON THE USE AND ABUSE OF SOME POLITICAL TERMS (1832) 40; MARKBY, ELEMENTS OF LAW, 6th ed. (1905) § 31; MERRIAM, HISTORY OF THE THEORY OF SOVEREIGNTY SINCE ROUSSEAU (1900) 155, 218; POLLOCK A FIRST BOOK OF JURISPRUDENCE, 6th ed. (1929) 272; Ritchie, "On the Conception of Sovereignty," (1891) 1 AM. ACAD. POL. SCI. ANNALS 385 at 392; WILLOUGHBY, THE NATURE OF THE STATE (1928) 291; McIlwain, "Sovereignty Again," (1926) 6 ECONOMICA 253 at 256; COHEN, RECENT THEORIES OF SOVEREIGNTY (1937) 36, 84; EASTWOOD AND KEETON, THE AUSTINIAN THEORIES OF LAW AND SOVEREIGNTY (1929) 62, 67; EMERSON, STATE AND SOVEREIGNTY IN MODERN GERMANY (1928) 255, 259; Chafee, Book Review, (1919) 32 HARV. L. REV. 979 at 980.

legal and the political sovereigns is one of the chief problems of a sound legal system and of good government.

Much confusion might have been avoided if the term sovereignty had been treated as an exclusively legal conception. It was first developed in the law. It has a genuine and, in most modern governments, an indispensable utility in describing the legal system of the state. It meets the need for certainty and precision as to the authoritative source of rules of law. Its use in political science has no particular value. The term "public opinion" or some similar phrase would be fully as descriptive, and would enable the student to grasp the meaning of the word without the careful reading of the context which is now necessary.

Sovereignty as a legal conception has sometimes been viewed as having two aspects: one external and one internal. The external sovereignty is the independence of the state in relation to other nations. The internal sovereignty is the relation of the sovereign within the state to the individuals and associations within the state. The purpose of this discussion is to consider the latter type of sovereignty. As a matter of strict legal theory it seems hard to regard a mere internal or external sovereignty as a full sovereignty. From the point of view of constitutional law, the so-called internal sovereign has unlimited law-making power. Hence as a question of municipal law, the lawyer will concern himself only with the rules laid down by the internal sovereign irrespective of their compliance with international law. Only in a case before an international tribunal would the lawyer look to the limitations on the so-called internal sovereignty laid down by international law. Viewed as a question of constitutional law, the internal sovereign would be regarded as supreme both externally and internally by the English and American lawyers. As Jellinek says, the so-called external sovereignty is merely a reflex of the internal sovereignty.[11] Thus from the point of view of constitutional law an amendment relating to territory outside of the nation would be valid.

As a matter of fact, it is sometimes confusing to admit the use of the term sovereignty in international law. Etymologically the word means "superiority." Historically it is descriptive of the relation existing between a state and its subjects. "Properly interpreted, sovereignty is a term of constitutional law and political science and not of international law, and it implies nothing more than the legal right of the state to determine its own internal life, regulate its own purely domestic affairs and make laws for its own subjects within its own territory."[12]

[11] DIE LEHRE VON DEN STAATENVERBINDUNGEN (1882) 23–24. Oppenheim says: "Sovereignty in the strict and narrowest sense of the term implies, therefore, independence all round, within and without the borders of the country." 1 OPPENHEIM, INTERNATIONAL LAW, 4th ed. (1928) § 64.

As to the relation between municipal law and international law, most Anglo-American writers assert the ultimate supremacy of the former as viewed from the standpoint of constitutional law. PICCIOTTO, THE RELATION OF INTERNATIONAL LAW TO THE LAW OF ENGLAND AND THE UNITED STATES OF AMERICA (1915); WRIGHT, THE ENFORCEMENT OF INTERNATIONAL LAW THROUGH MUNICIPAL LAW IN THE UNITED STATES (1916). The Continental writers are divided. See ANZILOTTI, IL DIRITTO INTERNAZIONALE NEI GIUDIZI INTERNI (1905); KAUFMANN, DIE RECHTSKRAFT DES INTERNATIONALEN RECHTS UND DAS VERHÄLTNITZE DER STAATSGESETZGEBUNGEN (1899); KELSEN, DAS PROBLEM DER SOUVERÄNITÄT UND DIE THEORIE DES VÖLKERRECHTS (1928) 120 ff.; KRABBE, THE MODERN IDEA OF THE STATE, translation (1922) 233 ff.; TRIEPEL, DROIT INTERNATIONAL ET DROIT INTERNE (1920) 132–152. A decade ago the German, Austrian, and Esthonian constitutions provided that international law should form a part of the national law. See also MATTERN, CONCEPTS OF STATE, SOVEREIGNTY AND INTERNATIONAL LAW (1928) 71; COHEN, RECENT THEORIES OF SOVEREIGNTY (1937) 57–92.

[12] Garner, "Limitations on National Sovereignty in International Relations," (1925) 19 AM. POL. SCI. REV. 1 at 6; Willoughby, "The Juristic Conception of the State," (1918) 12 AM. POL. SCI. REV. 192 at 202, takes the same view. Clark points out that "as a matter of juristic literature, independence *ab extra* has often been confused under the same title with the notion of a permanent *internal* superior, probably because of the practical indispensability of the latter, which I have previously pointed out, to any lasting external relations whatever." CLARK, PRACTICAL JURISPRUDENCE (1883) 173–174. "As a substantive, *sovereign* is a term expressing the relation between part of a given political society, or state, and the remainder. . . ." Ibid. 174. "Indeed, the term *sovereignty* altogether, as used to express external independence of a state, is going out of use." Ibid. 175. Unfortunately, almost fifty years after the above statements were

Legal sovereignty, or simply sovereignty, as it will hereafter be designated, it seems to the writer, has perhaps five leading characteristics. In the first place, it is a matter of fact, or of fact and law (although admittedly this tends to confuse the distinction from political sovereignty). The law of a state may expressly or impliedly recognize the sovereign as such, but such recognition is not essential. The sovereign of a state exists as such as a matter of fact, although in the long run it also exists as a matter of law. For example, in England Parliament is sovereign, although there is no law to that effect. To say that sovereignty rests on law would be inconsistent, since the sovereign is the creator of law.

A second characteristic ascribed to the sovereign by many writers is that it is absolute. It can pass a law on any subject it chooses, and such a law will be regarded as valid, in the sense that the courts of the state will enforce it. From the point of view of the lawyer, *qua* lawyer, it is sufficient that the sovereign has passed the law, and he will look no further as to its authority. If the body thought to be sovereign can legislate only on a limited range of subjects, it is not sovereign. In fact, the chief content of sovereignty is that its scope is unlimited.[13] That is, the sovereign is distinguished from any other legislative body in that it determines the limits of its own competence. If there is any other superior body or group

written the term is still much used in international relations, as shown for example in the objections raised in the Senate to the League of Nations and the Permanent Court.

From the point of view of international law, an internal limitation on the legal capacity of the state or its organ does not impair its independence in relation to other states. But from the point of view of constitutional law, there would seem to be a real limitation on sovereignty if the limitation is regarded as enforceable. As Salmond says, "all questions as to civil and supreme power are questions as to what is possible within, not without, the limits of the constitution." SALMOND, JURISPRUDENCE, 7th ed. (1924) 531.

[13] "The theory of sovereignty says nothing about the content of the command. The only question is whether it issues from a proper source; an imperative issuing from an authoritative source *is* law." KRABBE, THE MODERN IDEA OF THE STATE (1922), p. xlvi of the Introduction by Sabine and Shepard.

which can repeal or modify the laws it passes, or which can take away or even alter the limits of its competence, it is not sovereign, even though the superior group seldom acts. The mere potentiality of its action is enough to strip the inferior body of its claim to sovereign powers. Sovereignty is defined as unlimited legislative power. If power is given to another group to legislate with respect to certain topics, the original sovereign no longer has absolute law-making powers. It can legislate only in the fields which it did not give up, and this violates the essence of sovereignty, that the extent of its action has no limits as to subject matter.[14] It may be that the first group and the latter group each has a range of powers which the other cannot disturb. But that alone is insufficient. What each group has is simply governmental power, and not sovereign power. Otherwise it would be proper in certain cases to speak of municipal corporations as being sovereigns, when the Constitution provides for "Home Rule," as in some state constitutions in the United States.

In the third place, sovereignty is generally asserted to be indivisible. There is no inherent reason why this should be the case. It is a unit merely by definition. Sovereignty is an abstract conception and not a universal found in all countries at all times.

The fourth characteristic of sovereignty is that from the point of view of the lawyer the law passed by the sovereign need not be enforced, in particular cases at least. Looked at from a strictly juristic standpoint, the promulgation of a rule by the sovereign is enough to make the rule good law. Austin seems to have made obedience a prime factor in his definition of sovereignty: "If a *determinate* human superior, *not* in the habit of obedience to a like superior, receive *habitual* obedi-

---

[14] Willoughby seems to have underestimated the distinction between governmental and constituent power when he says that they are "two classes of functions that differ not as to kind, but only as to the subject matter with which they deal." WILLOUGHBY, THE NATURE OF THE STATE (1928) 206. Yet he later admits that "the amending clauses may fairly be said to be the most important clauses of any constitution." Ibid. 401.

ence from the *bulk* of a given society, that determinate superior is sovereign in that society, and the society (including the superior) is a society political and independent."[15] But jurists since Austin seem to have given less emphasis to enforcement, and regard it as a problem outside of the law. It is indeed the chief distinguishing mark of the political sovereign, but only a postulate of the legal sovereign.[16] In the long run, the legal sovereign must receive obedience to be such, but isolated violations of its laws do not detract from its character as sovereign.

The fifth characteristic attributed to the sovereign by most writers is that it is determinate. Who the political sovereign is, is generally not determinate, since public opinion is a force which operates indirectly and circuitously. But unless the alleged legal sovereign can be ascertained, it must be concluded that there is no such sovereign. To Austin must go the credit for having made determinateness a requisite of the sovereign.[17] The Anglo-American lawyer is accustomed to viewing law as something commanded or permitted by the

[15] 1 Austin, Jurisprudence, 4th ed. (1873) 226.

[16] "Sovereignty is authority, not might." McIlwain, "Sovereignty Again," (1926) 6 Economica 253 at 256.

The lawyer's "sole and ultimate standard of good law is the formal command of sovereign force supposed to be irresistible and unlimited." Harrison, "The English School of Jurisprudence," (1878) 30 Fortnightly Rev. 475 at 485. "The consideration of the limits on the sovereign power carries us outside of law courts, and therefore outside of law. If the sovereign be really sovereign, it will be able to compel its own law courts to enforce its own laws. Therefore, *to the lawyer, and for purposes of law,* the sovereign is unlimited. Any limitations on this sovereignty lie wholly outside the lawyer's province." Ibid. 490. John Dickinson says: "Legally a sovereign may well promulgate laws which actually he is unable to enforce." Dickinson, "A Working Theory of Sovereignty: II," (1928) 43 Pol. Sci. Q. 32 at 43. See also Bryce, Studies in History and Jurisprudence (1901) 509; Harrison, On Jurisprudence and the Conflict of Laws (1919) 24.

[17] "But Austin not only serves us by presenting in a typical form one theory of sovereignty, with its logical consequences worked out; he also, as it seems to me, points in the right direction in his emphasis upon determinateness." Dewey, "Austin's Theory of Sovereignty," (1894) 9 Pol. Sci. Q. 31 at 51. "Except as sovereignty secures for itself definite and definable modes of expression, sovereignty is unrealized and inchoate. Constitutional development has consisted precisely in creating definite ways in which sovereignty should exercise its powers." Ibid. 52.

sovereign. Unless this sovereign can be isolated, one cannot be sure that a law is valid, since it may turn out that it was not prescribed by the sovereign. In the words of Frederic Harrison:

"But there are no limits to the absolute power of the sovereign within the range of *municipal law;* or, in other words, *to the lawyer,* there are none. . . . *Law, for the purposes of the lawyer,* is a species of command issued by such a political supreme authority, to its political inferiors or subjects habitually obeying it. Nothing that is not a *command* is *law;* and nothing commanded by anything but the supreme authority, as already defined, is law."[18]

Sovereignty and law are thus inseparably linked. The sovereign having been located, the lawyer simply accepts his orders as law, without further consideration. This makes for simplicity and certainty in the law, and reduces sovereignty to a comparatively simple proposition as it relates to the problem of law.

The meaning of determinateness is not to be too narrowly circumscribed. It may mean a single person or a group of persons. Austin himself attributed sovereignty to a specific person, or a specific group; or to the person or group which comes within a certain class. Thus in England sovereignty rests in the King in Parliament, that is in those persons who at the time happen to be the King, the members of the House of Lords, and the members of the House of Commons. Where the sovereign is a single person, it is easier to understand the

---

[18] Harrison, "The English School of Jurisprudence," (1878) 30 FORTNIGHTLY REV. 475 at 484. Laski, "The Theory of Popular Sovereignty," (1919) 17 MICH. L. REV. 201 at 214, says: "For the lawyer, all that is immediately necessary, is a knowledge of the authorities that are legally competent to deal with the problems that arise. For him, then, the idea of sovereignty has a particular and definite meaning. It does not matter that an act is socially harmful or unpopular or morally wrong; if it issues from the authority competent to act, and is issued in due form, he has, from the legal stand-point, no further problems." See also, Ritchie, "On the Conception of Sovereignty," (1891) 1 AM. ACAD. POL. SCI. ANNALS 385; WILLOUGHBY, THE NATURE OF THE STATE (1928) 293-294.

fact of his being sovereign. But a group, as long as it is definitely ascertainable, no matter how numerous, may also be sovereign according to the writers. Although it is combined for action according to artificial rules, it nevertheless is sovereign. When the group acts, it acts corporately. This would seem to answer the objection of Dewey, who asks: "Admit, however, that sovereignty can be thus latent, then is every individual who composes this possible electorate a sharer in sovereignty?"[19] The sovereign may regulate the individual members of the group at will, and still be sovereign, as each person when acting does not exercise an individual bit of sovereignty but the corporate sovereignty which belongs to the whole group.

It has been seen that by sovereignty is meant unlimited law-making power. There have been many who have asserted that such a power must reside somewhere within every state.[20] Instead of being an abstract conception, applicable only to certain types of modern states, it has been thought to be a universal. Sovereignty has been placed in the King or Emperor. In England it is asserted to be in Parliament. In France (up to 1940 at any rate) it has been thought of as being in the Constituent Convention. In the United States it is con-

---

[19] Dewey, "Austin's Theory of Sovereignty," (1894) 9 POL. SCI. Q. 31 at 39. John Chipman Gray also seems to have overlooked the corporate nature of the exercise of sovereignty. GRAY, THE NATURE AND SOURCES OF THE LAW (1909) § 176. And likewise, BLISS, OF SOVEREIGNTY (1885) 125.

[20] "However they began, or by what right soever they subsist, there is and must be in all of them a supreme, irresistible, absolute, uncontrolled authority, in which the *jura summa imperii*, or the rights of sovereignty, reside." 1 BLACKSTONE, COMMENTARIES (1756) 49. See also Ritchie, "On the Conception of Sovereignty," (1891) 1 AM. ACAD. POL. SCI. ANNALS 385; WILLOUGHBY, THE NATURE OF THE STATE (1928) 183, 195, 206.

John Dickinson rests sovereignty not on an imperative theory of law, but "on the need for a single source of authoritative formulation." Dickinson, "A Working Theory of Sovereignty," (1927) 42 POL. SCI. Q. 524 at 525, note. "*Sovereignty in the legal sense* is after all nothing more or less than a logical postulate or presupposition of any system according to law." Ibid. 525. See also, MARKBY, ELEMENTS OF LAW, 6th ed. (1905) § 36; EMERSON, STATE AND SOVEREIGNTY IN MODERN GERMANY (1928) 272; COHEN, RECENT THEORIES OF SOVEREIGNTY (1937) 145.

stantly reiterated that it is in the people of the United States. A group of French publicists of the early nineteenth century, Cousin, Guizot, and Constant, asserted the sovereignty of reason.[21]

Closer analysis reveals, however, that there is no inherent necessity that a sovereign exist within a state. A study of early civilization reveals that many states have existed where there was no unlimited law-making power, and where custom or religion furnished the chief sources of the law. The kings and emperors of the Middle Ages regarded themselves as subject to the Law of God and the Law of Nature. With the establishment of the modern independent states of Europe, however, there came to be a real sovereign within each state. But the federal or composite state still presented the possibility of there being no sovereign in the state. If the framers of the Constitution had omitted any provision for amendment, as they might have done, it is difficult to see that there would be any sovereign in the United States.[22] Possibly an implied power to make amendments in the same manner that the Constitution was adopted would be inferred. But even this possibility might have been anticipated by an express provision of the original Constitution that there should never be any amendments. Under this state of affairs the federal government would be confined to the powers granted to it, and the states to all other powers except those expressly denied to the states or those reserved to the people. Thus there could

---

[21] MERRIAM, HISTORY OF THE THEORY OF SOVEREIGNTY SINCE ROUSSEAU (1900) 75–79. Bliss would eliminate the concept of sovereignty altogether. BLISS, OF SOVEREIGNTY (1885) 57, 173, 175. Edwin D. Dickinson says that sovereignty "has been an excuse for vanity, a subterfuge for selfish ambition, and a screen for ignorance in international relations. Rarely if ever has it expressed a legal principle or standard unmistakably relevant to the substance of the particular problem or controversy." Dickinson, "New Avenues to Freedom," (1931) 25 MICH L. REV. 622 at 625.

[22] DICEY, LAW OF THE CONSTITUTION, 8th ed. (1915) 143; BROWN, THE AUSTINIAN THEORY OF LAW (1906) 157, note; EASTWOOD AND KEETON, THE AUSTINIAN THEORIES OF LAW AND SOVEREIGNTY (1929) 70.

be no redistribution of powers among the states and the federal government and the people. Inasmuch as the essence of sovereignty according to the usual definition consists in the ability to fix the sovereign's own competence, and that of the inferior groups, there would demonstrably be no sovereign.

B. LOCATION OF SOVEREIGNTY IN THE UNITED STATES

It is conceivable that there might be no sovereign in the United States. But if there be one, it is a matter of the first importance to the lawyer to locate it, since it lies within the theoretical power of that sovereign to alter every rule which he is accustomed to regard as law. In the United States, powers are first divided between the federal government and the states. These powers in turn are subdivided between the executive, legislative, and judicial departments of each government. Outside of all these are the powers forbidden to the federal government, or to the state governments, and the powers reserved to the people. Apart even from these is the amending capacity itself, which can only be exercised by the federal government and the states jointly.

A theory which seems to have been the prevalent one during the period immediately after the Constitutional Convention was that sovereignty was divided between the states and the nation.[23] But sovereignty by definition is indivisible. The states and the federal government simply had plenary powers

---

[23] 1 STORY, COMMENTARIES ON THE CONSTITUTION OF THE UNITED STATES, 3d ed. (1858) §§ 207, 208; Cooley, "Sovereignty in the United States," (1892) 1 MICH. L. J. 81. Willoughby refers to all the legislative organs of the state, as well as the amending body, as exercising sovereign powers. He says that "all organs through which are expressed the volitions of the State, be they parliaments, courts, constitutional assemblies or electorates, are to be considered as exercising sovereign power, and as constituting in the aggregate the depository in which the State's Sovereignty is located." WILLOUGHBY, THE NATURE OF THE STATE (1928) 307. See also BRYCE, STUDIES IN HISTORY AND JURISPRUDENCE (1901) 507. It would seem more accurate, however, to say that ordinary legislative bodies merely exercise powers which have been delegated to them by the sovereign.

as to specific matters, and neither party could interfere with the powers of the other. Neither could determine its own legal competence. Both were subject to the amending body. Both the states and the federal government began later to claim exclusive sovereignty, and in the end all the disputants came to agree that sovereignty was a unit and indivisible.

A second theory, made popular chiefly through the efforts of John Calhoun, was that sovereignty resides in the states. So firmly was the theory held that it largely brought on the Civil War. But when the tests of sovereignty described above are applied, it becomes evident that the view has no sound basis. The clauses of the original Constitution itself show the limitations which were placed on the so-called sovereignty of the states. Article One, section 10, forbids the states to make treaties, coin money, emit bills of credit, pass any bill of attainder, ex post facto law, or law impairing the obligation of contracts, to lay duties on imports or exports, to lay tonnage duties, to keep troops or warships in time of peace, to enter into any agreement with another state, or with a foreign power, or to engage in war unless actually invaded. The Civil War Amendments and the recent amendments stripped them of further powers. A single state cannot amend the Constitution. The amending body is superior to it, and the state is bound by an amendment even though it does not ratify it.[24]

[24] It has frequently been pointed out that the subjection of the states to the amending power makes the United States a nation, instead of a confederacy. State ex rel. McCready v. Hunt, (1834) 2 Hill L. (S. C.) 1 at 171, 172, 179 (argument of Blanding); Madison in the debates of the Virginia Convention ratifying the Constitution, 3 ELLIOT, DEBATES ON THE ADOPTION OF THE FEDERAL CONSTITUTION (1937 reprint of 1836 2d ed.) 93–97; 1 CURTIS, CONSTITUTIONAL HISTORY OF THE UNITED STATES (1899) 613; 2 ibid. 19, note; 9 DANE, A GENERAL ABRIDGMENT AND DIGEST OF AMERICAN LAW (1829), Appendix 38; 1 BURGESS, POLITICAL SCIENCE AND COMPARATIVE CONSTITUTIONAL LAW (1891) 144; HART, INTRODUCTION TO THE STUDY OF FEDERAL GOVERNMENT (1891) 18; JAMESON, CONSTITUTIONAL CONVENTIONS, 4th ed. (1887) §§ 38, 57; POMEROY, CONSTITUTIONAL LAW, 10th ed. (1888) § 111; WILLOUGHBY, THE NATURE OF THE STATE (1928) 263. The same argument was made as to the status of the states in Germany. EMERSON, STATE AND SOVEREIGNTY IN MODERN GERMANY (1928) 99.

The state therefore fails as to both tests of sovereignty: it has no unlimited law-making power, and it is subject to a superior, the amending body.

During and immediately after the Civil War, the theory of sovereignty veered to the other extreme, and it was alleged that sovereignty was in the nation or in the federal government. Assuming that there is such a thing as external sovereignty, it is perhaps substantially correct to say that it is vested in the federal government. Yet the treaty-making power is subject to limitations, so that the government does not have even a complete external sovereignty. As to internal powers, the federal government has only the powers expressly or impliedly conferred on it, and all other powers not prohibited to the states are reserved to the states or to the people. Thus from one point of view the federal government has even less power than the states. Moreover, the federal government, like the states, cannot amend the Constitution, and is itself subject to the amending body. It should be noted, however, that the recent decisions on the child labor amendment look in the direction of making Congress in effect the sovereign by an application of the doctrine of political questions.[25]

The doctrine of the Supreme Court and of many of the leading commentators on constitutional law has been, and still seems to be, that sovereignty is located in the people.[26] This doctrine is ambiguous, perhaps conveniently so. As someone has pithily remarked, its "only force lies in the reputation of its advocates." Savigny has pointed out that in gen-

---

[25] Coleman v. Miller, (1939) 307 U. S. 433, 59 S. Ct. 972; Chandler v. Wise, (1939) 307 U. S. 474, 59 S. Ct. 992.

[26] ". . . the people, in their collective and national capacity, established the present constitution. It is remarkable, that in establishing it, the people exercised their own rights, and their own proper sovereignty, and conscious of the plenitude of it, they declared with becoming dignity 'We, the people of the United States, do ordain and establish this Constitution.' Here we see the people acting as sovereigns of the whole country; and in the language of sovereignty, establishing a constitution by which it was their will, that the state governments should

eral "people" may have at least four meanings.[27] It may in its broadest sense include all the persons living within the state during the whole time of the existence of the state. Obviously it is difficult to view a legal rule as proceeding from such a group. In the second place, it may mean the sum of all the individuals as an organized group living within the state

be bound, and to which the state constitutions should be made to conform." Jay, C. J., in Chisholm v. Georgia, (1793) 2 Dall. (2 U. S.) 419 at 470–471. See also the opinion of Wilson, J., at 454.

"The people of the United States, as one great political community, have willed that a certain portion of the government . . . should be deposited in and exercised by a national government; and that all matters of merely local interest should be deposited in and exercised by the state governments." Bradley, J., dissenting in Keith v. Clark, (1878) 97 U. S. 454 at 476.

"The sovereignty of a state does not reside in the persons who fill the different departments of its government; but in the people from whom the government emanated, and who may change it at their discretion. Sovereignty, then, in this country, abides with the constituency and not with the agent." Spooner v. McConnell, (C. C. Ohio 1838) 1 McLean 337 at 347, F. Cas. No. 13245.

"But in the last analysis the people are the sovereigns, and both the states and the United States are only serving instrumentalities. Whatever limitations are on such sovereignty are self-imposed." Feigenspan v. Bodine, (D. C. N. J. 1920) 264 F. 186 at 191.

See also McCulloch v. Maryland, (1819) 4 Wheat. (17 U. S.) 316; Cohens v. Virginia, (1821) 6 Wheat. (19 U. S.) 264 at 413; Yick Wo v. Hopkins, (1886) 118 U. S. 356, 6 S. Ct. 1064. Sovereignty was asserted to be in the people of the states and not of the nation by McLean, J., in Worcester v. Georgia, (1832) 6 Pet. (31 U. S.) 515; and Taney, C. J., in Ableman v. Booth, (1858) 21 How. (62 U. S.) 506 at 524. Jameson asserts that the view of popular sovereignty is accepted by "nearly all the writers, judges and lawyers who have expressed opinions on the subjects in the United States." Jameson, "National Sovereignty," (1890) 5 POL. SCI. Q. 193 at 194. This is also the view of WOODROW WILSON, THE STATE (1906) 610. See also Willis, "The Doctrine of Sovereignty under the United States Constitution," (1929) 15 VA. L. REV. 437.

If sovereignty be dropped as a legal term and viewed solely as a term of political science and philosophy, the views of the Supreme Court and the writers are doubtless correct. It has been asserted that state sovereignty "is primarily not a legal, but a philosophical conception." Brierly, "The Shortcomings of International Law," BRITISH YEAR BOOK (1924) 4 at 12. Pittman B. Potter says that it was a doctrine "which political scientists invented." Potter, "Political Science in the International Field," (1923) 17 AM. POL. SCI. REV. 381 at 385. Walter Thompson states that "it is doubtful if sovereignty can be retained as a purely legal concept." Book Review, (1938) 32 AM. POL. SCI. REV. 128 at 129.

[27] 1 SAVIGNY, SYSTEM DES HEUTIGEN RÖMISCHEN RECHTS (1840) § 10; see also Briggs, "Sovereignty and the Consent of the Governed," (1901) 35 AM. L. REV. 49.

at the same time. The third view is that it means the latter individuals with the exception of the government. In the fourth place, it may mean in republican states that particular organized assembly of individuals in which, according to the Constitution, the highest power really exists.[28] Possibly this is what the Supreme Court has meant when it referred to the people as being sovereign. But its language has been altogether too indefinite to make this clear.

With particular reference to the United States, by people may be meant either the people of the United States or the people of the individual states. The view of the Supreme Court has been that it means the former. Even accepting the former as being correct, it is not clear whether that means simply the electorate, or all citizens of the United States,[29] or the people as a politically organized mass,[30] or the people as an inorganic mass.

The Constitution nowhere expressly refers to the people as sovereign. The assertions in the Declaration of Independence of the inalienable rights of the people to liberty and the pursuit of happiness and the right to alter and abolish the government are nowhere repeated. Virtually the only mention of the people is in the Preamble and in the Ninth and Tenth Amendments. According to the Preamble the people of the

[28] "In the United States, indeed, the 'people' are the one original source of law, but it is the people in their entirely definite, aggregate, political, that is constitutional organization that is meant here." 2 VON HOLST, CONSTITUTIONAL HISTORY OF THE UNITED STATES (1879) 75.

[29] "The words 'people of the United States' and 'citizens' are synonymous terms, and mean the same thing. They both describe the political body who, according to our republican institutions, form the sovereignty, and who hold the power and conduct the Government through their representatives. They are what we call familiarly the 'sovereign people' and every citizen is one of this people, and a constituent member of this sovereignty." Dred Scott v. Sanford, (1856) 19 How. (60 U. S.) 393 at 404.

[30] "But who are the people? In the true sense of the term, it means the political society considered as a unit, comprising in one organization the entire population of the state, of all ages, sexes, and conditions." JAMESON, CONSTITUTIONAL CONVENTIONS, 4th ed. (1887) § 568.

United States ordain and establish the Constitution. But it is a remarkable fact that the Preamble as originally drawn named each of the thirteen states individually and that a change was made only because it was not known which states would ratify the Constitution.[31] Moreover the Preamble has no legal force. Even if the people were sovereign when they drew up the Constitution, they must be regarded as having given up their sovereignty when they provided for amendment by others than themselves. The Ninth Amendment provides: "The enumeration in the Constitution, of certain rights, shall not be construed to deny or disparage others retained by the people." The Tenth provides: "The powers not delegated to the United States by the Constitution, nor prohibited by it to the States, are reserved to the States respectively, or to the people." Neither amendment confers any affirmative powers on the people, nor clarifies the meaning of the word. Sovereignty or the power to amend can scarcely be derived from them. The Supreme Court has recently denied the right of popular referendum on amendments.[32]

It would seem clear that sovereignty does not lie in the corporate mass of the people of the United States, or in the organized citizenry. They have not the power to amend the Constitution. They do not even participate in the election of those who do have the amending power. The only sovereignty which they can be said to have is of a strictly nonlegal character, that of the force of public opinion and physical force. If such a test is adopted, there is no state now, and there has been no time in history when the people were not sovereign.

It is, to be sure, somewhat closer to the truth to speak of the electorate as sovereign. But even that group does not meet the test of sovereignty. It cannot determine its own competence,

[31] 5 ELLIOT, DEBATES (1836) 376.
[32] Hawke v. Smith, (1920) 253 U. S. 221, 40 S. Ct. 495.

and it is subject to a superior power. It simply elects those who do exercise the amending capacity. But election does not take place by a simple majority of the nation, or by a three-fourths majority. The election occurs within the limits of each state, and it is three-fourths of the states and not of the aggregate people that adopt amendments. The amending body is not the agent or the trustee of the electorate.[33] Once elected, the members of Congress and the state legislatures are free to adopt what amendments they will. They are ultimately politically accountable to the people, but not legally so. The mere act of voting for those who exercise the amending capacity is not the passing of a law. It is a mere ministerial act at the most and does not bring into being a rule of law. Even the exercise of the voting capacity occurs in most cases biennially.[34] In the event of the proposal of amendments by a national convention or ratification by state conventions, the electorate would as a matter of fact exercise considerable influence on particular constitutional changes, since election would be on the basis of the candidate's attitude towards the proposed amendments. But when proposal is by Congress and ratification by the legislatures, so many issues are involved in the election that the candidate's attitude concerning proposed amendments is likely to be overlooked or ignored. Only in the event that Article Five was amended so that the

[33] DICEY, THE LAW OF THE CONSTITUTION, 8th ed. (1915) 45; Ritchie, "On the Conception of Sovereignty," (1891) 1 AM. ACAD. POL. SCI. ANNALS 385 at 392; LEWIS, SOME REMARKS ON THE USE AND ABUSE OF SOME POLITICAL TERMS (1832) 43; BRYCE, STUDIES IN HISTORY AND JURISPRUDENCE (1901) 510, 538. D. O. McGovney seems in error when he argues that sovereignty "resides in the whole people of the United States conceived of as one nation" since the amending "machinery consists throughout of representatives of the people." McGovney, "Is the Eighteenth Amendment Void Because of Its Contents?" (1920) 20 COL. L. REV. 499 at 506. Bruce Williams adopts the same line of reasoning in "The Popular Mandate on Constitutional Amendments," (1921) 7 VA. L. REV. 280 at 283.

[34] "How can a people be sovereign when, e. g., they may pass upon public matters only once in four years, or may have their legislative acts revoked by juristic review?" WARD, SOVEREIGNTY (1928) 32.

electorate actually voted on a proposed amendment could it be said that the electorate was sovereign; and if each state were counted as a unit, as it is now, sovereignty would be regarded as in the electorates of the states and not of the nation. Even then it would be necessary to say that sovereignty is in the electorate together with the body which proposed the amendment. Not until the electorate is given both the initiative and the referendum on amendments will it be strictly accurate to speak of it as sovereign.[35] Even then, if the other modes of proposal and ratification are retained, there will remain the possibility of the exercise of sovereignty by other groups besides the people.

The people of the United States as an aggregate mass may perhaps be regarded as having been truly sovereign at only one time. This was when they adopted the Constitution.[36] This act of sovereignty was, however, a revolution and had no legal basis. Under the Articles of Confederation sovereignty was located in each state, and amendment of the Articles was valid only when every state concurred through ratification by its legislature after proposal by Congress. The Constitution was proposed by a Convention, was ratified by conventions, and was considered as established between the ratifying states when nine states had ratified. The people of the United States may be regarded as having acted in a sovereign capacity by having ignored the Articles of Confederation and perhaps their own state constitutions. When critically

[35] "The legal assumption that sovereignty is ultimately vested in the people affords no legal basis for the direct exercise by the people of any sovereign power whose direct exercise by them has not been expressly or impliedly reserved. Thus the people possess the power of legislating directly only if their constitution so provides." ROTTSCHAEFER, CONSTITUTIONAL LAW (1939) 8.

[36] "The people themselves in their natural, inherent sovereignty, but rarely interpose and decide,—never but in making or altering a constitution." 9 DANE, A GENERAL ABRIDGMENT AND DIGEST OF AMERICAN LAW (1829), Appendix 65. It has been asserted that the true sovereign has acted only three times in the United States: when it adopted the Declaration of Independence, the Articles of Confederation, and the Constitution. Radin, "The Intermittent Sovereign," (1930) 39 YALE L. J. 514 at 525.

examined, however, their alleged acts of sovereignty dwindle in scope. The electorate which participated in the elections of the state ratifying conventions was perhaps about a twentieth of the entire population.[37] Moreover, Congress and the state legislatures gave their stamp of approval to the Constitution. Thus the sole revolutionary act was ratification by less than a unanimous vote. Even the effect of this violation was considerably mitigated by providing that the Constitution should be binding only on those states which ratified it. It should also be noted that the members of the Constitutional Convention were elected by states and voted by states during its session. Ratification also occurred by states, and not by an aggregate popular vote or by a national convention of the people of the United States.

If the people of the United States ever had sovereignty, they must be regarded as having surrendered it by the adoption of Article Five.[38] All future changes were to be made not by the people but by the amending body. The original sover-

[37] BEARD, AN ECONOMIC INTERPRETATION OF THE CONSTITUTION OF THE UNITED STATES (1935) 250. 1 AUSTIN, JURISPRUDENCE, 4th ed. (1873) 329–330, says: "In a few societies political and independent (as, for example, in the Anglo-American States), the sovereign political government has been determined at once, and agreeably to a scheme or plan. But, even in these societies, the parties who determined the constitution (either as scheming or planning, or as simply voting or adopting it) were merely a slender portion of the whole of the independent community, and were virtually sovereign therein before the constitution was determined; insomuch that the constitution was not constructed by the whole of an inchoate community, but rather was constructed by a fraction of a community already consummate or complete." See also BROWN, THE AUSTINIAN THEORY OF LAW (1906) § 417.

[38] The Constitution "is supreme over the people of the United States, aggregately and in their separate sovereignties, because they have excluded themselves from any direct or immediate agency in making amendments to it, and have directed that amendments should be made representatively for them. . . ." Dodge v. Woolsey, (1855) 18 How. (59 U. S.) 331 at 348. When the people adopted the Constitution, "they delegated the power of amendment to their representatives, designating them and prescribing the function of each. . . . This delegated power the people have never retaken. Having so delegated the power of amendment, it cannot be executed in any way other than prescribed, nor by any instrumentality other than there designated." Feigenspan v. Bodine, (D. C. N. J. 1920) 264 F. 186 at 199.

eign created a minor sovereign, the amending body, somewhat lesser than itself. This amending body was subjected to three limitations, two of which have expired, so that today the only limitation on the power is the equal suffrage clause. On the view that the power which may impose such a limitation is sovereign, the people may be regarded as the sovereign and the amending body as the agent of the original people. But even this limitation may be destroyed by a unanimous vote of the states, and in the case of the deprivation of a particular state of equality in the Senate by the consent of that state. Perhaps even this would not be necessary if the doctrine of political question were applied. Thus it is difficult to see how a body so powerful as the amending body can be regarded as the legal agent of the people. Even on the assumption that it can be regarded as the agent of the people, this can only mean the agent of the original people, and as they are all dead, the agency can have no practical importance. The present amending body, which theoretically can strip the people of any of the rights which they have, political, property, or personal, must be regarded as an independent body, and the people as mere subjects in strict legal theory.

It has sometimes been thought that sovereignty resides in the Supreme Court of the United States. There is no question that, except in the case of political questions, the acts of the other branches of the federal government and of all branches of the state governments are subject to ultimate review by it when such acts are in conflict with the Constitution. The Supreme Court has been called the master of the Constitution.[39] It exercises a power not included within the jurisdiction of the English courts, that of reviewing the acts of the legislature. But the alleged difference between the Supreme Court and the courts of other nations is not so great as at first blush appears. Congress is not sovereign; Parliament is. If an act

[39] DICEY, THE LAW OF THE CONSTITUTION, 8th ed. (1915) 170–171.

of Congress violates a clause in the Constitution, the Supreme Court may declare it invalid when a case is brought before it. But when the amending body changes a clause in the Constitution, the Supreme Court has no power in the matter. True enough, the amendment must have been adopted according to the proper procedure. But where the proper procedure has not been followed, it cannot be said that the sovereign has acted. An alleged act of Parliament would not be regarded as law by an English court unless Parliament actually adopted it in its regular mode. The Supreme Court may also ascertain the conformity of the amendment to the equal suffrage clause, but this is probably its only power as to the content of the amendment. It would not even have this power where every state ratified, or when the state deprived of its equal suffrage ratified the amendment so depriving it.

The amending body may nullify a decision of the Supreme Court. Such was the effect of the Eleventh and the Sixteenth Amendments. Such would be the effect of the child labor amendment. It might even abolish the Supreme Court itself. John Dickinson asserts:

"Should the Supreme Court declare a law unconstitutional, it remains open to the amending power to reverse this result by so changing the Constitution as to bring the law into conformity therewith. But even in case this is done, the last word remains with the Court through its power to establish authoritatively the validity and meaning of the amendment."[40]

Perhaps this is true in actual practice. But as a matter of legal theory it is not. The justices of the Supreme Court take an oath to support the Constitution. The court is a mere agent of the United States like the President and Congress. It derives its being from the Constitution, and hence must con-

---

[40] Dickinson, "A Working Theory of Sovereignty," (1927) 42 POL. SCI. Q. 524 at 540–541.

form its action to the terms of the instrument. An amendment adopted according to the proper procedure and not in violation of the equality clause is as much a part of the Constitution as any other clause in the original document. An amendment in unequivocal terms abolishing the Supreme Court would be as binding on it as any other amendment. It would seem to be a case of clear usurpation should the court regard as invalid an amendment which clearly came within the scope of the amending power. The members of the Supreme Court are subject to impeachment. The membership of the court may be increased by Congress. Its decisions may be reversed by a later court. It has greatly limited its own jurisdiction by laying down the doctrine of "political questions." In fact, it has recently done so as to certain phases of the amending process in the child labor amendment cases.[41] As a matter of fact, though not of law, the Supreme Court would be very chary in running counter to the will of the amending body. As yet it has never set up its view as against that of the amending body.

The tremendous prestige enjoyed by the Constitution may lead some to think that the document itself must be regarded as sovereign. Harrington's aphorism about "government of laws and not of men" is almost a banality in the law of Great Britain and the United States. But sovereignty, by definition, must be vested in a person or in a group. Consequently, to say that sovereignty is in the Constitution is equivalent to saying that no sovereignty exists. The Constitution was not handed down on a mountain top like the Ten Commandments. A determinate group adopted it, and they must at the time, at least, have been its superior and the then sovereign. The death of its makers did not leave the Constitution sovereign, because

[41] Coleman v. Miller, (1939) 307 U. S. 433, 59 S. Ct. 972; Chandler v. Wise, (1939) 307 U. S. 474, 59 S. Ct. 992.

it at once became subject to alteration by the amending body. The Constitution itself cannot redistribute the powers of the federal and the state governments, and being subject to a superior power, fails in all respects to meet the tests of sovereignty. The Constitution by itself is incapable of action. Just as the so-called unwritten constitution of Great Britain is subject to change by Parliament, so the written Constitution of the United States may be reviewed or abolished by the amending body. Thus, in one sense, it is as proper to speak of the Constitution of the United States as having only the force of morality as it is to speak thus of the constitutional law of Great Britain.

The development of the theory of the corporate personality of the state has resulted in the location by some of sovereignty in the state. W. Jethro Brown says:

"The *possibility* of the location of the sovereignty in the State itself is implicitly recognized in all modern theories which state legal limitations upon the power which ranks highest in the hierarchy of State institutions. The sovereign is the source of all law, and so cannot be limited by law; where a legal limitation is held to exist upon a power claimed to be sovereign, we are compelled to infer that legal theory looks beyond the pretended sovereign to the State itself as true sovereign and ultimate source of law."[42]

But this theory does not seem to be especially helpful. In the first place it necessitates a definition of a state. A bog of controversy must be waded through before agreement can be reached on its juristic meaning. Austin says:

"*The* state is usually synonymous with '*the* sovereign.' It denotes the individual person, or the body of individual per-

[42] BROWN, THE AUSTINIAN THEORY OF LAW (1906) § 541. See also EASTWOOD AND KEETON, THE AUSTINIAN THEORIES OF LAW AND SOVEREIGNTY (1929) 67, 76; WARD, SOVEREIGNTY (1928) 39–44; EMERSON, STATE AND SOVEREIGNTY IN MODERN GERMANY (1928) 51–59; Rockow, "The Doctrine of the Sovereignty of the Constitution," (1931) 25 AM. POL. SCI. REV. 573 at 580.

sons, which bears the supreme powers in an independent political society." [43]

The state is thus made identical with the sovereign. But to say that the state is the sovereign manifestly does not help in the search for the sovereign, and merely begs the question.

Gray attacks Austin's definition, asserting that the sovereign is merely an organ of the state. [44] But to view sovereignty as vested in the abstract conception of the state is, so far as law is concerned, to make sovereignty an even more metaphysical conception than it now is. Sovereignty can only be exercised through concrete organs. Unless there is some organ, either in being or dormant, which can legally pass a given measure, it is futile to look to a mere legal fiction to accomplish the result. It is not difficult to conceive of a constitution with so limited an amending capacity that certain measures can only be passed by revolutionary methods. Doubtless it

---

[43] 1 AUSTIN, JURISPRUDENCE, 4th ed. (1873) 249, note. Burgess says that "in the transition from one form of state to another, the point of sovereignty moves from one body to another, and the old sovereign body, i. e. the old state, becomes, in the new system, only the government, or a part of the government." 1 BURGESS, POLITICAL SCIENCE AND COMPARATIVE CONSTITUTIONAL LAW (1891) 68.

The amending clause has a very important bearing on the juristic theory of the state from the point of view of constitutional law. It is sometimes maintained by those who have viewed the state in its internal as distinct from its external aspect that an essential characteristic of the state is that it have a sovereign. Willoughby says: "But to speak of a State as not being completely organized in its government, seems as much an absurdity as to say that a man is not completely organized in his physical frame." WILLOUGHBY, THE NATURE OF THE STATE (1928) 206. "An organized community of men either constitute or do not constitute a State, according to whether there is or is not to be discovered a supreme will acting upon all persons or other bodies within its limits." Ibid. 224.

The existence of the amending capacity thus supplies the sovereignty which is necessary to the full and perfect existence of the state. As Burgess says: "The state, however, was not organized in the confederate constitution; i. e., it could not *legally* speak the sovereign command." 1 BURGESS, POLITICAL SCIENCE AND COMPARATIVE CONSTITUTIONAL LAW (1891) 101.

[44] GRAY, THE NATURE AND SOURCES OF THE LAW (1909) § 150. Willoughby, who stresses the juristic status of the state, almost concedes that the state and the sovereign are identical. "In fact, it is almost correct to say that the sovereign will is the State, that the State exists only as a supreme controlling will, and that its life is only displayed in the declaration of binding commands, the enforcement of which is left to mere executive agents." WILLOUGHBY, THE NATURE OF THE STATE (1928) 302.

would be convenient to have a body which could legally adopt any proposed measure according to legal forms. But from the point of view of the lawyer this is not at all a necessity. In a federal state such as the United States where it is so difficult to ascertain what the state is, it seems better for the law to ignore the conception of a state and to emphasize the existence of a sovereign in the form of an amending body, which, if need be, may possibly be viewed as the juristic state.

Another theory which once attracted considerable support was the view that sovereignty is in the states united. By this is not meant sovereignty in the states severally, nor sovereignty in the federal government, but sovereignty in the aggregate of the states. This was the view of Austin:

"And, lastly, I believe that the sovereignty of each of the states, and also of the larger state arising from the federal union, resides in the states' governments *as forming one aggregate body*: meaning by a state's government, not its ordinary legislature, but the body of its citizens which appoints its ordinary legislature, and which, the union apart, is properly sovereign therein."[45]

John C. Hurd has written a bulky volume in support of this view.[46] The theory is, however, subject to two criticisms. It regards the electorates of the states united as sovereign. As has been pointed out, this is a confusion of political sovereignty with legal sovereignty, inasmuch as the voters have no direct voice in the creation of constitutional law. In the second place, it omits Congress from the sovereign power. It is a mistake to regard the states as sovereign simply because amendments are ultimately ratified by them.[47] The power of Congress in

[45] 1 AUSTIN, JURISPRUDENCE, 4th ed. (1873) 268.

[46] HURD, THE THEORY OF OUR NATIONAL EXISTENCE (1881), esp. 140, 374. This book is "Dedicated in Homage to the Sovereign: Whoever He, She, or They, May Be." The same view is taken by BROWNSON, THE AMERICAN REPUBLIC (1866) 220–221. See also Richman, "From John Austin to John C. Hurd," (1901) 14 HARV. L. REV. 353.

[47] Dicey omits to include Congress as a part of the Sovereign. DICEY, THE LAW OF THE CONSTITUTION, 8th ed. (1915) 144–145.

the matter is at least equal to that of the states. An amendment is never brought about without prior initiation by Congress. Even when a constitutional convention is applied for by the state legislatures, the call must go forth from Congress. Congress, moreover, has the power to select the mode of ratification. Looked at from one angle, Congress has a dual capacity in proposing amendments. It actually initiates the amendment, while, at the same time, its vote in favor of it is in a way a vote of ratification, inasmuch as, without it, the amendment cannot even go before the states. It is in Congress that amendments have been buried. The initiatory powers of the state legislatures have never as yet been brought to a successful fruition. It thus appears that the powers of the federal government with reference to amendments are fully equal to those of the states. A true sovereign must therefore embrace both governments. The states are sovereign neither individually nor aggregately.

In the last analysis, one is brought to the conclusion that sovereignty in the United States, if it can be said to exist at all, is located in the amending body. The amending body has often been referred to as the sovereign, because it meets the test of the location of sovereignty.[48] As Willoughby has said:

"In all those cases in which, owing to the distribution of governing power, there is doubt as to the political body in

[48] "In a government controlled and limited by a written Constitution as is ours, the test of actual sovereignty is to be found in the power to amend the Constitution. When you ascertain where, and how, and by whom that power is exercised, you have located the source of sovereignty." Potter, "The Method of Amending the Federal Constitution," (1909) 57 U. Pa. L. Rev. 589 at 592. See also State ex rel. McCready v. Hunt, (1834) 2 Hill L. (S. C.) 1 (an early case with a valuable discussion of the relation of sovereignty to the amending power) at 61 (argument of Grimke), 127 (of M'Willie), at 165, 166, 169, 172 (of Blanding), at 108 (of Smith, Attorney General), at 221 (opinion of O'Neall, J.), at 259, 260, 263 (dissenting opinion of Harper, J.); Bliss, Of Sovereignty (1885) 114, 124 ff.; Dewey, "Austin's Theory of Sovereignty," (1894) 9 Pol. Sci. Q. 31 at 39; Dicey, The Law of the Constitution, 8th ed. (1915) 5, 144–145; Hart, Introduction to the Study of Federal Government (1891) 12; Lansing, "Notes on Sovereignty in a State," (1907) 1 Am. J. Int. Law 105 at 126, who says, however, that the English doctrine

which the Sovereignty rests, the test to be applied is the determination of which authority has, in the last instance, the legal power to determine its own competence as well as that of others."[49]

In Germany, where the problem of the location of sovereignty has also been complicated by the existence of a composite state, the publicists have similarly developed what is known as the Kompetenz-Kompetenz theory.[50] Hobbes, the first Englishman with whom the theory of sovereignty is prominently associated, expressed the same view when he said that "the legislator is he, not by whose authority the law was first made, but by whose authority, it continues to be a law."[51]

Applying the criteria of sovereignty which were laid down at the beginning of this chapter, the amending body is sovereign as a matter of both law and fact. Article Five expressly creates the amending body. Yet in a certain manner of speaking the amending body may be said to exist as a matter of fact since it could proceed to alter Article Five or any other part of the Constitution. While it is true that the sovereign cannot act otherwise than in compliance with law, it is equally true that it creates the law in accordance with which it is to act.

of sovereignty is incapable of "being usefully applied" to constitutions like that of the United States; SALMOND, JURISPRUDENCE, 7th ed. (1924) 531, note k; POLLOCK, A FIRST BOOK OF JURISPRUDENCE, 6th ed. (1929) 278; SIDGWICK, THE ELEMENTS OF POLITICS (1891) 17, 602; Williams, "The Popular Mandate on Constitutional Amendments," (1921) 7 VA. L. REV. 280 at 293, who asserts that the implication of Hawke v. Smith, (1920) 253 U. S. 221, 40 S. Ct. 495, is "that legal sovereignty in the United States rests in those bodies which are capable of altering or amending the Constitution"; WILLOUGHBY, THE NATURE OF THE STATE (1928) 260 ff., 304.

[49] WILLOUGHBY, THE NATURE OF THE STATE (1928) 197. See also Radin, "The Intermittent Sovereign," (1930) 39 YALE L. J. 514 at 523, 526; Pennock, "Law and Sovereignty," (1937) 31 AM. POL. SCI. REV. 617 at 632; Uhl, "Sovereignty and the Fifth Article," (1936) 16 SOUTHWESTERN SOCIAL SCI. Q., No. 4, p. 1 at 15.

[50] MERRIAM, HISTORY OF THE THEORY OF SOVEREIGNTY SINCE ROUSSEAU (1900) 190—196. See also EMERSON, STATE AND SOVEREIGNTY IN MODERN GERMANY (1928).

[51] HOBBES, LEVIATHAN (1651), c. xxvi, par. 9.

And the doctrine of political questions in effect lessens the legal restraints on sovereignty. In practice most sovereigns come into being as a matter of fact. Thus originally the Constitution was adopted as a revolutionary act, and the amending body, resting as it does on a part of the Constitution, was at first a de facto sovereign. The passage of time has made people forget that the Constitution was in its origin anything but legal, so that today the amending body may be viewed as sovereign in law and in fact.

In the second place, the amending body has absolute lawmaking power, unless factual limitations be also viewed as legal limitations. At any rate it is possible to go as far as Bentham, who says that the sovereign has indefinite lawmaking power.[52] The amending body may strip the federal government of all its powers, or it may consolidate all the states into a single unitary state. It may place the powers of all three departments of government in a single department. It may legislate, as by passing a prohibition amendment. It may act as a court, as by overruling a decision of the Supreme Court. It may add to or subtract from the powers reserved to the people. It may alter the very amending body itself. It may revise not only the rules of constitutional and criminal law, but those of property and contract. It may strip the individual of personal liberty which he may have regarded as inalienable. That it will attempt to do all or even a small part of these things is unlikely. The outcome doubtless would be a revolution. But that it has an indefinite power to do any particular one of these things cannot be denied. As DeLolme says of Parliament, so it may be said of the amending body, that it "can do everything but make a woman a man, and a man a woman."

[52] BENTHAM, A FRAGMENT ON GOVERNMENT, 1st ed. (1776), c. iv, par. xxiii.

From one point of view, the power of the amending body is even more despotic than that of the British Parliament. The common view is that one Parliament is not bound by the laws of a previous Parliament. That is, in actuality, there is an implied limitation on sovereignty with reference to time. But in the United States the amending body might arguably by express provision forbid any future change of a clause in the Constitution. For instance, the Corwin amendment provided that the Constitution should never be amended so as to abolish slavery.[53] However, this, like the equality provision, could probably be repealed by a unanimous vote of the states. The original Constitution forbade any amendment with reference to the slave trade or the imposition of a direct tax without apportionment prior to 1808. The equal suffrage clause is still a limitation on the ordinary amending power. The amending body might amend the amending clause or might arguably abolish itself, so that legally there would be no possibility of amendment. It might provide for an altogether different type of amending body, so that an entirely different kind of sovereign would come into being. Sovereignty, viewed in the broadest sense, may be regarded as the power to make a law on any subject binding for all time in all places. This capacity theoretically exists in the amending body. However inexpedient such an amendment might be, it would seem that that would be the view of many American lawyers.[54] There are not many who assert that the ordinary amending body could abolish the equal suffrage clause. It would seem that under the prevailing legalistic interpretation of the Constitution an absolute prohibition against amendment could be overcome only by revolution.[55]

[53] H. J. R. 80, CONG. GLOBE, 36th Cong., 2d sess. (1861) 1263.

[54] Austin, however, is of the view that the sovereign cannot bind its successor. 1 AUSTIN, JURISPRUDENCE, 5th ed. (1885) 263–264.

[55] But Professor ROTTSCHAEFER, CONSTITUTIONAL LAW (1939) 9–10, states: "There has been found no case in which the power to amend has been employed

From a legal standpoint it is not a necessary concomitant of this absolute law-making power that every amendment be enforceable. The lawyer is interested only in the source of the act, and that source being authoritative, he will ask no more questions. The lack of enforcement of the Fifteenth and Eighteenth Amendments did not detract from their legal character. Of course, if the whole Constitution was ignored over a considerable period, there would probably be a change in the sovereign. But for ordinary purposes, when the amending body has acted, the lawyer accepts its command as law.

The amending body is determinate. It has been pointed out that sovereignty may reside in a group as well as in a person. Moreover, this group need not be a single organized body meeting at one place, but may be composed of several groups viewed as a corporate unit. As John Dickinson says, "sovereignty can be exercised by a system of organs properly geared together no less than by a single organ." [56] Hence it is that sovereignty may be regarded as being in the amending body though that body is composed of both federal and state units meeting at forty-nine different places. All the units are viewed as one single corporate or collegiate body, and each when it acts does not exercise its own sovereignty but exercises the corporate sovereignty. Doubtless the three-fourths majority of the states that combine to adopt one amendment will be di-

to directly or indirectly modify a constitutional provision expressly excepted from that power. The issues that such an attempt would raise could not be settled by any reasoning derived by logical processes from prevailing conceptions of sovereignty, and those based on considerations of convenience and expediency point to the solution that such attempts to limit the power of amendment should be held futile. The necessities of orderly government do not require that one generation should be permitted to permanently fetter all future generations."

[56] Dickinson, "A Working Theory of Sovereignty," (1927) 42 POL. SCI. Q. 524 at 539. This would seem to meet the objection of Bliss, who argues that an amendment requires "the action of the federal State and of the several local States, each in its own sphere. There is no one sovereignty, or one sovereign people, or aggregate of peoples, that can make the change." BLISS, OF SOVEREIGNTY (1885) 114.

vided as to another. But this does not detract from the sovereign character of the amending power any more than in the case of Parliament, which also acts by a majority.[57] Sovereignty is not in any specific three-fourths of the states, but it is clear that it always is in any three-fourths of them that unite in ratifying an amendment. Similarly it is never clear whether proposal of amendments will be by Congress or by a convention, nor whether ratification will be by the state legislatures or by conventions. Yet when these have acted, it appears that the sovereign has acted. The sovereign is a real sovereign, though one fluctuating in its composition. It is known only after it has acted. The groups in whom the possibility of amending resides are the potential sovereign, and in that sense it may be said that sovereignty resides in the full quota of all possible amending groups. But the exercise of sovereignty, which is of more interest to the lawyer than its residence, is by the actual amending power at a given time. The larger group is merely a container of the smaller, and there is no difference as to the legal effects of their acts. The larger group is merely the political group from which over a long period every state at some time or other will be a part of the amending power.

There is one type of situation where prima facie it seems that a minority is sovereign in the United States. A minority of the states may block an amendment. A single state may defeat the abolition of the equal suffrage clause. But a true sovereign must have no superior and must have affirmative law-making power. A minority is superior only in a negative way. As Gray admits, "this minority cannot be called Sovereign; except as an obstacle to amending the Constitution, it is powerless."[58]

---

[57] "The Austinian sovereign acts only by a majority, never in fact by its total membership. . . ." Jameson, "National Sovereignty," (1890) 5 POL. SCI. Q. 193 at 200. See also MAINE, EARLY HISTORY OF INSTITUTIONS (1888) 331-332.

[58] GRAY, THE NATURE AND SOURCES OF THE LAW (1909) § 177.

It is a peculiarity of the American sovereign that who it is can never be known precisely until it has acted.[59] This does not detract from its sovereign character, as it is enough that it is definitely known when it has acted. There are four possible combinations of the amending body in the United States. In every instance except one the power has been made up of Congress and the state legislatures. In the case of the Twenty-First Amendment it was made up of Congress and the state conventions. It may also be made up of two-thirds of the state legislatures applying for a convention, Congress in calling the Convention, the Convention, Congress in selecting the mode of ratification, and the state legislatures in ratifying. A fourth possible combination is of the legislatures in applying for a convention, Congress in calling it, the Convention, Congress in selecting the mode of ratification, and state conventions in ratifying. Congress thus must participate in any amendment, and has the power of selecting which group shall be the ratifying part of the sovereign. The group within the group that acts as part of the sovereign may also fluctuate. The two-thirds of Congress which proposes one amendment will vary from the group which proposes another. Similarly the three-fourths majority of the states which ratifies one amendment will differ from the majority which ratifies another.

The amending body as a corporate unit is responsible to no one. But the groups of which it is composed have no such freedom. The amending body may abolish or strip any of the groups of its powers. The result of abolishing either the federal or the state groups would, however, be to destroy the federal character of the United States. If the state groups were destroyed, the United States would in effect become a unitary state. On the other hand, if the federal group were abolished,

---

[59] "We come here, as before to an insoluble contradiction; sovereignty is not determinate until after it has been exercised—until the vote has been taken." Dewey, "Austin's Theory of Sovereignty," (1894) 9 Pol. Sci. Q. 31 at 40.

the Union would be on its way to a mere confederation. While it would be legal to change the composition of the sovereign, the suggested changes would mean the destruction of the federal status.

It has sometimes been thought that the sovereign must be constantly in session or must act frequently.[60] From a legal standpoint this is not necessary. A latent potential sovereign is enough. The dissolution of the House of Commons makes Parliament nonetheless the sovereign. An Asiatic despot is sovereign even when asleep. A half a century elapsed between the passage of the Twelfth and the Thirteenth Amendments, so that the amending power was regarded as so dormant a sovereign as not to be worthy of the name. The three Civil War Amendments were adopted within a five-year span. Forty years passed with no further changes. But within the seven-year period from 1913 to 1920, four amendments of outstanding importance were adopted, and a child labor amendment was shortly thereafter proposed to the states. The Twentieth and Twenty-First Amendments were adopted in the early 1930's. The sovereign has become so vigorous that there are now many who would seek to curb it. The formerly prevalent view as to the weakness of the sovereign has now either swung to the opposite extreme, or maintains that it has just the proper degree of strength. During periods of non-action it may perhaps be said, with some equivocation, that

[60] "Suppose a generation has passed away since any amendment has been passed, or since any legislature has acted upon any amendment proposed by Congress; where is the portion or class constituting the sovereign to be found?" Dewey, ibid. at 39. "Under a federal as under a unitarian system there exists a sovereign power, but the sovereign is in a federal state a despot hard to rouse. He is not, like the English Parliament, an ever-wakeful legislature, but a monarch who slumbers and sleeps. . . . But a monarch who slumbers for years is like a monarch who does not exist." DICEY, THE LAW OF THE CONSTITUTION, 8th ed. (1915) 145. See also BROWN, THE AUSTINIAN THEORY OF LAW (1906) 148, note at 153; BRYCE, STUDIES IN HISTORY AND JURISPRUDENCE (1901) 539; WILLOUGHBY, THE NATURE OF THE STATE (1928) 305; EMERSON, STATE AND SOVEREIGNTY IN MODERN GERMANY (1928) 271, note 6; Chafee, Book Review, (1919) 32 HARV. L. REV. 979 at 980.

the sovereign commands what it permits.[61] Legal sovereignty may be in abeyance. The theory of sovereignty does not have the same significance in the United States as it does in England, inasmuch as it is an organization behind that of the regular government and because so large a majority is required for it to act. Under such circumstances it is easily explicable why so little thought is devoted to the alleged sovereign and why so much attention is given to the powers of the organs of government as distributed under the existing Constitution. The events of recent American history are likely to result in the study the subject deserves.

Perhaps the leading obstacle to the recognition of sovereignty in the amending body is the limitation imposed by the equal suffrage in the Senate clause.[62] In reply it must be noted that the proviso has no practical significance as to most amendments that might be proposed. Strictly speaking, it is doubtless correct to say that the existence of the clause precludes the ordinary amending body from being regarded as sovereign. But even that clause is not an absolute limitation on the amending power, as has been pointed out in Chapter IV. The two earlier absolute limitations which existed until 1808 are

---

[61] SIDGWICK, THE ELEMENTS OF POLITICS (1891) 602, says: "Suppose that the body which *can* dismiss the otherwise supreme government does not dismiss it and gives no directions. Is it still supreme?—assuming that its inactivity is not due to fear. I think we must say that the power of dismissal—or any other power of giving orders—is still *possessed* though it is not *exercised*; assuming that the inactive organ would be obeyed if it gave orders. . . . I think we must attribute supreme power to any individual or body completely capable of corporate action, which admittedly can withdraw power at will from a government otherwise supreme." Markby says that though "the ultimate sovereign power was generally dormant, and was only called into active existence on rare and special occasions," this is "not inconsistent with sovereignty, or with our conception of a political society; but it is a peculiarity." MARKBY, ELEMENTS OF LAW, 6th ed. (1905) § 33.

[62] BRYCE, STUDIES IN HISTORY AND JURISPRUDENCE (1901) 540; GRAY, THE NATURE AND SOURCES OF THE LAW (1909) §§ 178–180; LASKI, THE PROBLEM OF SOVEREIGNTY (1917) 267; Ritchie, "On the Conception of Sovereignty," (1891) 1 AM. ACAD. POL. SCI. ANNALS 385 at 397; SALMOND, JURISPRUDENCE, 7th ed. (1924) 531, note k; State ex rel. McCready v. Hunt, (1834) 2 Hill L. (S. C.) 1 at 84 (argument of Finley).

gone, so that today there is no limitation whatever on the amending power when every state is included.[63] The requirement of unanimous consent makes the sovereign no less such.[64] Moreover, possibly the doctrine of "political questions" applies so that even the ordinary amending body could act without restraint. The provisions of Article Five as to procedure are not to be regarded as limitations, since the sovereign cannot be said to be acting when the proper procedure is not followed.[65] Here again the doctrine of "political questions" applies, at least to some phases of the amending procedure.

In conclusion it seems well to consider what should be the attitude of the lawyer to the sovereign in the form of the amending body. First of all, it seems that the lawyer should welcome its definite location, since he as much as anyone should be interested in the body which has in its power the ultimate determination of what shall be the law. At first blush it may seem to hark back to the days of despotism to accept a body with such unlimited power. But if there be such a power it is desirable to know in whom it is vested. When the force of public opinion can be focused on a body with definite powers, it may perhaps be more readily held morally accountable.[66] Moreover, as W. Jethro Brown points out, "one

[63] Ritchie, "On the Conception of Sovereignty," (1891) 1 AM. ACAD. POL. SCI. ANNALS 385 at 398, says that "Austin, in his search for determinate persons, must wander about till he finds George Washington, James Madison, and a large number of other persons who (a Scotchman may be permitted, and expected, to remark) are now dead." But the possibility of amendment by all the states avoids the necessity of imputing sovereignty to the makers of the Constitution.

[64] "But the fact that it is so formally limited does not mean that the power does not exist, any more than it is claimed that the Polish assembly had not the legislative power because of the existence of the *liberum veto*." WILLOUGHBY, THE NATURE OF THE STATE (1928) 264.

[65] "Even the manner in which, or the determination of the person by whom, the Legal Sovereign is chosen is a matter distinct from the nature and scope of his authority. He is none the less Sovereign in the contemplation of law because he reigns not by his own right but by the choice of others. . . ." BRYCE, STUDIES IN HISTORY AND JURISPRUDENCE (1901) 510.

[66] "It is much better that the law in all its harshness and its makers in all their legal irresponsibility should stand out clearly before the eyes of those who

of the great advantages of having a legal sovereign is to make a revolution under the forms of law possible." [67]

In the second place, there need be no fear of possible tyrannical acts of the sovereign. An extraordinary majority is required for it to act. Both the federal governments and the states are represented in all its acts, and each holds an absolute veto over the other. Moreover, the electorate which chooses Congress and the state legislatures has constantly increased in the ratio of its number to that of the people as a mass.[68] Election takes place so frequently that while those who exercise the amending capacity cannot be held legally responsible, they are held politically accountable.

Finally it must be seen that the status of the amending body has an important bearing on the controversy over the nature and extent of the powers of the federal government and the states, and on the general doctrine of sovereignty. Sovereignty rests in neither the federal government nor in the states, but, if it may be said to reside anywhere, in the amend-

are required to obey. For then there is most likelihood of the moral responsibility of the legal sovereignty being stringently enforced." Ritchie, "On the Conception of Sovereignty," (1891) 1 AM. ACAD. POL. SCI. ANNALS 385 at 401.

[67] BROWN, THE AUSTINIAN THEORY OF LAW (1906) 167, note at 168. Willoughby says: "The value of *constitutional* government is not that it places Sovereignty in the hands of the people, but that it prescribes definite ways in which this sovereign power shall be exercised by the State." WILLOUGHBY, THE NATURE OF THE STATE (1928) 302. Radin states: "revolution is the sovereign act par excellence." Radin, "The Intermittent Sovereign," (1930) 39 YALE L. J. 514 at 526.

[68] "Lawyers are apt to speak as though the legislature were omnipotent, as they do not require to go beyond its decisions. It is, of course, omnipotent in the sense that it can make whatever laws it pleases, inasmuch as a law means any rule which has been made by the legislature. But from the scientific point of view, the power of the legislature is of course strictly limited. It is limited, so to speak, both from within and from without; from within, because the legislature is the product of a certain social condition, and determined by whatever determines the society; and from without, because the power of imposing laws is dependent upon the instinct of subordination; which is itself limited. If the legislature decided that all blue-eyed babies should be murdered, the preservation of blue-eyed babies would be illegal; but legislature must go mad before they could pass such a law, and subjects be idiotic before they could submit to it." STEPHEN, THE SCIENCE OF ETHICS (1882) 143.

ing body. The amending capacity demonstrates neither the supremacy of the states nor of the federal government. At one time it may operate in favor of the states, and at another in favor of the federal government. That the rights of neither will be impaired is guaranteed by their joint action in the amending process. Both are but agents of the composite states. In the amending body we discover both the sovereign and the state.

The nature of the federal amending process demonstrates the futility of the concept of sovereignty. It has been pointed out that its use in international law is doubtful, and that its use if proper at any time is only so in constitutional law. Its use in constitutional law has resulted in great confusion in the United States. It has been seen that the only body to which the characteristic can logically be attributed is the amending body. The chief time when the question of sovereignty becomes important is when the validity of the substance of an amendment is challenged. It is this fact alone which has induced the extensive discussion of the subject. For other purposes it is sufficient to examine the powers which have been conferred on the federal and state governments and their departments.

The involved explanations made necessary and the metaphysical difficulties encountered in ascribing sovereignty to the amending body show the barren aridity of the term. The equality in the senate clause prevents a strictly correct application of the term to the ordinary amending body. The original limitations expiring in 1808 show that there was no sovereign whatever up to that year, though possibly unanimous action by the states would have sufficed. The excessive majorities required for proposal and adoption of amendments prevent frequent action by the sovereign. During two periods of approximately half a century each no amendments were adopted. Until the amending body acts it can never be known in advance who the sovereign will be. Forty-nine bodies meeting at different places act on the matter, and each of these bodies in turn is divided, except in Nebraska, into a lower and upper house. Unless the procedure of amendment prescribed in Article Five is pursued, the sovereign has not acted at all, and the action of the amending group is mere *brutum fulmen*. The recent doctrine as to political questions perhaps somewhat alters this, however. Each part of the amending body is subject to law, and may be altered or abolished. The amending body itself may be altered through the amending process, and limitations on the future amending capacity may be imposed. The amending body is an artificial sovereign deriving its being from a law in the form of Article Five. The amending groups hold office for but a short time, and may be supplanted by others in the elections in which an increasingly larger electorate participates. The theory of sovereignty, moreover, presupposes the continued orderly existence of the government. In case of a revolution the commands of the sovereign would be disregarded, and authority could not longer be ascribed to the amending body either in fact or in law. The moral, religious, physical, and other factual limitations on the supposed sovereign are so important that it may perhaps be correct to say that they are also legal limitations, as there comes a time when law and fact shade into one another. Finally, when it is remembered that throughout all history, American as well as European, there never has been a consensus as to the meaning of sovereignty, it seems that the term should be used only with the greatest circumspection.[69]

[69] Saying all this, we should still bear in mind the words of the great English historian, W. S. Holdsworth: "The great achievements of the doctrine of sovereignty were the mastering of the lawlessness of the mediaeval state, and the provision, in the modern territorial state, of an organism which, by keeping the peace, has made social and political progress possible. The measure of its achievement is the contrast between the state of Europe in 1500 and in 1700. We are so accustomed to the efficient manner in which lawlessness and crime are suppressed, that we are apt to forget that this result has been achieved through the ceaseless efforts of the ministers of the state, using powers and machinery which owe their origin and their force to the sovereignty of the

state. I think that those who go about to deny or minimize this sovereignty have forgotten this fact. They have forgotten that in the smaller matters of government, which concern the daily intercourse of man and man, it is the fact of the state's sovereignty which causes the machinery to run smoothly; and that in a time of crisis they may have reason to be thankful for its existence. As Dicey, writing in 1914, has well said, 'Crises arise from time to time in the history of any great state when, because national existence or national independence is at stake, the mass of a whole people feel that the authority of the nation is one patent and one certain political fact.' . . . At the present day, when some have maintained that the doctrine of sovereignty should be discarded as an outworn doctrine, English law firmly maintains the sovereignty of the king in Parliament." HOLDSWORTH, SOME LESSONS FROM OUR LEGAL HISTORY (1928) 137–139, 140, quoting from DICEY, THE LAW OF THE CONSTITUTION, 8th ed. (1915) xliii.

Also to be remembered are the words of Rupert Emerson: "That actual highest power may temporarily rest elsewhere than with the normatively defined sovereign is a fact which is too obvious to require statement; but on the other hand there can equally be no doubt that the modern constitutional State has brought about a closer practical coincidence between the legal sovereign and the actual possessor of and wielder of highest power than has ever before been possible. . . . To discard the principle of sovereignty is to accept the contingent threat of chaos that appears whenever two or more formally equal powers stand opposed to each other with no highest power authorized to decide between them." EMERSON, STATE AND SOVEREIGNTY IN MODERN GERMANY (1928) 257, 272.

Chapter VI

The Reform of the Amending Clause

INCREASINGLY in recent years, culminating in 1938 in extensive hearings before a subcommittee of the Senate Committee on the Judiciary,[1] proposals have been made to alter and improve the process of amending the federal Constitution. The adoption of the Eighteenth Amendment stimulated much discussion concerning the ease or difficulty of amendment. The proposed Wadsworth-Garrett amendment[2] of Article Five received much attention in the 1920's. President Roosevelt's proposal in 1937 concerning an increase in the size of the Supreme Court attracted attention to the efficacy of the amending process. The uncertainties arising from the doctrine of political questions laid down in the 1939 decisions of the Supreme Court may cause a movement for clarification.[3] From 1911 to 1928 eighteen amendments were offered in Congress to change Article Five, and in the 1937 sessions five such amendments were offered.[4]

The various proposals may best be discussed as they affect the two methods of proposal and the two methods of ratification provided under Article Five of the Constitution and discussed in Chapter III.

A. REFORM OF PROPOSAL OF AMENDMENTS

1. *Proposal by National Convention*

There has been comparatively little discussion of the reform of proposal of amendments by a national convention.[5]

[1] HEARINGS ON S. J. RES. 134, 75th Cong., 3d sess. (1938) 1–85 ("Ratification of Constitutional Amendments by Popular Vote").

[2] See citations in note 72, infra.

[3] (1940) 24 MINN. L. REV. 393 at 406.

[4] HEARINGS ON S. J. RES. 134, 75th Cong., 3d sess. (1938) 37.

[5] An account of the efforts up to 1889 to obtain a national convention is set out in AMES, THE PROPOSED AMENDMENTS TO THE CONSTITUTION OF THE

Of the four modes of proposal and ratification this has seemed the one most likely not to be used. While there has been agitation for individual amendments, and such individual amendments have sometimes been of great importance, there have been no widespread tangible evidences of a desire for complete or even substantial revision of the Constitution.[6] It is true that under the wording of Article Five such a convention might propose ordinary individual amendments. In fact, Article Five provides for the call of a "convention for proposing amendments," and does not refer in express terms to a revision or to the adoption of an entirely new constitution. It has, however, been usual both in the experience of the states and of the nation to view the initiation of specific amendments as the function of a legislative body and that of revision as the function of a convention. Moreover, because of the additional expense and because of the increased legal complications and delays involved, it is unlikely that the convention method will often be resorted to for ordinary amendments.

Assuming, however, that there is a popular demand for revision of the Constitution, is the present machinery adequate? Probably the true reason that there has been no national convention since the Constitutional Convention itself is that there has been no real demand for it. But at least a partial reason may be the difficulty of obtaining applications from the legislatures of two-thirds of the states. It would seem that the applications must be reasonably contemporaneous in time. It is by no means easy to obtain applications by thirty-two legislatures for a convention within approximately the same interval. Possibly, too, the applications must be ad-

UNITED STATES DURING THE FIRST CENTURY OF ITS HISTORY. (1897) 281–284. The recent attempts are discussed by Wheeler, "Is a Constitutional Convention Impending?" (1927) 21 ILL. L. REV. 782; "How Long is a State Petition for a Constitutional Convention Good?" (1931) 17 A. B. A. J. 143, embodying a report to the New York State Bar Association also appearing in 74 CONG. REC. (1931) 2924 and S. Doc. 78, 71st Cong. 2d sess. 1930).

[6] A somewhat plausible, though not convincing, argument is made in MACDONALD, A NEW CONSTITUTION FOR A NEW AMERICA (1921).

dressed to the calling of a convention for general revision. Hence if one application is for the purpose of securing an amendment to abolish polygamy and another to achieve woman suffrage, perhaps these applications cannot be counted together, especially where, as has been the case, the latter is afterwards obtained under the usual amending process.[7]

The suggested number of reforms of this part of Article Five has not been large. Most of them have looked in the direction of making it easier to secure the call of a convention. During the Civil War period and previously, although there was much discussion of holding a convention, the constitutional difficulties of securing such a convention were too great. It has been suggested that application by the legislatures of a majority of the states should be sufficient.[8] Some have advocated an even lesser number of applications, such as those of twelve states.[9] In defense of these changes it may be said that whereas proposal by Congress is one important step of two, involving the initiation of an actual specific amendment, the application of the legislatures is simply one step of three, the others being the call of a convention which really proposes the amendment, and the subsequent ratification by the states. Gouverneur Morris suggested at the Constitutional Convention that Congress be permitted to call a federal convention whenever it chose.[10] Another change which might be desirable

[7] See supra, chap. III.

[8] Senator Henderson, of Missouri, S. J. R. 16, 38th Cong., 1st sess. (1864) CONG. GLOBE, 38th Cong., 1st sess. (1864) 145, 553 (committee report), 1313, (debated); Rep. Berger of Wisconsin, H. J. R. 71, 62d Cong., 1st sess. (1911); Senator Owen of Oklahoma, 58 CONG. REC., (1919) 5700; Rep. Lea of California, H. J. R. 168, 71st Cong., 2d sess. (1929), and Tuller, "A Convention to Amend the Constitution—Why Needed—How It May be Obtained," (1911) 193 No. AM. REV. 369 at 385; Rep. Porter of Virginia, H. J. R. 180, 42nd Cong., 3d sess. (1873) (or the application of legislatures of any number of states embracing three-fifths of the enumerated population of the several states).

[9] Rep. Chandler of New York, H. J. R. 315, 64th Cong., 2d sess. (1916), one-fourth of the states.

[10] 5 ELLIOT, DEBATES ON THE ADOPTION OF THE FEDERAL CONSTITUTION, 2d ed. (1937) (reprint of 1836 ed.) 498. It has been suggested that Congress

would be to provide some method to force Congress to issue the call when the requisite number of states have applied, or to drop out Congress and provide that some executive official issue the call, since there seems to be no legal remedy if Congress fails to act. Under the Wadsworth-Garrett amendment, the convention would also be empowered to select the mode of ratification, whether by legislatures or by conventions, whereas under Article Five this power is vested in Congress. Burgess has proposed that in view of the tendency of legislative bodies to confuse matters of a statutory nature with matters of fundamental constitutional law, the legislative mode of proposing amendments should be done away with entirely and only a national convention should be allowed to propose.[11] It has been suggested that it might be desirable to have federal conventions periodically to revise the Constitution.[12] Former Attorney General Homer Cummings regards the national convention method as too cumbersome for prac-

already has this power. MacDonald, A New Constitution for a New America (1921) 115. It was held, however, in Hawke v. Smith, (1920) 253 U. S. 221, 40 S. Ct. 495, that the modes of ratification stipulated in Article Five are exclusive, and the same reasoning would probably apply to the modes of proposal. Rep. Porter of Virginia, H. J. R. 180, 42d Cong., 3d sess. (1873), proposed that a three-fifths majority of Congress should be empowered to call a convention. Rep. Berger of Wisconsin would allow a majority of each House of Congress to call a convention, H. J. R. 246, 68th Cong., 1st sess. (1924); H. J. R. 274, 69th Cong., 1st sess. (1926), and H. J. R. 281, 70th Cong., 1st sess. (1928).

[11] Burgess, Recent Changes in American Constitutional Theory (1923) 107 and 112. The first proposal at the Constitutional Convention was to leave Congress out of the process, for fear that it might ignore the wishes of the people. 5 Elliot, Debates (1836) 128. The committee of detail, in its first draft of the instrument, proposed that a convention should be called by Congress upon application of two-thirds of the states. Ibid. 381. But nothing was said as to whether the legislatures were to propose and the convention to adopt, or whether the convention was to do the whole thing. Lincoln in his first inaugural address stated that proposal by a convention was preferable to that by Congress, since the people should have the power to originate as well as to approve amendments.

[12] Needham, "Changing the Fundamental Law," (1921) 69 U. Pa. L. Rev. 223 at 236 (every ten years). Rep. Chandler of New York, H. J. R. 315, 64th Cong., 2d sess. (1916), proposed that conventions be held every thirty years.

tical service.[13] Senator George W. Norris proposed in 1937 to abolish the method altogether, though considerable objection was taken at the hearings on his proposal.[14]

2. *Proposal by Congress*

Until recent years most of the amendments offered to Article Five have been directed at the mode of proposing amendments by Congress. This is easily understandable in view of the fact that it is at this stage that most proposed amendments have failed.[15] Of some three thousand amendments introduced in Congress only twenty-six were actually submitted to the states and only five of these failed of ratification in the states. The obstacle of having to pass both houses of Congress has resulted in the failure of comparatively few amendments up to 1923, sixteen having passed the Senate and not the House, and the same number having passed the House and not the Senate. Relative to the total number of amendments adopted, however, this total is high. The criticism is often made that the excessive majority required for proposal, namely, two-thirds of each House, is an insuperable barrier. In fairness, however, two things should be observed. In the first place, it has been held that only two-thirds of a quorum and not two-thirds of the members elected is sufficient.[16] Of even greater importance is the fact that many of the amendments offered would not command even a majority of Con-

---

[13] Cummings, "Nature of the Amending Process," (1938) 6 GEO. WASH. L. REV. 247 at 250. Former Attorney General Mitchell suggests that a convention is suitable only for general revision of the Constitution. Mitchell, "Methods of Amending the Constitution," (1932) 25 LAWY. & BANKER 265.

[14] HEARINGS ON S. J. R. 134, 75th Cong., 3d sess. (1938) 3–4, 65, 79, 84.

[15] The amendments proposed from 1789 to 1889 are set out in AMES, THE PROPOSED AMENDMENTS TO THE CONSTITUTION (1897), while those offered after that date up to July 2, 1926, are to be found in S. Doc. 93, 69th Cong., 1st sess. (1926) (Tansill, "Proposed Amendments to the Constitution of the United States"). See Ames, "The Amending Provision of the Federal Constitution in Practice," (1924) 63 AM. PHIL. SOC. PROC. 62 at 63.

[16] National Prohibition Cases, (1920) 253 U. S. 350, 40 S. Ct. 486, 588.

gress.[17] That is to say most of the amendments offered have been killed in committee and have never come to a vote of the entire house sitting as such. Such liberals as Senator Norris have found no objection to the present mode of proposal.[18]

Nevertheless it is entirely conceivable that amendments desirable in every respect will fail to obtain the necessary two-thirds majority, although a simple majority might be obtained. Certainly it is clear that, in the case of the ratification of treaties by the Senate and the overriding by Congress of the presidential veto, there are numerous instances of failures where there would have been approvals if only a simple majority had been required. The matter of amending the Constitution is not so fundamentally different from these matters that, over a long period of time at least, the same failures will not occur. Even under the Articles of Confederation apparently a majority might propose. It is not surprising, therefore, that there have been many proposals, both in Congress and by commentators, that a lesser majority be required.[19] Most of the alternatives offered have agreed on a simple majority of each House of Congress as enough.[20] The

[17] Of more than 1800 proposals introduced from 1789 to 1889 more than half never got beyond their reception and reference to a committee. The rest were either reported or received further discussion, but only a very small percentage of these were brought to a vote.

[18] 65 CONG. REC. (1924) 4942; letter of June 10, 1931, to the author of this book; S. J. R. 134, 75th Cong., 1st sess. (1937).

[19] A simple majority in two successive sessions of Congress:—Smith, "Shall We Make Our Constitution Flexible?" (1911) 194 NO. AM. REV. 657 at 667; Johnstone, "An Eighteenth Century Constitution," (1912) 7 ILL. L. REV. 265 at 283. A simple majority of Congress as an aggregate group in two successive sessions: 1 BURGESS, POLITICAL SCIENCE AND COMPARATIVE CONSTITUTIONAL LAW (1891) 152. See also Cummings, "The Nature of the Amending Process," (1938) 6 GEO. WASH. L. REV. 247 at 253.

[20] Senator Henderson of Missouri, S. J. R. 16, 38th Cong., 1st sess. (1864); Senator Owen of Oklahoma, S. J. R. 42, 62d Cong., 1st sess. (1911); Rep. Crumpacker of Indiana, H. J. R. 375, 62d Cong., 3d sess. (1913); Senator Thompson of Kansas, S. J. R. 9, 63d Cong., 1st sess. (1913); Senator Owen, S. J. R. 20, 63d Cong., 1st sess. (1913); Rep. Lafferty of Oregon, H. J. R. 60, 63d Cong., 1st sess. (1913); Senator LaFollette of Wisconsin, S. J. R. 24, 63d Cong., 1st sess. (1913) (or upon application of ten states); Rep. Chandler of New York, H. J. R. 95, 63d Cong., 1st sess. (1913) (or by one-fourth of the

state constitutions generally permit proposal by a simple majority of each house of the legislature. Sometimes the proposition is that a simple majority of a quorum of each house shall be the required majority, while at other times it is that it be a majority of the members elected to each house. Possibly it would be wise to safeguard the amending process by departing from the rule governing the passage of ordinary legislation that only a majority of a quorum is necessary, and laying down the latter rule.[21] However, that might, on occasion, make the amending process even more difficult than it now is, since two-thirds of a quorum may be less than a majority of all the members elected to Congress. To illustrate, two-thirds of a quorum of the Senate would be thirty-three, whereas a majority of the members elected to the Senate would be forty-nine.

Under the present system each house of Congress votes separately as to proposal. Burgess has suggested that the two houses sit together as a single body when proposing amendments, a majority of the aggregate group to be sufficient to adopt.[22] In France the constitution up to 1940 was actually

states having at least one-fourth of population of United States); Rep. Bryan of Washington, H. J. R. 422, 63d Cong., 3d sess. (1915); Senator Owen, S. J. R. 9, 64th Cong., 1st sess. (1915) (or upon application of legislatures of majority of states); Rep. Chandler of New York, H. J. R. 315, 64th Cong. 2d. sess. (1916); Senator Owen of Oklahoma, S. J. R. 8, 65th Cong., 1st sess. (1916), S. J. R. 33, 66th Cong., 1st sess. (1919), S. J. R. 14, 67th Cong., 1st sess. (1921), and S. J. R. 27, 68th Cong., 1st sess. (1923). A proposal by Senator Brookhart was voted down in the Senate, 65 CONG. REC. (1924) 4929, and see speech at 4556. See also, Potter, "The Method of Amending the Federal Constitution," (1909) 57 U. PA. L. REV. 589 at 609; Thompson, "The Amendment of the Federal Constitution," (1912) 3 ACAD. POL. SCI. PROC. 65 at 75, with alternative of proposal by a majority vote of one house in two successive Congresses; Edward S. Corwin, letter of May 27, 1931, to the author of this book.

[21] Senator Henderson of Missouri, S. J. R. 16, 38th Cong., 1st sess. (1864); Senator Owen of Oklahoma, 58 CONG. REC. (1919) 5700; Senator Brookhart of Iowa, 65 CONG. REC. (1924) 4564. Rep. Porter of Virginia introduced an amendment for proposal by three-fifths of Congress—H. J. R. 180, 42d Cong., 3d sess. (1873). Edward S. Corwin, in a letter of May 27, 1931, to the author of this book, favors the former rule.

[22] I BURGESS, POLITICAL SCIENCE AND COMPARATIVE CONSTITUTIONAL LAW (1891) 152.

amended by such a joint session. The wisdom of adopting such a plan in the United States, however, is questionable because of the federal nature of our government. The states are represented according to population in the House of Representatives and as states in the Senate. Hence to combine the two bodies for amending purposes would be to decrease the influence of the less populous states. Moreover, Article Five provides that no state shall be deprived of its equal suffrage in the Senate without its consent. It is therefore arguable that such a provision would be in violation of the equal suffrage clause. Since, however, Congress might be dropped out of the amending process, since each state would still have its two senators, and since under the Twelfth Amendment the two houses sit jointly to count the electoral vote, this argument is not thoroughly convincing. The more fundamental objection, then, is that already stated,—the violation of the federal concept.

Because of the difficulties of obtaining the concurrence of both houses of Congress, it has occasionally been suggested that a proposal by one house should be effectual. These proposals almost invariably contemplate that the resolution must pass the house proposing twice, in two consecutive sessions, before the amendment can go to the states.[23] It prevents hasty action, it permits an indirect popular referendum by requiring action by a subsequently elected house, and it prevents the dominance of one house of Congress over another, especially where the house not concurring is affected by the amendment. For example, the Seventeenth Amendment providing for the popular election of Senators passed the House of Representatives several times before it was finally approved by the Senate. As has been previously pointed out, sixteen

---

[23] Senator Owen of Oklahoma, S. J. R. 20, 63d Cong., 1st sess. (1913), and 58 Cong. Rec. (1919) 5700; Thompson, "The Amendment of the Federal Constitution," (1912) 3 Acad. Pol. Sci. Proc. 65 at 75; Carman, "Why and How the Present Method of Amending the Federal Constitution Should be Changed," (1938) 17 Ore. L. Rev. 102.

resolutions have passed the Senate but failed in the House, and a similar number have passed in the House but failed in the Senate. Such a provision is not found in the state constitutions, but it is employed in another federal constitution, that of Australia. Under the Australian Constitution if an amendment twice passes one house of Parliament and is twice rejected by the other house, the second rejection occurring at least three months after the first one, the amendment is then to be submitted by the Governor-General to the states.[24]

Under the present Article Five, Congress is vested with a considerable degree of power in connection with both the submission and adoption of amendments. As was seen in the discussion of national conventions, there have been a number of suggestions looking in the direction of taking away some of those powers. The seeming lack of any way to compel Congress to call a convention, even though there have been applications by the requisite number of legislatures, has been the subject of strictures.[25] Objection has also been raised to the power of Congress to select the mode of ratification even though proposal is by a convention. It has been suggested that the only mode of proposal should be by convention. Under the decision of *Dillon v. Gloss*,[26] Congress may prescribe a reasonable time limit for the ratification of an amendment by the states, although the decision of the court was really dictum since the amendment there involved itself contained a time limit proviso. In *Coleman v. Miller*,[27] it was held that the time limit involved a political question. There have been numerous suggestions that Article Five be amended

[24] Constitution of Commonwealth of Australia, § 128.

[25] On Jan. 19 and 28, 1861, Mr. Florence of Pennsylvania proposed that "the power of the people in three-fourths of the states to call and form a convention to alter, amend, or abolish the Constitution . . . shall never be questioned." CONG. GLOBE, 36th Cong., 2d sess. (1861) 479, 598.

[26] (1921) 256 U. S. 368, 41 S. Ct. 510, commented on by Freund, "Legislative Problems and Solutions," (1921) 7 A. B. A. J. 656.

[27] (1939) 307 U. S. 433, 59 S. Ct. 972.

so as to fix a definite time limit, such as six, eight or ten years. A provision for automatic proposal of an amendment has been made by Representative Doolittle of Kansas that whenever any law of the United States be declared invalid by the decree of any court the law shall be submitted along with a proposed constitutional amendment covering the same, acceptance of the law and amendment to be by the legislatures of three-fourths of the states.[28] It has recently been suggested that the legislatures of the majority of the states be permitted to propose an amendment.[29]

3. Proposal by Initiative

While most of the suggestions looking toward direct popular participation in the amending process have been with respect to ratification, there have been a number of proposals that the people themselves should be allowed to initiate amendments or that the legislatures should be allowed to apply for specific amendments as well as for a national convention.[30] It is claimed that the people participated, at least in-

[28] H. J. R. 221, 63d Cong., 2d sess. (1914).

[29] Carman, "Why and How the Present Method of Amending the Federal Constitution should Be Changed," (1938) 17 ORE. L. REV. 102.

[30] Senator Cummins of Iowa in 1913 suggested proposal by legislative resolutions of sixteen states, certified to the President of the United States, or on the petition of fifteen per cent of the voters in twenty-four states. His proposal was adversely reported to the Senate by the Senate Judiciary Committee in 1914. 51 CONG. REC. (1914) 1560; S. J. R. 26, 63d Cong., 1st sess. (1913). See later proposal, S. J. R. 33, 64th Cong., 1st sess. (1915). Senator LaFollette of Wisconsin the same year advocated proposal on the application of ten state legislatures, or by the application of ten states through a popular vote provided a majority of the electors voting on the question favored the amendment or by a majority of both houses of Congress, in addition to the existing modes of proposal. S. J. R. 24, 63d Cong., 1st sess. (1913). Previously on Aug. 5, 1912, S. J. R. 131, 62d Cong., 2d sess., he had advocated proposal on the application of ten states. Rep. Jackson of Kansas suggested proposal on the application of the legislature of one state, H. J. R. 350, 62d Cong., 2d sess. (1912). See also Rep. Chandler of New York, H. J. R. 95, 63d Cong., 1st sess. (1913) (one-fourth of the states having at least one-fourth of population of United States); Rep. Doolittle of Kansas, H. J. R. 220, 63d Cong., 2d sess. (1914) (legislature of one state); Senator Owen of Oklahoma, S. J. R. 9,

directly, when the Constitution itself was proposed by a national convention instead of by Congress. The use of the initiative among the states, not only with respect to statutes but also constitutional amendments, has naturally resulted in a demand for its use in national politics. It has been suggested that a petition signed by some such number as 500,000 voters should operate as the proposal of an amendment to be voted on at the next general election, while a petition signed by a somewhat larger number, such as a million voters, should be acted on even earlier.[31] This plan ignores the federal scheme by neglecting to provide that such petitions must be somewhat uniformly scattered throughout the states, though this is not particularly serious since the amendment still remains to be voted on. A number of other proposals require that the petitions be concurred in by a certain percentage of the voters in a certain number of states.[32] It is notable that another federal country, Switzerland, provides for the use of the constitutional initiative; its experience has shown that, while the initiative is not a universal panacea, on the other hand it has not been productive of serious ills. The experience of the states in our own

64th Cong., 1st sess. (1915) (legislatures of majority of states); Rep. Gray of Indiana, H. J. R. 294, 64th Cong., 1st sess. (1916) (legislatures of two-thirds of states, or majority vote in two-thirds of states); Senator Owen, S. J. R. 27, 68th Cong., 1st sess. (1916) (majority of state legislatures); Rep. Lea of California, H. J. R. 168, 71st Cong., 2d sess. (1929) (majority of state legislatures).

[31] Rep. Gray of Indiana, H. J. R. 294, 64th Cong., 1st sess. (1916) (majority vote in two-thirds of states); Senator Pomerene of Ohio, S. J. R. 22, 66th Cong., 1st sess. (1919) (proposal on petition of 500,000 voters); Rep. Emerson of Ohio, H. J. R. 60, 66th Cong., 1st sess. (1919) (proposal on petition of 500,000 voters), and H. J. R. 123, 66th Cong., 1st sess. (1919) (proposal on petition of 500,000 voters, to be submitted at next congressional election, or proposal on petition of 1,000,000 voters to be submitted to voters at special election); Rep. Morin of Pennsylvania, H. J. R. 110, 67th Cong., 1st sess. (1921), the same; Rep. Berger of Wisconsin, H. J. R. 281, 70th Cong., 1st sess. (1928), the same.

[32] Rep. Berger of Wisconsin, H. J. R. 79, 62d Cong., 1st sess. (1911) (five per cent of the voters in each of three-fourths of the states); Rep. Igoe of Missouri, H. J. R. 319, 63d Cong., 2d sess. (1914) (ten per cent of voters of majority of states).

country has not been such that one can lay down dogmatically that the popular initiative is either desirable or undesirable.[33] Doubtless in some states at some times the use of the initiative has resulted in hasty, ill-considered and excessive constitutional changes. Recent use in connection with labor legislation has not been wholly satisfactory.[34] On the other hand, one can point to many cases where it has been used but moderately and in a deliberate way and for desirable reforms. Certainly no state which does not provide for its use can claim to be truly democratic. The possibility of a resort to it means that there can be no real weight to the charge that it is impossible to secure changes which the people really want, and may spur Congress to act more promptly than it otherwise would. After all the evidence is in, it seems hard to conclude that the experience of the states with the initiative has been so unsatisfactory that its introduction into the federal system would work great mischief. In fairness it should be said, however, that the problems of a nation as large and heterogeneous as the United States may be so different that the experience of the states, limited and controversial as it has been, may hardly serve as a fair basis for recommending its introduction into the federal system.[35] For instance, the federal initiative might result in lack of deliberation. Possibly recent world events indicate that there are practical limits on democracy. If the people are given a vote on the ratification of amendments, it may be argued that that is a sufficient degree of democracy for practi-

[33] Dodd, The Revision and Amendment of State Constitutions (1910) 292: "The popular initiative is open to many objections, both theoretical and practical, but the people should have power independently of the legislature, to force changes in their constitutions when such changes are desired. Perhaps the greatest value which the initiative will have is not the direct results which may come from its use, but in its influence in causing legislatures to act upon matters upon which action is desired by the people." See also Radin, "Popular Legislation in California," (1939) 23 Minn. L. Rev. 559.

[34] See Preliminary Report of Committee on Labor, Employment and Social Security, (1939) 64 A. B. A. Rep. 531 at 545, 568.

[35] Ames, The Proposed Amendments to the Constitution (1897) 286.

cal purposes. If Congress be given the power to propose amendments by a simple majority, that, too, would seem fairly to assure the submission of measures desired by the people.

B. REFORM OF RATIFICATION OF AMENDMENTS

1. *Ratification by State Conventions*

Next to proposal of amendments by a national convention, the least discussed phase of Article Five is that providing for ratification of amendments by state conventions at the option of Congress. Congress thus far has but once chosen to select this mode of ratification, though the original Constitution was thus ratified. An Illinois constitutional convention sought to ratify the Corwin amendment although Congress had submitted it to the state legislatures.[36] It has been asserted that certain types of amendments, such as those impinging on the police power of the state or impairing alleged inalienable individual rights, must be ratified by state conventions. The Supreme Court, however, in 1931 decided that all amendments are on the same basis with respect to the mode of ratification.[37] Hence it now is clear that conventions may ratify only when Congress sees fit to select that mode of ratification.

There has until recently been no substantial criticism of the convention mode of ratification. In fact, efforts were made

[36] Senator Adams of Colorado, whose general conclusions are favorable, however, 65 CONG. REC. (1924) 4804, said: "The weakness is this, that the initiation of measures submitted under the initiative comes from small groups, groups having no authority whatsoever. That is, one may sit down in his office and frame an amendment to the Constitution, or a law, and then, through the process of petition circulation, initiate it."

[37] United States v. Sprague, (1931) 282 U. S. 716, 50 S. Ct. 220, overruling (D. C. N. J. 1930) 44 F. (2d) 967, noted in (1932) 27 ILL. L. REV. 72; (1931) 29 MICH. L. REV. 777, and (1931) 79 U. PA. L. REV. 807. See also, United States v. Panos, (D. C. Ill. 1930) 45 F. (2d) 888; United States v. Thibault, (C. C. A. 2d, 1931) 47 F. (2d) 169; speech of Rep. J. J. McSwain, 74 CONG. REC. (1931) 3002; brief of Edmund B. Dunford, 74 CONG. REC. (1931) 5819.

when the recent amendments were submitted to induce Congress to make use of this mode. Likewise at the time when the Civil War Amendments were proposed in Congress, attempts were made to secure their submission to direct popular vote—quite clearly unconstitutional under *Hawke v. Smith*[38]—or at least submission to conventions. In all of these cases it seems, however, that the reason prompting such demands was not so much that of consulting the wishes of the people as of securing the defeat of the amendments.

It seems desirable at this point to consider the arguments in favor of and against the use of the state convention method of ratification. First to be considered are the defects, for defects there admittedly are. Precedent is against its use, since it has been used only once, namely, with respect to the Twenty-First Amendment. It is more expensive than the legislative mode since special machinery must be set up. It is likely to involve more delay than the legislative mode for the same reason. It is likely to involve certain legal complications not found in the legislative mode, as, for example, whether the power to regulate the election, place of meeting, procedure, etc. of state conventions is in Congress or the state legislatures. It is not likely to secure such full and careful deliberation as the legislative method; the experience with respect to the Twenty-First Amendment showed that convention members felt themselves bound by the popular will.[39] It should be noted, however, that many persons feel that legislators should vote the way they think the majority of their constituents wish them to, and that in these days of straw votes and mass writing to legislators, the legislators do not need to wait for an election to find out what the people back home think. Finally, if the object of reforming the

[38] (1920) 253 U. S. 221, 40 S. Ct. 495.
[39] BROWN, RATIFICATION OF THE TWENTY-FIRST AMENDMENT TO THE CONSTITUTION (1938) 6; Martig, "Amending the Constitution," (1937) 35 MICH. L. REV. 1253 at 1284.

amending process is to secure more democracy, the logical procedure is to provide directly for a popular vote: the convention method is nothing but a step in that direction, and if the convention merely follows the popular will, it is but a futile ceremony.

On the other hand, there are a number of outstanding merits in the convention method, at least in comparison with the legislative method. It is more likely to represent the popular will,[40] since conventions are selected subsequent to submission of an amendment while frequently legislatures are not. It is also more likely to represent the popular will since it is selected for only one issue, while a legislature, even though selected after submission, is likely to be selected for its views on several and unrelated issues. The members of a convention are likely to vote more independently of wrongful influences since they do not face the temptation of legislators to vote with an eye to reelection. An abler group of persons is likely to be chosen as members of the convention than of the legislature, particularly if the convention is small in number. Since a convention is unicameral, it may proceed more quickly than the legislatures, which are bicameral except in Nebraska. The convention method is deemed preferable to a popular referendum by those who distrust the intelligence of the masses, particularly if the popular referendum occurred at a general election so as to confuse the voter, or if the referendum were hastily taken after submission so that there was no adequate time for deliberation. On the other hand, where speed was desirable a convention might be quickly summoned, whereas many proposals for popular referenda contemplate action only at general elections.

It has sometimes been argued that the present mode of ratification is entirely satisfactory because of the possibility that

[40] Brown, "The People Should be Consulted as to Constitutional Changes," (1930) 16 A. B. A. J. 404; Needham, "Changing the Fundamental Law," (1921) 69 U. Pa. L. Rev. 223 at 228ff.

the convention mode may be used.[41] Experience thus far scarcely justifies this belief since Congress has but once resorted to its use even though efforts were made both as to the Civil War Amendments and the most recent amendments.[42] Because Congress itself is a legislative body, because of the expenses and delay of using the convention mode, and because of the inertia due to usage, it seems unlikely that Congress will often resort to the use of conventions of its own free will. If the convention mode is to be frequently used it will probably be necessary to amend the Constitution so as to provide that Congress may submit amendments only to conventions. Burgess, who is opposed to the use of the regular governmental machinery in the amending process, favors such a rule.[43] Each convention under his plan would have the relative weight that the population of the state bears to the population of the nation.

2. Ratification by State Legislatures

It is at the legislative mode of ratification that most proposals for the reform of the amending process have been directed in recent years. The reasons for this are interesting. The fatal step in the amending process for most propositions has been that of proposal, a fact which is easily demonstrable when it is realized that twenty-one of the twenty-six amendments which have been submitted by Congress have been ratified, with the status of the child labor amendment still

[41] Ames, "The Amending Provision of the Federal Constitution in Practice." (1924) 63 AM. PHIL. SOC. PROC. 62 at 74.

[42] Senator Dixon, CONG. GLOBE, 40th Cong., 3d sess. (1869) 1040.

[43] BURGESS, RECENT CHANGES IN AMERICAN CONSTITUTIONAL THEORY (1923) 107, 112ff. See proposal of Senator Wadsworth, of New York, S. J. R. 109, 68th Cong., 1st sess. (1924), for ratification by conventions chosen by the people or by popular vote; Senator Shields of Tennessee, 65 CONG. REC. (1924) 4801–4802; Rep. Garrett of Tennessee, 66 CONG. REC. (1924) 2160. See also Williams, "The Popular Mandate on Constitutional Amendments," (1921) 7 VA. L. REV. 280 at 298.

in doubt. The proponents of an easier amending process are scarcely pursuing the logical course of action, therefore, when they urge the alteration of the ratifying process rather than that of the process of proposal. The real reasons, however, are not far to seek. Many of these proposals are for a direct popular referendum on amendments. They are based on the notion that the people should participate directly in fundamental changes in law and government, both because it is the truly democratic method and because measures thus ratified are more likely to be enforced. Many of the proponents of this change have a more selfish motive, however. They favor a popular referendum because they believe that it will make the Constitution more difficult to amend. The enemies of the Eighteenth Amendment, for instance, argued that that amendment was railroaded through the legislatures by the well organized propaganda of a minority. This pressure, it is argued, cannot in the nature of things be brought to bear on the people themselves. It should be observed that the most strenuous opponents of making amendment easier have generally coupled their proposals for popular ratification with clauses providing for legislative participation as well, thus really adding another step to the existing amending process. Manifestly the prime motive of such a scheme is to impede the process rather than to consult the wishes of the people.

One of the changes suggested in the legislative mode is to require something less than the legislatures of three-fourths of the states. Two out of five amendments submitted by Congress which failed of ratification failed by the vote of a single state. One of the chief defects of the Articles of Confederation was the requirement of unanimity of the states in the adoption of amendments. A single state could therefore veto the wishes of all the other states and so the amending process was rendered well nigh useless. The adoption of the Constitution hence became a revolutionary act, since it was made to go into effect when ratified by three-fourths of the states. The present requirement of a three-fourths majority was one of the compromises of the Constitutional Convention. Sherman proposed that every state must concur in the ratification of amendments.[44] James Wilson proposed ratification by two-thirds of the states.[45] It is significant that Wilson's proposal failed by a five to six vote. His later motion providing for a three-fourths majority was then accepted. Patrick Henry, in opposing the ratification of the Constitution by the Virginia Convention, argued that the negative power given to one-fourth of the states made amendment impossible.[46] The first proposal for altering the method of amendment was made by the Rhode Island Convention when it ratified the Constitution on May 29, 1790. The proposition was that after the year 1793 no amendment to the Constitution should be made "without the consent of eleven of the states heretofore united under the Confederation."[47] There seem to have been two motives behind the proposals: to make it more difficult to amend, and to insure the preponderance of the original thirteen colonies.

The Rhode Island proposal seems to have been the only one looking in the direction of increasing the majority of states required. Subsequent proposals have all gone in the other direction. On January 11, 1864, in connection with the resolution for the abolition of slavery, Senator Henderson of Missouri introduced a resolution allowing ratification by two-thirds of the states.[48] The constitution of the Confederate States provided for a similar majority.[49] In 1873,

---

[44] 5 ELLIOT, DEBATES, 2d ed. (1836).

[45] Ibid.

[46] 3 ibid. 49.

[47] FOSTER, MINUTES OF THE RHODE ISLAND CONSTITUTIONAL CONVENTION OF 1790 (1929) 96–97.

[48] S. J. R. 16, 38th Cong., 1st sess. (1864).

[49] Article V, § 1. Similar proposals were made by Rep. Crumpacker of Indiana, H. J. R. 375, 62d Cong., 3d sess. (1913), and Senator Cummins of Iowa, S. J. R. 26, 63d Cong., 1st sess. (1913).

Mr. Porter of Virginia proposed that amendments were to be valid, "when approved and ratified by a majority of the electors in the several states voting thereon and qualified to vote for representatives in Congress."[50]

A number of proposals have suggested ratification by simple majority of the states.[51] Such proposals, however, are almost invariably accompanied by a provision for submission of amendments to direct popular vote. In addition, it is generally provided that there be both a majority of the states and a majority of the votes of the entire nation in favor of the amendment.[52] That is the rule in both Switzerland and Australia. Were only a majority of the popular vote in the entire country required, less than a majority of the states might approve.[53] This could scarcely be acceptable except to those who are prepared to cast aside the federal concept of governmental relations. On the other hand, to permit ratification by a mere majority of states might easily result in the passage of an amendment contrary to the wishes of a majority of the electors.[54] Indeed, even under the present system it

[50] H. J. R. 180, 42d Cong., 3d sess. (1873).

[51] Senator LaFollette of Wisconsin, S. J. R. 131, 62d Cong., 2d sess. (1912) and S. J. R. 24, 63d Cong., 1st sess. (1913); Senator Thompson of Kansas, S. J. R. 9, 63d Cong., 1st sess. (1913); Rep. Lafferty of Oregon, H. J. R. 60, 63d Cong., 1st sess. (1913) (or majority vote of electors in the several states).

[52] Rep. Igoe of Missouri, H. J. R. 319, 63d Cong., 2d sess. (1914); Smith, "Shall We Make Our Constitution Flexible?" (1911) 194 No. AM. REV. 657 at 668; Johnstone, "An Eighteenth Century Constitution," (1912) 7 ILL. L. REV. 265.

[53] For such proposals, see that of Senator Owen of Oklahoma, S. J. R. 20, 63d Cong., 1st sess. (1913); Rep. Lafferty of Oregon, H. J. R. 60, 63d Cong., 1st sess. (1913) (or majority of state legislatures); Senator Pomerene of Ohio, S. J. R. 22, 66th Cong., 1st sess. (1919); Rep. Emerson of Ohio, H. J. R. 123, 66th Cong., 1st sess. (1920); Rep. Morin of Pennsylvania, H. J. R. 110, 67th Cong., 1st sess. (1921); Rep. Boylan of New York, H. J. R. 133, 68th Cong., 1st sess. (1924); Rep. Dyer of Missouri, H. J. R. 229, 70th Cong., 1st sess. (1928); Professor Edward S. Corwin, letter of May 27, 1931, to the author of this book.

[54] For such proposals, see Senator LaFollette of Wisconsin, S. J. R. 24, 63d Cong., 1st sess. (1921); Rep. Chandler of New York, H. J. R. 315, 64th Cong., 2d sess. (1916).

has been pointed out that it is possible to secure ratification by the less populous states representing an actual minority of the population. On the other hand, it is to be remembered that an amendment may be defeated by the twelve least populous states, and that the concurrence of such twelve, while not likely, is fully as probable as the concurrence of the thirty-six least populous states in ratifying. Moreover, the amendment must have been previously concurred in by two-thirds of Congress, the lower house of which is elected on the basis of population. Senator Owen has proposed ratification by a majority of congressional districts and a majority of the aggregate vote.[55] Most of the state constitutions provided for ratification by a majority of the popular vote. Both of these two last proposals would be out of harmony with the federal principle, so that the farthest an adherent of the latter principle could go in the direction of majority rule is to accept the Swiss and Australian plan of accepting a majority of the states plus a majority of the electors of the entire country.

Perhaps a more conservative plan would be to permit ratification by two-thirds of the states.[56] It is noteworthy that

---

[55] S. J. R. 9, 64th Cong., 1st sess. (1915). See also his other proposals: S. J. R. 42, 62d Cong., 1st sess. (1911) (acceptance by a majority of congressional districts and a majority of the states); S. J. R. 8, 65th Cong., 1st sess. (1917), (majority vote in majority of congressional districts); S. J. R. 14, 67th Cong., 1st sess. (1921) (majority vote in majority of congressional districts).

[56] Senator Cummins of Iowa, S. J. R. 26, 63d Cong., 1st sess. (1913), proposed adoption by two-thirds of state legislatures or by majority vote in two-thirds of states; Rep. Bryan of Washington, H. J. R. 422, 63d Cong., 3d sess. (1915); Senator Cummins, S. J. R. 33, 64th Cong., 1st sess. (1915) (same as earlier proposal, supra); Rep. Lea of California, H. J. R. 168, 71st Cong., 2d sess. (1929) (majority of people of the nation and a majority of the people in two-thirds of the states ratifying); Senator Norris of Nebraska, S. J. R. 134, 75th Cong., 3d sess. (1937).

"It seems evident, then, that where the check is sought in numbers, a majority is too small, and a unanimous vote too large, for either practicability or safety. A mean must be sought not liable to these objections, and that not from *a priori* considerations, but from experience." JAMESON, CONSTITUTIONAL CONVENTIONS, 4th ed. (1887) 553.

the more recent proposals, except that of Senator Norris in 1937,[57] have accepted the existing rule requiring the approval of three-fourths of the states, and have stressed rather the idea of a popular referendum.[58] In fact, under the Wadsworth-Garrett amendment an amendment might have to be ratified not only by the legislatures of three-fourths of the states but also by the popular vote of three-fourths of the states.[59] And even under the Jones amendment to the latter amendment the legislatures would still act as advisory bodies, and would have to vote on an amendment before the popular vote was taken.[60] In view of the comparative ease of securing ratification after an amendment has been submitted, especially as seen in the cases of the last six amendments, it is

[57] S. J. R. 134, 75th Cong., 3d sess. (1937).

[58] Rep. Chandler of New York, H. J. R. 95, 63d Cong., 1st sess. (1913); Rep. Gray of Indiana, H. J. R. 294, 64th Cong., 1st sess. (1916) (majority of electors in three-fourths of states or by legislatures in three-fourths of states); Senator Fletcher of Florida, S. J. R. 182, 65th Cong., 2d sess. (1918); Rep. LaGuardia of New York, H. J. R. 430, 65th Cong., 3d sess. (1919), and H. J. R. 12, 66th Cong., 1st sess. (1919); Rep. Griffin of New York, H. J. R. 35, 66th Cong., 1st sess. (1919); Rep. Siegel of New York, H. J. R. 36, 66th Cong., 1st sess. (1919); Senator Harrison of Mississippi, S. J. R. 48, 66th Cong., 1st sess. (1919); Senator Frelinghuysen of New Jersey, S. J. R. 126, 66th Cong., 1st sess. (1919); Rep. Johnston of New York, H. J. R. 306, 66th Cong., 2d sess. (1920); Rep. MacGregor of New York, H. J. R. 332, 66th Cong., 2d sess. (1920); Rep. Griffin of New York, H. J. R. 12, 67th Cong., 1st sess. (1921); Rep. MacGregor, H. J. R. 21, 67th Cong., 1st sess. (1921); Rep. Siegel of New York, H. J. R. 29, 67th Cong., 1st sess. (1921); Rep. Kissel of New York, H. J. R. 118, 67th Cong., 1st sess. (1921); Rep. Cullen of New York, H. J. R. 162, 67th Cong., 1st sess. (1921); Rep. Vare of Pennsylvania, H. J. R. 34, 68th Cong., 1st sess. (1923); Rep. Griffin of New York, H. J. R. 37, 68th Cong., 1st sess. (1923); Senator Ashurst of Arizona, S. J. R. 17, 68th Cong., 1st sess. (1923); Rep. Griffin of New York, H. J. R. 18, 69th Cong., 1st sess. (1924); Rep. Griffin, H. J. R. 68, 70th Cong., 1st sess. (1927); Rep. Lea of California, H. J. R. 168, 71st Cong., 2d sess. (1929); Rep. Andresen of Minnesota, H. J. R. 348, 71st Cong., 2d sess. (1930) (popular vote or conventions as Congress shall prescribe) [and see 72 CONG. REC. (1930) 10,930]; Rep. Griffin, H. J. R. 362, 71st Cong., 2d sess. (1930); see article by Senator Ashurst, "Making Amendments," SATURDAY EVENING POST, April 25, 1929, reprinted in 72 CONG. REC. 3066 (1930); Senator Norris, in a letter of June 10, 1931, to the author of this book.

[59] See citations in note 72, infra.

[60] 65 CONG. REC. (1924) 4802. Argument of Senator Dixon of Connecticut, CONG. GLOBE, 40th Cong., 3d sess. (1869) 706.

doubtful that there will be any reduction in the number of states required to concur, however desirable that may be theoretically.

Another change which has frequently been suggested in the legislative mode is that ratification be only by legislatures the more numerous branch of which have been elected after the submission of the amendment.[61] Since state senators are frequently elected for a longer term than state representatives, the principle of subsequent election is generally confined in the proposals to the House of Representatives. In the case of some of the Civil War Amendments, it was suggested that Congress provide in its resolution of proposal and submission that the amendment be submitted only to subsequently elected legislatures. Four or five states have constitutional or statutory provisions providing for ratification of federal amendments only by such legislatures, but these provisions have recently been held unconstitutional.[62] All of the recent amendments have been ratified by legislatures which were in existence when they were proposed, and this was true even of the Bill of Rights. An existing legislature might of course of its own accord by a sort of self-denying ordinance fail to act on an amendment. The pressure is generally so

[61] Senator Buckalew of Pennsylvania, CONG. GLOBE, 40th Cong., 3d sess. (1869) 828 (as part of the Fifteenth Amendment); Senator Davis of Kentucky, CONG. GLOBE, 40th Cong., 3d sess. (1869) 1309 (as part of the Fifteenth Amendment); Senator Hendricks of Indiana, CONG. GLOBE, 40th Cong., 3d sess. (1869) 543, 1311 (as part of the Fifteenth Amendment); Rep. Woodward of Pennsylvania, CONG. GLOBE, 40th Cong., 3d sess. (1869) 1226; Rep. Garrett of Tennessee, H. J. R. 69, 67th Cong., 1st sess. (1921), and H. J R. 429, 67th Cong., 4th sess. (1923); Senator Wadsworth of New York, S. J. R. 4, 68th Cong., 1st sess. (1923); 65 CONG. REC. 89, 3549, 3675, 3942, 4420, 4488, 4556, 4717, 4800, 4929, 4995, 5009, reported with amendments, debated and recommitted; Rep. Garrett, H. J. R. 68, 68th Cong., 1st sess. (1923), debated, reported back, 65 CONG. REC. 10,414; Rep. Garrett, H. J. R. 15, 69th Cong., 1st sess. (1925); Senator Wadsworth, S. J. R. 8, 69th Cong., 1st sess. (1925); Rep. Garrett, H. J. R. 143, 70th Cong., 1st sess. (1928); Ames, "The Amending Provision of the Federal Constitution in Practice," (1924) 63 AM. PHIL. SOC. PROC. 62 at 74; Jacob Tanger, letter of June 17, 1931, to author of this book.

[62] Leser v. Garnett, (1922), 258 U. S. 130, 42 S. Ct. 217.

great, however, for immediate action, often involving even special sessions, that the only way to secure ratification by a subsequent legislature is to provide for it in the federal Constitution.[63] The chief argument of the proponents of this reform is that the sentiment of the people will be more directly reflected, since the legislators will be elected on the basis of their attitude towards the amendment. Moreover, greater time for deliberation will be provided. The arguments on the other side, however, seem more convincing. Doubtless to some extent a subsequently elected legislature will better represent popular opinion. The chances are, however, that the legislators are elected on their attitudes towards other issues. If the popular will is to be truly reflected, this can be much better accomplished by the use of conventions elected with reference to the single issue involved. Or even better, why not provide for a popular referendum if the real object is to consult the people? As the late Senator Borah said, "Let us not have homeopathic doses!"[64] The amending process is already difficult enough. To require ratification by later legislatures is simply to add one more obstacle, as a delay of at least one and generally two years will be required. Couple this delay with a provision for a popular referendum in addition to the action of the legislature, as did the Wadsworth-Garrett amendment, and an almost insuperable barrier against amendments is set up. It is hard to escape the conclusion that the proponents of action by subsequent legislatures

[63] Senator Morton of Indiana introduced a resolution, S. J. R. 32, 41st Cong., 1st sess. (1869), prescribing the procedure to be followed by the legislatures in ratifying. See supra, chap. 3, note 86. And see AMES, THE PROPOSED AMENDMENTS TO THE CONSTITUTION OF THE UNITED STATES (1897) 290. Mr. Shanks of Indiana introduced the same amendment in the House, H. J. R. 57, 41st Cong., 1st sess. (1869). Mr. Juul of Illinois, H. J. R. 242, 66th Cong., 1st sess. (1919), introduced a resolution regulating voting strength in state legislatures when ratifying amendments.

[64] 65 CONG. REC. (1924) 4562.

are more interested in preventing amendment than they are in securing popular representation.[65]

A problem that has arisen on several occasions is whether or not a state may rescind its action on an amendment. If three-fourths of the states have ratified an amendment, it then seems clear that there can be no effective repudiation of prior action. On the other hand, at any time prior to such ratification the rule is in greater doubt.[66] The Supreme Court has recently ruled that a political question is involved.[67] A number of proposals have been made that until the necessary majority of acceptances have been obtained, a state should be free to change its prior action whether such action was affirmative or negative.[68] This is one of the provisions of the Wadsworth-Garrett amendment. But that amendment goes a step further and provides that repudiation by more than one-fourth of the states shall bar the further consideration of the amendment by the legislatures. The latter provision seems undesirable. It is designed to add to the difficulties of the already existing process. To allow thirteen states to kill an amendment will obviously mean that the opponents of an amendment will concentrate on a small number of states early in the fight and perhaps kill the amendment before it has had a chance for consideration.[69] It is bad enough to allow thirteen legislatures to hold up an amendment under any conditions. It is simply making matters worse to let them destroy it at the outset. At least until some provision is made permitting rati-

[65] Senator Norris, 65 CONG. REC. (1924) 4941, said: "Some people want to make it difficult to amend the Constitution. Others want to simplify it. There is argument on both sides. I concede absolutely that there is good argument each way, but I can not conceive of any argument that simply calls for delay, and that is what I think we have done with this amendment."

[66] See supra, chap. III.

[67] Coleman v. Miller, (1939) 307 U. S. 453, 59 S. Ct. 972.

[68] Rep. Garrett, H. J. R. 143, 70th Cong., 1st sess. (1928).

[69] See the argument of Senator Heflin of Alabama, 65 CONG. REC. (1924)

fication by a lesser majority of the states, it would seem that the proposals should be rejected.

3. *Ratification by Popular Referendum*

The chief proposal for the alteration of the amending process to receive serious consideration in the past two decades has been that for a popular referendum.[70] It is felt that the people themselves should participate at some stage in the amending process. Some of the proposals go so far as to say that the people should be allowed even to initiate amendments, as is done in Switzerland and in some of our states. These proposals, however, have not been strongly pressed and attention has been increasingly centered on securing confirmation by the people. Popular suffrage has been vastly extended from what it was when the Constitution was drafted. Although popular referenda were unknown in 1787, the states have used the popular referendum as the exclusive mode of ratification of amendments to and revision of the state constitutions ever since about 1830. The extension of suffrage to the negroes by the Fifteenth Amendment and to women by the Nineteenth Amendment, both under the federal Constitution, has kept the idea of popular participation in government in the public eye. The provision of the Seventeenth Amendment for the popular election of senators more than almost anything else has stimulated the demand for popular participation in the amending process. The suggestions for ratification only by subsequently elected legislatures is indicative of the trend, as is that for the abolition of the electoral college. But perhaps the most immediate impetus which has been given to the movement came from the adoption of the Eighteenth and Nineteenth Amendments, particularly the

---

[70] The use of the popular referendum under the present terms of Article Five was held unconstitutional in Hawke v. Smith, (1920) 253 U. S. 221, 40 S. Ct. 495. See Taft, "Can Ratification of an Amendment to the Constitution Be Made to Depend on a Referendum?" (1920) 29 YALE L. J. 821.

Eighteenth. It is argued with enough plausibility to convince a great many people that the Eighteenth Amendment was railroaded through the legislatures by means of powerful lobbies and a species of intimidation.[71] It is asserted that, if the legislators had really voted as they felt, the amendment would never have been ratified. It is pointed out that a number of legislatures ignored previous popular referenda rejecting the amendment, and that in a number of cases subsequent popular votes under what the courts later found to be invalid or inapplicable provisions for referenda on federal amendments showed that the popular will was not in accord with that of the legislature. The Democratic party in 1924 adopted a plank advocating a popular referendum on federal amendments. Certainly the tendency of the past century has been towards more democracy in government. It is the frequently repeated doctrine of the Supreme Court that the people are sovereign, that they adopted the Constitution and may alter that document. If this doctrine is to be given anything but lip service, it would seem that the time has come when the people should be given the right to vote on whether an amendment should be adopted.

In the effort to secure a popular referendum, one must be careful to see that something else is not foisted upon one. The substitute may be so bad as to make the continuance of the present clause preferable. The provision for a referendum may be so hedged about with clauses which clog the amending process as to merit the defeat of the entire proposal.[72] Such was the situation with respect to the Wadsworth-Garrett

---

[71] Senator Ashurst, 58 Cong. Rec. (1919) 5694, said: "I believe that the two amendments which were last proposed for ratification, viz., the one providing for woman suffrage and the other for prohibition—and I am earnestly in favor of both those amendments—were not forced upon the people, but that they were submitted in response to a demand made by the people. At the same time I am not oblivious to the fact that there are millions of citizens of high character who believe that lobbies intimidated the legislatures of the various States and even intimidated Congress into submitting those amendments."

[72] Miller, "Amendment of the Federal Constitution: Should It Be Made More Difficult?" (1926) 10 Minn. L. Rev. 185.

amendment.[73] This proposal permitted in certain cases, but did not require that an amendment be subjected to a popular referendum. It provided "that any state may require that ratification by its legislature be subject to confirmation by popular vote." If the state failed to make such provision, there could be no popular referendum. It was argued that the states would immediately make such provision. This was effectively answered by pointing out that there was no good reason why the amendment should not directly provide for such ratification to make a popular referendum absolutely certain. The legislatures themselves would scarcely feel disposed to give up their present exclusive right of ratification, and it might take a great deal of time and effort to incorporate such a provision into the state constitution. Moreover, there was only to be a referendum if the legislature ratified the amendment. If the legislature rejected, that ended the issue, and the people were left entirely without voice in the matter. Such a provision naturally made rejection very easy and acceptance even more difficult than it already is. Furthermore, the then existing legislature might reject, but could not accept.[74]

A number of senators of more liberal views perceived these objections to the Wadsworth-Garrett amendment, and in fact the Senate Judiciary Committee reported out a revised proposal by Senator Walsh of Montana, popularly referred

[73] Rep. Garrett of Tennessee, H. J. R. 69, 67th Cong., 1st sess. (1921); Senator Wadsworth of New York, S. J. R. 40, 67th Cong., 1st sess. (1921); Senator Wadsworth, S. J. R. 271, 67th Cong., 4th sess. (1923); Rep. Garrett, H. J. R. 429, 67th Cong., 4th sess. (1923); Senator Wadsworth, S. J. R. 4, 68th Cong., 1st sess. (1923); Rep. Garrett, H. J. R. 143, 70th Cong., 1st sess. (1928). See speech by Senator Wadsworth, 65 CONG. REC. (1924) 4491, 4495, and S. J. R. 21, 67th Cong., 1st sess. (1921), making both legislative and popular vote mandatory.

[74] These arguments were very clearly brought out by Mr. Huddleston of Alabama, 67 CONG. REC. (1926) 7203, who advocated ratification by popular vote. See also Rep. Griffin of New York, 66 CONG. REC. (1925) 4205.

to as the Walsh substitute.[75] The principal feature of Walsh's proposal was that amendments should be referred directly to the people for ratification. The long delays and the increased difficulties of amendment under the Wadsworth-Garrett amendment were pointed out. Senator Jones of Washington then offered an amendment to the Walsh substitute, taking a position intermediate between that of Senators Wadsworth and Walsh.[76] Unlike Wadsworth's proposal it provided for a referendum when the legislature rejected an amendment as well as when it ratified. Also unlike Wadsworth's proposal, this plan contemplated the mandatory use of the popular referendum in all cases. It did agree with Wadsworth's proposal, however, in the fact that the legislature still remained a part of the amending procedure. But it became a purely advisory body. That is to say, no matter how the legislature voted, a popular referendum automatically followed; the result of the legislative vote, whether for or against the amendment, was immaterial.

The proponents of the Jones amendment argued that the people would receive the benefits of the legislative discussions. If a popular vote alone were taken, such a vote might come so soon after proposal by Congress that there would be no time for deliberation. On the other hand, it was argued that this plan turned the legislature into a mere debating society, and that since its action was mere *brutum fulmen* it would not take its function seriously enough to make its discussions of any value to the people. In fact, it would strip the legislature of its dignity to make it a mere advisory body. There would be unnecessary delay involved since the people

[75] S. Rep. 202 on S. J. R. 4, 68th Cong., 1st sess. (1924), 65 CONG. REC. (1924) 3675. For defenses of Walsh's substitute, see Adams, 65 CONG. REC. (1924) 4497, 4802, 4804, 4998; Brandegee, ibid. 4497, 4565, 4931; Borah, ibid. 4561, 4563, 4564; Robinson, ibid. 4800; Walsh, ibid. 4931; Gerry, ibid. 4935; Norris, ibid. 4941.

[76] 65 CONG. REC. (1924) 4802, 4929.

could act only after the legislature had acted, and moreover only a subsequently elected legislature itself could act. As to the possibility of undue haste and lack of knowledge on the part of the voters, it was pointed out that it is virtually impossible to secure the proposal by Congress by the necessary two-thirds vote without long preliminary popular agitation and discussion. Senator Walsh and a number of other senators who favored a popular referendum objected vigorously to the Jones amendment, and declared they preferred the existing system to it.

It is true that the Jones amendment did present a rather evenly balanced proposal, on the one hand making a considerable delay necessary and yet on the other hand providing for a popular referendum in all cases, such referendum to be absolutely decisive irrespective of the action of the legislature. It was subject to the further objection that in case the legislature took no action at all then no referendum could occur. The Senate at first accepted the amendment,[77] only shortly later to reject it.[78] The Walsh substitute finally died on the calendar. The House Judiciary Committee twice reported favorably on the Wadsworth-Garrett amendment, but no vote was ever taken on it. Senator Brandegee twice proposed that Congress should have the option of submitting amendments to be ratified according to either of the present modes or by a popular referendum.[79]

Assuming that there is to be a popular referendum, there is still the question of when it should be held. The most usual proposal is that it shall be held at the next general federal election, in other words at the next election of members of

---

[77] 65 CONG. REC. (1924) 4940, by a vote of 34 to 29.

[78] Ibid. 5003, by a vote of 39 to 35.

[79] S. J. R. 90, 65th Cong., 1st sess. (1917), and S. J. R. 41, 66th Cong., 1st sess. (1919), twice reported favorably by the Senate Judiciary Committee, 58 CONG. REC. (1919) 4265, 5694–5700. See also Smith, "Shall We Make Our Constitution Flexible?" (1911) 194 No. AM. REV. 657.

the House of Representatives.[80] This means that the amendment will be voted on by the people at some time less than two years after it was submitted by Congress. It also means that all of the states would be passing on the amendment on one uniform date, excepting, of course, Maine, which votes earlier. If the amendment were rejected, that would seem to cut off another referendum without a new submission by Congress. Hence we would dispose of the problem whether or not a given amendment is still pending. Other proposals have been that it shall be voted on at the next general state election held within the state.[81] General state elections are held usually every two years, and in some states annually, so that amendments would be voted on at approximately the same time. A third conceivable plan would be to allow each state to hold its election when it chose.[82] This, however, would do away with uniformity of time of ratification and still leave unsolved the problem of whether or not a given amendment is still pending. Perhaps the most satisfactory stipulation is that first mentioned, providing for a vote at the same time that the lower house of Congress is being elected.

It has been suggested that to permit a popular vote at so early a date may result in action on the amendment before there has been an opportunity for public discussion and deliberation on the amendment. Congress might submit an amendment only a few months before the election. Doubtless there is some force in this objection. Possibly it might be well to prescribe a minimum period, such as one year or

---

[80] Senator Pomerene of Ohio, S. J. R. 22, 66th Cong., 1st sess. (1919); Rep. Emerson of Ohio, H. J. R. 60 and 123, 66th Cong., 1st sess. (1919); Rep. Lea of California, H. J. R. 168, 71st Cong., 2d sess. (1929). In Australia an amendment is submitted to popular vote within not less than two or more than six months after it has been proposed. Constitution of Commonwealth of Australia, § 128.

[81] Senator Norris, in a letter of June 10, 1931, to the author of this book.

[82] Speech by Senator Wadsworth, 65 CONG. REC. (1924) 4495; S. J. R. 134, 75th Cong., 3d sess. (1938).

six months, between the date of submission and that of the popular referendum.[83] The present amendments have been ratified in most cases by the then existing legislatures, in some cases on receipt of telegraphic information of the approval by Congress. No amendment has taken as much as three years to ratify, and the tremendous pressure brought to bear on the legislatures has been such as to induce prompt action, in some cases through special sessions. Moreover, as Senator Walsh has pointed out, the bare fact of approval by Congress in itself indicates that a measure has received long prior discussion, so that the populace does not need a long period of time in which to make up its mind.[84]

If Article Five be amended to provide for ratification of amendments by a popular referendum, questions may arise concerning what majority shall be necessary to carry an amendment and who shall be the judge of whether or not an amendment has been adopted by the requisite majority. By a majority do we mean a majority of the qualified electors of the state, or a majority of the electors voting on the amendment? The same doubt has arisen as to similarly phrased clauses in state constitutions. Perhaps the sounder legal view is that simply a majority of the electors voting on the amendment is sufficient, yet the adjudicated cases split about evenly on the matter. To prevent any controversy it seems best to provide expressly that ratification be by a majority of the qualified electors voting on the proposed amendment.[85] The

[83] Carman, "Why and How the Present Method of Amending the Federal Constitution Should be Changed," (1938) 17 Ore. L. Rev. 102.

[84] 65 Cong. Rec. (1924) 4558; Borah, ibid. 4564; Norris, ibid. 5002.

[85] Mr. Porter of Virginia, H. J. R. 180, 42d Cong., 3d sess. (1873); Senator Owen of Oklahoma, 58 Cong. Rec. (1919) 5700. See speech by Senator Robinson of Arkansas, 65 Cong. Rec. (1924) 3676; speeches by Senators Harrison and George, ibid. 4999; proposal by Senator Reed of Missouri, supported by Norris, ibid. 5003, 5006; letter of June 10, 1931, by Senator Norris to author of this book. Professor Edward S. Corwin, in a letter of May 27, 1931, to the author of this book suggests ratification by an absolute majority of the number voting in the most recent presidential election.

Wadsworth-Garrett amendment is doubly ambiguous in providing simply for "confirmation by popular vote." Usage, however, would seem to indicate that by this is meant a simple majority rather than a two-thirds or a three-fourths or some other majority.

In the recent congressional debates argument arose over which was to control the matter of whether or not an amendment has been adopted,—the federal government or the states. Under the present legislative mode, the courts will not look behind the legislative rolls to decide whether an amendment has been adopted after it has been certified to the secretary of state by the state officials. But ratification by popular vote does not involve a precisely analogous situation, and so question might arise as to whether or not the federal government might attempt to regulate the conduct of the election, the qualifications of voters, and the counting of the ballots, etc. It was after some acrimonious debate on this as well as other controversial issues that the Walsh substitute was recommitted to committee for clarification.[86]

Another point which has frequently been raised is that of how long an amendment remains open for ratification after it has been submitted by Congress. As a matter of common sense, an amendment proposed a generation or more previously should not remain open to ratification.[87] A time limit set out in an amendment on a specific subject would govern the ratification of that amendment. But the Supreme Court has gone even further and said that Congress has the implied power to prescribe a reasonable time limit for ratification,[88] and that the question of time is a political one.[89] A number of

[86] Senator Swanson of Virginia, 65 CONG. REC. (1924) 5007–5009.

[87] Senator Ashurst of Arizona, 55 CONG. REC. (1917) 5556–5557; Senator Norris, letter of June 10, 1931, to the author of this book; BURDICK, THE LAW OF THE AMERICAN CONSTITUTION (1922) 39.

[88] Dillon v. Gloss, (1921) 256 U. S. 368, 41 S. Ct. 510.

[89] Coleman v. Miller, (1939) 307 U. S. 433, 59 S. Ct. 972.

proposals have therefore been made for specific time limits, such as five,[90] six,[91] seven,[92] or eight[93] years. Where action by both the legislatures and the voters is contemplated, naturally a longer period should be provided, and such changes were offered when the Wadsworth-Garrett amendment was discussed in Congress. If ratification were to be exclusively by a popular referendum, especially if the vote were taken at a uniform date, there would seem to be no need for providing a limitation, unless the referendum provision be construed to permit another referendum without another submission by Congress. In connection with time limitations, perhaps it might be well to limit the time during which an application by a legislature for a national constitutional convention is effectual.

One of the latest proposals to receive attention was Senate Joint Resolution 134 introduced by Senator Norris in 1937.[94] Under this proposed amendment there would be ratification by popular vote, the vote of only two-thirds of the states would be required, and the states would be deprived of their present right to propose amendments. Amendments would be submitted by each state to the electors thereof at the next

[90] Senator Chilton of West Virginia, S. J. R. 126, 63rd Cong., 2d sess. (1914); Mr. Igoe of Missouri, H. J. R. 137, 65th Cong., 1st sess. (1917).

[91] Senator Wadsworth of New York, S. J. R. 207, 64th Cong., 2d sess. (1917), and S. J. R. 88, 65th Cong., 1st sess. (1917); Senator Brandegee of Connecticut, S. J. R. 90, 65th Cong., 1st sess. (1917), and S. J. R. 41, 66th Cong., 1st sess. (1919); speech by Senator Ashurst of Arizona, 55 CONG. REC. (1917) 5556–5558; Senator Fletcher of Florida, S. J. R. 182, 65th Cong., 2d sess. (1918).

[92] Mr. Cullen of New York, H. J. R. 162, 67th Cong., 1st sess. (1921). See article by Senator Ashurst, "Making Amendments," SATURDAY EVENING POST, April 25, 1929, reprinted in 72 CONG. REC. (1930) 3066.

[93] Senator Wadsworth, S. J. R. 109, 68th Cong., 1st sess. (1924). Though advocating a time limit, no specific time is suggested by Platz, "Article Five of the Federal Constitution," (1934) 3 GEO. WASH. L. REV. 17 at 48.

[94] See "Ratification of Constitutional Amendments by Popular Vote," HEARINGS BEFORE A SUBCOMMITTEE OF THE COMMITTEE ON THE JUDICIARY OF THE UNITED STATES SENATE, ON S. J. RES. 134, 75th Cong. 3d sess. (1938).

See criticism of the proposal in editorial, (1938) 24 A. B. A. J. 298; Thomson, "Amending the Constitution," (1938) 42 LAW NOTES No. 1, p. 9.

general election held in the state after the date of proposal; but if a general election was to be held within sixty days after the date an amendment is proposed, it is to be submitted at the next succeeding general election. The electors were to have the qualifications requisite for electors of the state legislature. Each state was to conduct the election and determine the result thereof as the state law provided, or in the absence of such state law as the Congress shall provide. Congress was to have power to prescribe by a uniform law the form in which the question of the ratification should be submitted to the electors in the several states. The amendment was to be submitted to state conventions for ratification.

Beginning January 18, 1938, a subcommittee of the Committee on Judiciary of the Senate, consisting of George W. Norris of Nebraska, Chairman, Carl A. Hatch of New Mexico, Key Pittman of Nevada, Tom Connally of Texas and Warren R. Austin of Vermont conducted hearings on the proposal.

Federal Judge William Clark of New Jersey pointed out to the committee that in most of the countries of the world having a federal government, amendment involves action on the part of the federal legislature only and that the federal principle is preserved only by the requirement that the altering action be taken in a special manner, such as by a special majority of two-thirds or three-fourths, with or without a period of reflection, that is, repassage after a year.[95] Only the United States, Switzerland, Australia, and Germany insist on action elsewhere than in the federal legislature. Furthermore, in all these latter countries except the United States, the action is by popular vote and only in Australia is the vote by states. Senator Norris' amendment approximated that of the next most rigid amending process, that of Australia. Judge Clark argued that ratification by legislatures was objectionable for

[95] HEARINGS, supra, note 94, at p. 11.

three reasons:[96] (1) the ratifying legislature may have been elected before submission, hence may not be representative of the people's wishes; (2) the legislature, even if subsequently elected, may have been elected for their views on other issues; and (3) legislators vote with an eye to reelection. In his opinion, a convention was subject to none of these three objections, but a convention was still not as democratic a procedure as a popular referendum. Moreover, the experience with the Twenty-First Amendment showed that a convention was not deliberative and merely followed the people's instructions; it was simply an expensive form of referendum. He also advocated that ratification should be by only two-thirds of the states.

Most of the witnesses appearing objected to the proposed amendment. It was felt that the states should still retain the right to request Congress to call a national convention to amend the Constitution, since Congress might refuse to do so in defiance of public sentiment. It was thought that the voter was not competent to pass on the soundness of amendments. It was argued that a vote at a general election would be confusing because of the numerous and unrelated questions to be voted on. It was argued that there would not be sufficient time for deliberation if amendments could be voted on only sixty days after proposal.

The proposed amendment was also objected to on the ground that it did not correct the difficulties in securing *proposals* of amendments by Congress.[97] Mr. Bainbridge Colby, former Secretary of State, took exception on a number of grounds.[98] He pointed out that delay occurred at the stage of proposal rather than in ratification, that ratification by popular referenda was proposed as early as 1873, that many propo-

[96] Ibid. 12.
[97] Ibid. 48, 53.
[98] Ibid. 51–66.

nents of a popular referendum wished to retard the amending
process, that the people are not fitted to pass on many possible
amendments, that there will be too many other issues to vote
on at general elections, that many people will fail to vote
on amendments, that popular referenda would result in delay
in ratifying amendments since dissimilar to legislatures they
are limited to certain fixed time periods, and that to allow
ratification by only two thirds of the states would result in
political and geographical cleavages.

C. SUBSTANTIVE REFORMS

Virtually all the changes which have been suggested in the
amending process have been as to procedure. Although in the
last decade numerous assertions have been made that there
are certain implied limitations on the content of amendments,[99]
few suggestions have been made that express limitations be
inserted in the amending clause.[100] It is of course true that the
Constitutional Convention inserted three such limitations and
that a fourth limitation was suggested but rejected. Two of
these limitations, couched in absolute terms, so that apparently a unanimous vote of all the states could not destroy
them, expired in 1808. The first forbade Congress from pro-
hibiting the importation of slaves until 1808. Apparently,
however, an amendment forbidding such importation without
mention of Congress, in other words an amendment of a legislative nature such as the Eighteenth Amendment, would have
been valid. The second limitation expiring in 1808 was that

[99] See chap. IV, supra, pp. 87–126, for full discussion.

[100] But such a suggestion is made by Butler, "The Constitution One Hundred
and Forty Years After," (1928) 12 CONST. REV. 121 at 126. Westervelt,
"Amend Article V," (1931) 24 LAWY. & BANKER 166 at 169, would amend
Article Five so as to provide "that amendments dealing strictly with the organization of government might be submitted to the legislatures of the several
states for ratification and adoption, and that those dealing in any way with
the mass of governmental powers must be submitted to conventions of the
people."

no capitation or other direct tax shall be laid except in proportion to population. Although more doubtful, this too was only a limitation on Congress, so that an amendment legislating on the subject might have been adopted. Thus these limitations were such only on the powers that could be given to Congress. Nevertheless the principle remains clear that there were certain things that could not be done directly by the amending power, although very much the same result might be accomplished indirectly. The third limitation, and the only one now in existence, is that no state shall be deprived of its equal suffrage in the Senate without its consent. Hence, even though an amendment is adopted according to the regular procedure, it is invalid if it deprives a state of its equal suffrage unless the state affected consents. An amendment adopted by all the states, however, would wipe out even this clause. Although some of the proponents of limitations on the amending power have drawn a great deal of comfort from the equal suffrage clause, it would seem that the limitation is more nominal than real in its practical effect.[101]

A proposal which would have resulted in a substantial restriction on the amending power was that offered by Sherman at the Convention "that no state should be affected in its internal police."[102] Madison objected that this would pave the way for special provisos in behalf of the individual states, and Sherman's motion was lost. The last serious attempt to limit the content of amendments was made just prior to the Civil War when numerous proposals were made forbidding Congress to adopt any amendment abolishing slavery.[103] Congress actually submitted an amendment to this effect, known as the Corwin amendment, which was ratified by two states and by

[101] See supra, chap. IV, pp. 83–87; 96–99.

[102] See supra, chap. IV, pp. 86–87.

[103] Fourteen such proposals were made between Dec. 12, 1860, and April 8, 1864. See the list in AMES, THE PROPOSED AMENDMENTS TO THE CONSTITUTION OF THE UNITED STATES (1897) 356–368.

an Illinois constitutional convention which happened to be in session.[104] It should be observed, in passing, that this amendment would have restricted only Congress and not the amending power itself, so that an amendment directly abolishing slavery would have been valid. Only two state constitutions contain express limitations on the content of amendments.[105]

It would seem that the present federal amending power is practically unlimited in its scope. No question could arise over the validity of changes in the amending procedure itself, and none as to changes in content, provided that the equal suffrage clause is observed. Amendments limiting the substance of future amendments would possibly be valid under the American conception of the powers of the sovereign, though in England it has been asserted that one Parliament is not bound by the acts of another. Yet it would seem extremely unfortunate to impose any limitations on content, both because one generation cannot foresee the needs of another and because such restrictions make a revolution necessary to accomplish the change which is forbidden. Fortunately the proponents of a more difficult amending process have concentrated on changes in procedure, so that there is little prospect at the present time that any limitations on content will be added to Article Five.

D. POLICY FACTORS TO BE CONSIDERED

In concluding this study of the reform of the federal amending power, it seems not only proper but essential to summarize the underlying factors which are to be considered when amendment or revision of the Constitution is sought. One must beware of making an absolute of any one element, since here as in most other situations it is unlikely that there

[104] Ibid. 196, 286, 363.
[105] See chap. II, p. 24, note 65.

is any one fundamental principle entitled to exclusive emphasis.[106]

Before considering these various factors one must carefully distinguish between the policy and the legality of changes in the amending process. As has been seen, it is unquestionably legal to make any change that is desired in the amending procedure provided of course that the existing rules are followed in making that change. But it by no means follows that merely because a change can legally be made and is made that such a change is a desirable one. By the policy of a change, on the other hand, is meant the practical operation of the machinery in its effect on the life of the nation. In considering the reform of the federal amending power, it is the policy we are interested in rather than the legality.

First to be considered in examining the policy of a change suggested in the amending procedure is its effect on the maintenance of the federal system.[107] Will the change so operate as to bring about the destruction of the states, or substantially

---

[106] JAMESON, CONSTITUTIONAL CONVENTIONS, 4th ed. (1887) 549, says: "Provisions regulating the time and mode of effecting organic changes are in the nature of safety-valves,—they must not be so adjusted as to discharge their peculiar function with too great facility, lest they become the ordinary escape-pipes of party passion; nor, on the other hand, must they discharge it with such difficulty that the force needed to induce action is sufficient to explode the machine. Hence the problem of the Constitution-maker is, in this particular, one of the most difficult in our whole system, to reconcile the requisites for progress with the requisites for safety."

Mr. Huddleston of Alabama, 67 CONG. REC. (1926) 7203, stated that "the clause which lies nearest to its heart is the clause which permits a change in the Constitution. It is more vital and more fundamental than any other provision of the Constitution. For, by dealing with that clause, we may fix it so that the Constitution is absolutely rigid and may never be amended, or we may fix it so that it may be amended lightly and without sufficient thought. In other words, through that clause we reach toward every other clause in the whole Constitution, and that can not be said about any other clause of the Constitution.

"I can not go into that in detail. I merely want to bring the thought that unnecessary meddling with the Constitution becomes a more serious offense when we deal with an amendment to the particular clause, than if we were undertaking to deal with any other section."

[107] Martig, "Amending the Constitution," (1937) 35 MICH L. REV. 1253 at 1285.

to weaken them? It should be clear, however, that there is nothing sacrosanct in the maintenance of the federal system per se. The federal system is defensible only when it conduces to the greatest good of the nation and the states.[108] As soon as it becomes evident that the nation would be better off as a unitary state, such as France or Italy, then let it become such, and let the principle of the general welfare supersede that of states' rights. Similarly if a division of the nation into its component elements would operate for the general welfare of those concerned, let the union be dissolved. That either one of these situations now exists in the United States can scarcely be seriously asserted. We are still strongly committed to the notion of an "indestructible Union, composed of indestructible States."[109] There is little question that the trend in recent years has been toward centralization. The increasingly industrial character of the nation, the improvement of the means of communication, the disappearance of the frontier, and the past feeling of confidence which the federal government has inspired in the people have all combined with an irresistible force to strengthen the feeling of unity.[110] Yet one cannot deny the need of local self government, based on a real popular interest and popular knowledge of the local situation. The

[108] Cf., however, the statement as to the intent of the framers of the Constitution, in Goodnow, "Judicial Interpretation of Constitutional Provisions," (1912) 3 ACAD. POL. SCI. PROC. 49 at 52: "Finally, the confidence of the fathers in the existence of eternal political verities and the possibility that fallible humanity might ascertain and formulate them is seen in the difficulty if not impossibility of amending the constitution which resulted from the processes of amendment provided."

[109] Senator Reed of Pennsylvania, 65 CONG. REC. (1924) 4496; Frierson, "Amending the Constitution of the United States," (1920) 33 HARV. L. REV. 659; Dodd, "Amending the Federal Constitution," (1921) 30 YALE L. J. 321 at 348, 354; Ames, "The Amending Provision of the Federal Constitution in Practice," (1924) 63 AM. PHIL. SOC. PROC. 62 at 74; HORWILL, THE USAGES OF THE AMERICAN CONSTITUTION (1925) 220; Moschzisker, "Dangers in Disregarding Fundamental Conceptions When Amending the Federal Constitution," (1925) 11 CORN. L. Q. 1; Garrett, "Amending the Federal Constitution," (1929) 7 TENN. L. REV. 286 at 288.

[110] BRYCE, AMERICAN COMMONWEALTH, 4th ed. (1910) 403; THOMPSON, FEDERAL CENTRALIZATION (1923) 305-327.

Eighteenth Amendment has demonstrated that there are limitations on what can be accomplished by the federal government. The import of this is clear: since the federal principle is a valuable one, care must be taken that the states are consulted as such in the ratification of amendments and possibly in their proposal as well. When the states ratify as such, it is obvious that under the natural law of self-preservation they will safeguard their own interests. In view of the seemingly inevitable trend towards centralization, however, they must not be given an absolute veto, and the requirement of adoption by an excessive majority of states might well be somewhat relaxed. That is to say, the federal principle must be harmonized with the general welfare, since in the last analysis it is defensible only as conducing to the general welfare.[111]

A second factor of importance is that of the wisdom and efficiency of the amendments secured through the change in the amending process. Will the change be of such kind as to result in the adoption of amendments which will prove harmful to the country? Can a lesser majority than is now required be trusted to adopt amendments which may injure not only themselves, but the dissenting majority? Will the constitution not become unduly prolix and cluttered up with legislative provisions?[112] The mere fact that a simple majority, or even an extraordinary majority, desire a change by

[111] Possibly the doctrine of political questions laid down in Coleman v. Miller, (1939) 307 U. S. 433, 59 S. Ct. 572, leaving the ultimate decision to Congress as to certain phases of amending procedure violates the federal principle. It may be argued, however, that it does not since the Senate is peculiarly representative of the states.

[112] Freund, "Legislative Problems and Solutions," (1921) 7 A. B. A. J. 656 at 658, says that "when the people desire to accomplish through the constitution a direct result independent of legislative assistance, they overlook the fact . . . that there are few propositions of law that can be made sufficiently brief for constitutional formulation, and at the same time self-executing." See also BURGESS, RECENT CHANGES IN AMERICAN CONSTITUTIONAL THEORY (1923) 114; BURDICK, THE LAW OF THE AMERICAN CONSTITUTION (1922) 49.

no means demonstrates that the change will prove beneficial.[113] King Mob may be just as much a despot as a single
dictator. The discussions at the Constitutional Convention
show that the framers of the Constitution were frankly aristocratic in their views and deliberately set up a framework of
government and a charter to protect the rights of minorities.[114]
This is quite clearly shown in Article Five, which permits
amendment not by a majority of the states or a majority of the
people, but only by three-fourths of the states without any
direct popular participation in any stage of the amending
process. This made it certain that the rights given to mi-

[113] Miller, "Amendment of the Federal Constitution: Should It Be Made
More Difficult?" (1926) 10 MINN. L. REV. 185 at 188–190, says: "Generally
the votes which have been cast in state elections, and particularly in referendums
upon proposed constitutional amendments, have indicated an unwillingness
upon the part of the people to concern themselves with such questions. The
slogan, 'When in doubt, vote no!' has been applied with particular emphasis,
and from the evidence available it appears that usually the number and percentage of votes cast upon proposals for amendments have been the lowest cast
for any propositions or candidates on the ballot. The reason is that the voters
are unable or unwilling to give proper consideration to such questions. They
elect lawmakers for that purpose and have a right to expect that their representatives will take testimony, consider all of the evidence and, after due and
proper deliberation, render a reasoned decision. Many voters are not properly
trained to understand questions of the import involved in proposed constitutional amendments. . . ."

Walter F. Dodd, "Amending the Federal Constitution," (1920) 30 YALE
L. J. 321 at 354, says: "A serious question presents itself as to whether the
federal amending process should be so easy as to permit the introduction into
the Constitution of provisions which involve distinctly sectional or political
issues. Clearly the federal Constitution performs a function different from that
of the state constitution, and should be less flexible than the state constitutions
may properly be." See also JAMESON, CONSTITUTIONAL CONVENTIONS, 4th ed.
(1887) 552–553; Long, "Tinkering with the Constitution," (1915) 24 YALE
L. J. 573 at 586; Brown, "Irresponsible Government by Constitutional Amendments," (1922) 8 VA. L. REV. 157; Butler, "The Constitution One Hundred
and Forty Years After," (1928) 12 CONST. REV. 121 at 123. Cf., however,
the view of Smith, "Shall We Make Our Constitution Flexible?" (1911) 194
No. AM. REV. 657 at 669–670, that the dominating political party should be
able to introduce amendments.

[114] Senator Bruce of Maryland, 65 CONG. REC. (1924) 4557, says that
"they kept their eyes no more on the possibility of oppression in high places
than they did upon what they conceived to be the caprices, the passions, the
sudden gusts of impulse in one form or another to which men en masse are
subject. They believed in representative government rather than in pure
democracy."

norities under the Constitution would be taken from them only after the majority had made itself overwhelmingly strong. In other words, the theory is that a constitutional amendment is of much greater significance than a statute, and that it is much more likely to be a wise amendment when a large majority concur in it. The Eighteenth Amendment is frequently cited to show that even a large majority can make a mistake.

There is, however, another side of the picture. The amending process may be made so difficult as to prevent the adoption of amendments which are unquestionably sound. One must balance against the undesirable amendments checked by a difficult amending process the desirable ones not adopted because of such process.[115] It has been asserted that a more flexible amending process might have averted the Civil War. The enemies of the Eighteenth Amendment also appear to forget that a difficult amending process makes it almost impossible to repeal an unsatisfactory amendment. Making it easier to amend might result in the adoption of a number of undesirable proposals, yet such amendments might be repealed with the same ease. The doctrine of political questions may be regarded as a method of making the amending process easier. Moreover, it does so by placing authority in Congress instead of the people, thus assuring some deliberation.

A third factor, and one closely related to that just discussed is that of proper deliberation. The amending process should not be so changed that amendments can be adopted without an opportunity to discuss the arguments pro and con.[116] An

[115] Ernest C. Carman denies that it is better to do without good amendments rather than allow bad ones to be adopted. Carman, "Why and How the Present Method of Amending the Federal Constitution Should Be Changed," (1938) 17 ORE. L. REV. 102 at 104.

[116] "The great principle to be sought is to make the changes practicable, but not too easy; to secure due deliberation, and caution; and to follow experience, rather than to open a way for experiments, suggested by mere speculation or theory." 2 STORY, COMMENTARIES ON THE CONSTITUTION OF THE UNITED STATES, 3d ed. (1858) 634. See also Senator Wadsworth, 65 CONG. REC. (1924) 4495.

amendment should receive at least as much consideration as a statute. Under the present system, due deliberation is more than amply secured. The two-thirds majority required in Congress and the three-fourths required among the states insure adequate deliberation. A measure which must pass the scrutiny of thirty-seven legislative bodies, each in turn (except in Nebraska) divided into an upper and a lower house, can scarcely be said to have been rushed through. In fact, the agitation for some of the most recent amendments, such as the income tax and woman suffrage amendments, began seventy-five and fifty years ago, so that the process if anything must be said to be too slow. For this last reason it would seem that the proposals for ratification only by subsequently elected legislatures and permitting of a confirmation by popular vote of the legislative ratification should both be defeated.[117] The present provisions for securing deliberation are entirely adequate. In fact, some of the more recent proposals call for a lessening of the majorities required both for proposal and ratification. The proposal for a popular referendum also looks in the direction of less deliberation, since the amendment would be voted on conclusively by the people within one or two years after discussion.

The framers of the Constitution anticipated a frequent use of the amending power.[118] Practically all the critics of the present amending process, at least until the last two decades,

---

[117] In 1826 Rep. Herrick of Maine introduced a resolution to regulate the time for introducing amendments, proposal to be allowed only every tenth year. CONGRESSIONAL DEBATES, 19th Cong., 1st sess. (1826) 1554. Chief Justice Von Moschzisker of the Supreme Court of Pennsylvania suggested that if a popular referendum is to be provided for, only a limited number of amendments should be voted on at the same election. Moschzisker, "Dangers in Disregarding Fundamental Conceptions when Amending the Federal Constitution," (1925) 11 CORN. L. Q. 1 at 5–6. Senator Owen, 58 CONG. REC. (1919) 5700, proposed that there be mailed to each voter a copy of the proposals and a copy of the arguments, for and against, prepared by two committees composed of leading representatives of the opposing sides.

[118] Hamilton's remarks at the Constitutional Convention, 5 ELLIOT, DEBATES (1836) 530 and Madison in THE FEDERALIST, No. 43.

have agreed that the process should be made easier.[119] No amendments were adopted between 1804 and 1865, or between 1870 and 1913. The Progressive Party in 1912 adopted a plank favoring easier amendment. The adoption of the last six amendments has resulted in a reversal of opinion on the part of many, so that such proposals as the Wadsworth-

[119] Marshall C. J., in Barron v. Baltimore, (1833) 7 Pet. (32 U. S.) 24 at 249–250; Brown, J., in Holden v. Hardy, (1898) 169 U. S. 366 at 387, 18 S. Ct. 383; WILSON, CONGRESSIONAL GOVERNMENT (1885) 242; 1 BURGESS, POLITICAL SCIENCE AND COMPARATIVE CONSTITUTIONAL LAW (1891) 150; Potter, "The Method of Amending the Federal Constitution," (1909) 57 U. PA. L. REV. 589 at 592; THOMPSON, "The Amendment of the Federal Constitution," (1912) 3 ACAD. POL. SCI. PROC. 65 at 69; BRYCE, AMERICAN COMMONWEALTH, 4th ed. (1910) 359; Smith, "Shall We Make Our Constitution Flexible?" (1911) 194 No. AM. REV. 657; Johnstone, "An Eighteenth Century Constitution," (1912) 7 ILL. L. REV. 265; BEARD, AMERICAN GOVERNMENT AND POLITICS (1914) 62; DICEY, THE LAW OF THE CONSTITUTION, 8th ed. (1915) 145; John W. Davis, "Present Day Problems," (1923) 48 A. B. A. REP. 193 at 201; Senator Brookhart of Iowa, 65 CONG. REC. (1924) 4564, 4566; Rep. Huddleston of Alabama, 66 CONG. REC. (1925) 4572; Arneson, "Is It Easy to Amend the Constitution?" (1926) 60 AM. L. REV. 600; Miller, "Amendment of the Federal Constitution: Should It Be Made More Difficult?" (1926) 10 MINN. L. REV. 185.

Ames seems at first to have thought the amending process too difficult. AMES, THE PROPOSED AMENDMENTS TO THE CONSTITUTION OF THE UNITED STATES (1887) 300 ff. But more recently he has changed his opinion. "Although the speaker some years ago held the view that the amending process was too difficult, he has been led, in common with others, as a result of recent experience, to a modification of that opinion. He believes that a radical change in the method of amendment is neither necessary nor desirable." Ames, "The Amending Provision of the Federal Constitution in Practice," (1924) 63 AM. PHIL. SOC. PROC. 62 at 74.

DODD, THE REVISION AND AMENDMENT OF STATE CONSTITUTIONS (1910) 141, note, states that "it seems to be the general view that our federal constitution cannot be amended except in times of national crises." In "Amending the Federal Constitution," (1921) 30 YALE L. J. 321 at 348–354, he concludes that the present process is substantially satisfactory.

See also Maggs, "The Constitution and Recovery Legislation: The Rôles of Document, Doctrine and Judges," LEGAL ESSAYS IN TRIBUTE TO ORRIN K. McMURRAY (1935) 399 at 401; Dodd, "Adjustment of the Constitution to New Needs," (1936) 22 A. B. A. J. 126; Garrison, "The Constitution and Social Progress," (1936) 10 TULANE L. REV. 33; Howard, "Is Our Constitution Adequate for Present Day Needs?" (1937) 23 WASH. U. L. Q. 47 at 75; Clark, "Some Recent Proposals for Constitutional Amendment," (1937) 12 WIS. L. REV. 313 at 315; Fraenkel, "What Can Be Done About the Constitution and the Supreme Court?" (1937) 37 COL. L. REV. 212; Cummings, "The Nature of the Amending Process," (1938) 6 GEO. WASH. L. REV. 247 at 252; Powell, "Changing Constitutional Phases," (1939) 19 BOST. U. L. REV. 509 at 518.

Garrett amendment are designed to make it more difficult.[120] The weight of opinion, however, probably is that the present process is difficult enough, perhaps exactly to the proper degree.[121]

The controversy over adding members to the Supreme Court in 1937 raised the question as to the adequacy of the amending process to secure needed reforms. Many felt that it was too difficult to secure necessary amendments.[122] The recently enunciated doctrine of political questions may be in part a consequence of the difficulty of amendment.[123] Strange as it may seem, the first definite proposal to make the amending process easier did not come until the Civil War period. Up to 1911 approximately twenty-five amendments to the

[120] Brown, "The 'New Bill of Rights' Amendment," (1922) 9 VA. L. REV. 14; Lanier, "Amending the Federal Constitution," (1923) 9 VA. L. REG. (N. S.) 81; Mussman, "Is the Amending Process too Difficult?" (1923) 57 AM. L. REV. 694, and "The Difficulty of Amending our Federal Constitution: Defect or Asset?" (1929) 15 A. B. A. J. 505; Senator Edge of New Jersey, 65 CONG. REC. (1924) 4497, 4938; Klinglesmith, "Amending the Constitution of the United States," (1925) 73 U. PA. L. REV. 355 at 368; Cadwalader, "Amendment of the Federal Constitution," (1926) 60 AM. L. REV. 389; Butler, "The Constitution One Hundred and Forty Years After," (1928) 12 CONST. REV. 121; Garrett, "Amending the Federal Constitution," (1929) 7 TENN. L. REV. 286.

[121] Senator Bursum of New Mexico, 65 CONG. REC. (1924) 4420, stated: "It seems to me that consideration of amendments to the Constitution ought not to be considered the first business to take up. We have gotten along pretty well during the last 150 years without those amendments, and we might get along perhaps a few days longer."

Senator Walsh, in attacking the Wadsworth-Garrett amendment, ibid. 4561, stated: "I do not think there is any occasion for any amendment to the Constitution on this subject; but, if there is, I think that the obvious tendency of the times and the wisdom of our age suggests that the matter be submitted to the people of the State."

Cf. the view of Senator Pepper of Pennsylvania, ibid. 4569: "I am unable to share the view of the Senator from Montana [Mr. Walsh] that this subject is one unworthy of consideration at the present time. It seems to me that while the experiences incident to the adoption of recent amendments are fresh in our minds, and at a time when we are not distracted by the pendency of any great amendment involving a question of policy upon which the country is divided, is the ideal time to propose for consideration a measure designed to prevent in the future evils which have been incident to the process of amendment in the past."

[122] See note 118, supra.

[123] Coleman v. Miller, (1939) 307 U. S. 433, 59 S. Ct. 972.

amending process were offered, while since that time seventy-five proposals have been made, making a total of about one hundred amendments offered in Congress to Article Five. The fact that the last seventy-five proposals have been made in the last two decades possibly foreshadows a change. The writer predicts that with the defeat of the child labor amendment and an interval during which no amendments are adopted, the view that the process is too difficult will gain strength.

The need for an easier amending process can easily be overstated, however. The Constitution is of so elastic a nature that on many subjects the desired ends can be achieved without altering the Constitution.[124] The language of the Constitution is brief and couched in general terms. Moreover the liberal construction school of interpretation has triumphed over the strict constructionists, so that by a process of interpretation the terms of the Constitution may be made to cover

[124] AMES, THE PROPOSED AMENDMENTS TO THE CONSTITUTION OF THE UNITED STATES (1887) 302; BRYCE, THE AMERICAN COMMONWEALTH, 4th ed. (1910) 371; Goodnow, "Judicial Interpretation of Constitutional Provisions," (1912) 3 ACAD. POL. SCI. PROC. 49; Hall, " 'An Eighteenth Century Constitution'—A Comment," (1912) 7 ILL. L. REV. 285; Llewellyn, "The Constitution as an Institution," (1934) 34 COL. L. REV. 1 at 4, 21; Dodd, "Adjustment of the Constitution to New Needs," (1936) 22 A. B. A. J. 126; Coudert, "Judicial Constitutional Amendment," (1904) 13 YALE L. J. 331; Brandeis, J., quoted by Mason, "Mr. Justice Brandeis: A Student of Social and Economic Science," (1931) 79 U. PA. L. REV. 665 at 693; and Corwin, "Social Planning under the Constitution," (1932) 26 AM. POL. SCI. REV. 1 at 26.

Senator Walsh of Montana, 65 CONG. REC. (1924) 4494, has stated: "Of course, many features of this Constitution of ours are of doubtful wisdom theoretically. We can easily conceive that a whole flood of evils might possibly ensue by reason of extraordinary powers granted here, but some way or other, they never do."

Thayer, "Our New Possessions," (1899) 12 HARV. L. REV. 464 at 468, said: "That instrument, astonishingly well adapted for the purposes of a great, developing nation, shows its wisdom mainly in the shortness and generality of its provisions, in it silence, and its abstinence from petty limitations. As it survives fierce controversies from age to age, it is forever silently bearing witness to the wisdom that went into its composition, by showing itself suited to the purposes of a great people under circumstances that no one of its makers could have foreseen. Men have found, as they are finding now, when new and unlooked-for situations have presented themselves, that they were left with liberty to handle them."

most problems that arise. There are limits, however, on what can be accomplished by interpretation. The commerce clause, the war power, and the Fourteenth Amendment all admit of interpretation. But such provisions as those for the electoral college and the time of meeting of Congress itself do not. The amendment process should not be so difficult that strained interpretations causing loss of confidence in the judiciary must be resorted to.[125] Nor should it be so difficult that the federal judicial veto of legislation cannot be overcome.[126]

A fourth factor is that of popular democracy.[127] The nation has been a republic since it broke away from England. Beginning with the Jacksonian era the electorate has grown by leaps and bounds, so that there is almost universal manhood suffrage except in the South. The Fifteenth Amendment, nominally at least, increased the votes of the nation. Within our own times suffrage has been conferred on women. The Seventeenth Amendment provided for popular election of Senators, and very largely paved the way for agitation in behalf of popular participation in the amending process. The average of popular education is surely higher than it ever was, and should become even higher with the gradual assimilation of our immigrants. The Supreme Court, the commentators on the Constitution and our political orators make frequent reference to the sovereignty of the people. Yet the people do not participate in a single stage of the amending process. The Constitution was not directly adopted by the

[125] Potter, "The Method of Amending the Federal Constitution," (1909) 57 U. PA. L. REV. 589 at 595.

[126] Smith, "Shall We Make Our Constitution Flexible?" (1911) 194 No. AM. REV. 657 at 662.

[127] BORGEAUD, ADOPTION AND AMENDMENT OF CONSTITUTIONS IN EUROPE AND AMERICA (1895) 337; SMITH, THE SPIRIT OF AMERICAN GOVERNMENT (1907) 40; MACY and GANNAWAY, COMPARATIVE FREE GOVERNMENT (1915) 291; Eldridge, "Need for a More Democratic Procedure of Amending the Constitution," (1916) 10 AM. POL. SCI. REV. 683; Ames, "The Amending Provision of the Federal Constitution in Practice," (1924) 63 AM. PHIL. SOC. PROC. 62 at 70.

people, nor is it amendable directly by them. [128] The framers of the Constitution distrusted democracy.[129] The optional convention plan provided for in Article Five is never resorted to, and if it were it would not so accurately reflect the wishes of the people as a popular vote. It is indeed an anomalous situation where the people are given no participation in the most important of political matters—that of altering the Constitution. Even the indirect participation presented through the use of the legislatures can scarcely be called representative because of the excessive majorities required both for proposal and for adoption. Ordinarily one conceives of democracy as acting through simple majorities. Under the present system the representatives of thirteen states can check the wishes of both the people and the representatives of the other thirty-five.

Before we can correctly speak of the people as being sovereign in the United States, we must amend the Constitution so as to permit a majority of the electorate of the entire country to amend the Constitution. There would, however, be but a slight departure from this principle if we permitted ratification by a majority of voters in each of a majority of states, thus making the state still the unit of ratification, or if the provision were for ratification by a majority of the voters in each state as well as a majority of the electorate of the entire nation. The advocates of the democratic principle must bear in mind the other factors which have been previously

[128] BORGEAUD, ADOPTION AND AMENDMENT OF CONSTITUTIONS IN EUROPE AND AMERICA (1895) 333, in contrasting governmental with popular ratification, said: "The former springs historically from a semi-mediaeval conception of the state, by which sovereignty is divided between the prince and the representatives of the nation, and under the influence of which the constitutions have taken on the character of compacts between two parties. The latter is the one whose foundations were laid by the Revolution, and which has been developed in the democratic spirit of our time."

[129] Cummings, "The Nature of the Amending Process," (1938) 6 GEO. WASH. L. REV. 247 at 249, citing passages from the debates in the Constitutional Convention.

discussed. Obviously the maintenance of the federal principle will necessitate the preservation of the states as units in the amending process. Moreover, to permit amendment by a simple majority may result in the adoption of undesirable and excessive constitutional changes, without adequate deliberation. Events in Europe cast doubt on too sweeping an extension of the democratic principle. An amendment reflecting only the wishes of a majority may also encounter difficulties in enforcement.

It is of course easy to make a fetish of democracy. To a great many people Wilson's epigram about "making the world safe for democracy" has taken on a sardonic meaning. It is sun clear that political democracy is not a panacea for the ills of the nation. The dictatorships in Europe and elsewhere indicate a lapse back to more aristocratic forms of government and, according to some, a failure of democracy. Perhaps the use of the referendum will now and then result in the adoption of unwise changes. The experience of the states of this country has on the whole been favorable.[130] The electorate is on the whole as conservative or more conservative than the legislatures, so that possibly there would be fewer changes than previously if the popular referendum were adopted. At least, many of the proponents of a more difficult amending process will also often be found recommending ratification by popular vote. If mistakes are made, the people will recognize that the mistakes are their own. They will naturally take more interest in a document which is their own.[131]

[130] Dodd, The Revision and Amendment of State Constitutions (1910) 270–292; Radin, "Popular Legislation in California," (1939) 23 Minn. L. Rev. 559.

[131] Senator Borah, 65 Cong. Rec. (1924) 4562–4563 said: "The Constitution ought to be regarded as the people's law, the people's charter. I think just so nearly as is practicable and possible the judgment of the people, direct and immediate, should be taken as to what should be found in their Constitution. Certainly, if we were making a constitution or rewriting the Constitution and resubmitting it, we would feel under obligation to submit it as directly to the

Perhaps they will also be more willing to comply with the laws laid down by themselves. The demand for popular democracy should be heeded to the extent of allowing participation in the ratification of amendments and possibly even in initiation.[132]

A fifth factor is that of securing clarity and certainty in the amending process.[133] The doctrine of political questions laid down in *Coleman v. Miller*[134] leaves in doubt the line between political and justiciable questions. It leaves in doubt the procedure in Congress in deciding political questions and the effect of nonaction by Congress. It leaves open to argument whether a decision by Congress in a particular case will be a binding precedent in later similar situations. Orderly procedure in the adoption of important and often permanent

people as practicable, and I feel that in incorporating amendments we should observe the same rule.

"There are a number of reasons for this, but one of the reasons is largely what you might call a sentimental or psychological reason, that is, I feel that people ought to be permitted to feel that when the Constitution is completed from time to time, and as it stands, it is their expression, an instrument which they have made; that it is their charter, that upon them it depends largely for its existence, and I should therefore want to bring home to them as nearly as possible the changing of it or the amending of it or the modifying of it in any respect. . . .

"I was at one time very much disturbed over the question of the initiative and referendum, but as I have observed its working in Switzerland and elsewhere, I find, instead of its being a radical proposition, it is an extremely safe and conservative proposition."

[132]BORGEAUD, ADOPTION AND AMENDMENT OF CONSTITUTIONS IN EUROPE AND AMERICA (1895) 337, states that "it appears possible, after the comparative study we have just made, to determine precisely the principle which governs contemporary democracy in the exercise of its constituent powers. This principle is proclaimed in the immense majority of constitutional texts we have had occasion to examine, and dominates the entire development of the public law of those nations whose constitutional history has been the chief object of our investigation. It may be formulated as follows: The constituent power is wielded directly by the people for purposes of sanction; directly or indirectly through its representatives for purposes of initiation. In other words—considering sanction alone, which shows the essential characteristic—the imperative act which gives being to the fundamental law proceeds directly from the body of qualified voters, sole possessors of the sovereign rights of the nation."

[133](1940) 24 MINN. L. REV. 393 at 406.

[134](1939) 307 U. S. 433, 59 S. Ct. 972.

amendments is not as well assured as when decisions are by the courts. Therefore, provided that an easier method of amending the Constitution is substituted for the existing methods provided in Article Five, it might be well also expressly to provide in Article Five that all questions arising under Article Five are to be regarded as justiciable.

A sixth and last factor to be considered is that of enforcement. This factor has been almost entirely overlooked[135] until recently, not only in connection with amendments but also as to statutes in general. The Fifteenth Amendment and more recently the Eighteenth have very forcibly brought this question to the front. It is an unfortunate situation to have a law passed which is not enforced. It is a great deal more unfortunate to adopt an amendment to the national constitution which in large part remains a dead letter on the books.[136] In considering changes of the amending process, one is therefore by no means raising an academic question when one asks

[135] Arnold, "Law Enforcement—An Attempt at Social Dissection," (1932) 41 YALE L. J. 1–14.

[136] Moschzisker, "Dangers in Disregarding Fundamental Conceptions When Amending the Federal Constitution," (1925) 11 CORN. L. Q. 1; Brown, "The People Should Be Consulted as to Constitutional Changes," (1930) 16 A. B. A. J. 404.

Senator Underwood of Alabama pointed out in the Senate debate on the adoption of the Eighteenth Amendment, 55 CONG. REC. (1917) 5554: "The sound and underlying theory of democracy 'that a just form of government requires the consent of the governed' is often subject to perversion. President Hadley of Yale University says: 'Not content with saying that all just government is based on the consent of the governed, the enthusiastic advocates of democracy hold that if you could only find what a majority of the governed wanted you could easily incorporate it into law. Never was there a greater practical error. Public law, to be effective, requires much more than the majority to support it. It requires general acquiescence. To leave the minority at the mercy of the whims of the majority does not conduce to law or good government or justice between man and man. Even Rousseau, the leading apostle of modern democracy, saw this most clearly. He said in substance: "A majority of the people is not the people and never can be. We take a majority vote simply as the best available means of ascertaining the real wishes of the people in cases when it becomes necessary to do so."' . . .

"It does not forgive the error of government to be able to command majorities in legislative bodies when a vast number of people stand in opposition to statutes which they feel and believe trench on their personal rights and endanger their personal liberty."

whether it will make likely the adoption of amendments which will not be enforced. Because of the difficulties of enforcement, it may be desirable to require that something more than a simple majority of the legislatures or of the people must favor a change. While a simple majority may be adequate for a statutory change, a constitutional change should have something more substantial behind it. A simple majority may by changes in popular sentiment become a minority. Sumptuary legislation, even when favored by considerably more than a majority, may encounter such opposition as to breed a feeling of disrespect for law in general. The violation of the federal principle may also result in a falling down of enforcement because of the jealousy of the states. Altering the amending process in such a way as to permit of unwise or hasty changes also contributes to a failure of the law. The passage of amendments without consulting the people by a popular referendum may result in charges that the amendment was railroaded through the legislatures and is not representative of the real wishes of the people. It is evident, then, that the factor of enforcement is subject to the interaction of the other factors.

Great caution must be exercised, however, with respect to the conclusions one draws concerning the element of enforcement. Most amendments would not be so difficult to enforce as the Eighteenth Amendment. It has been pointed out that it is undesirable to alter the amending process in such a way that unenforceable or unenforced amendments will be adopted. On the other hand, an even worse situation develops when an amendment is adopted which it is practically impossible to repeal chiefly because of difficulties in the amending process. It seems that evils are bound to arise under either a facile or a difficult amending process. The reformer is seemingly between Scylla and Charybdis. Balancing the evils involved, is it not perhaps saner in the long run to make the amending process sufficiently easy so that an occasional mistake is made which may be corrected in the same easy fashion, rather than to make it so difficult that when a mistake is made such mistakes cannot be corrected except by revolution?[187] After all, the people or some large part of them must be permitted to make their mistakes and to do so within the limits of the Constitution. It would therefore seem undesirable to write into the Constitution limitations on the content of amendments, or to alter the procedure in such a way as to make amendment almost impossible. There is no scientific method of ascertaining beforehand whether or not an amendment can or will be enforced, and even after its adoption statements alleging nonenforcement may be hard to prove. As Thomas Jefferson has said, each generation must be permitted to make its own laws. It may be well to guard the people against themselves as to ordinary matters, but it is possible to go too far when it is sought to do this with respect to altering the Constitution. Society cannot go on without taking some chances. The interests of progress as well as order must be consulted, otherwise order itself will perish.[188]

[187] Arneson, "A More Flexible Constitution," (1927) 61 AM. L. REV. 99. Lunt, "Amending the Constitution," (1930) 23 LAWY. & BANKER 252 at 254 (summarized from the AMERICAN MERCURY), stated. "The problem is far from simple. It is doubtful if any workable system could be devised, based directly or indirectly upon popular acclaim, which would prevent the perpetration of such sumptuary errors as the Eighteenth Amendment and yet permit of the correction of the defects discovered in the functioning of the organic law and the inevitable adjustment to wholly unforeseen conditions."

See also the speeches of Mr. Huddleston of Alabama, 66 CONG. REC. (1925) 4573 and 67 CONG. REC. (1926) 7203. In the former speech he said: "But assuming that some one of the amendments which have been adopted is objectionable and should be repealed, those who advocate making it harder to amend the Constitution take an illogical position. They advocate making it harder to repeal an objectionable amendment than it was to secure its adoption."

[188] Professor Munroe Smith has said: "Sooner or later, however, it will be generally realized that the first article in any sincerely intended progressive programme must be the amendment of the amending clause of the Federal Constitution." Smith, "Shall We Make Our Constitution Flexible?" (1911) 194 No. AM. REV. 657 at 673.

Mr. Osmond K. Fraenkel stated during the Supreme Court controversy of 1937: "The . . . most desirable choice would be to make easier the method of amendment itself." Fraenkel, "What Can Be Done About the Constitution and the Supreme Court?" (1937) 37 COL. L. REV. 212 at 226.

Bibliography

[Includes treatises and articles but not comments, decision notes or miscellaneous references]

Abbot, Everett V., "Inalienable Rights and the Eighteenth Amendment," (1920) 20 *Col. L. Rev.* 183.

Adelson, Shirley—see Moore, James William.

Ames, Herman V., "The Amending Provision of the Federal Constitution in Practice," (1924) 63 *Am. Phil. Soc. Proc.* 62.

————*The Proposed Amendments to the Constitution of the United States During the First Century of Its History* (1897).

Anzilotti, Dionisio, *Il Diritto Internazionale Nei Giudizi Interni* (Bologna 1905).

Arneson, Ben A., "Is It Easy to Amend the Constitution?" (1926) 60 *Am. L. Rev.* 600.

Arnold, Thurman, "Law Enforcement—An Attempt at Social Dissection," (1932) 42 *Yale L. J.* 1.

Austin, John, *Lectures on Jurisprudence*, 4th ed. (1873) (2 vols.).

Bacon, Seldon, "How the Tenth Amendment Affected the Fifth Article of the Constitution," (1930) 16 *Va. L. Rev.* 771.

Bates, Henry M., "How Shall We Preserve the Constitution?" (1926) 44 *Kan. St. Bar Assn. Proc.* 128.

Beard, Charles A., *An Economic Interpretation of the Constitution of the United States* (1913).

Benton, T. H., *Abridgment of the Debates of Congress* (1857).

Blackstone, William, *Commentaries on the Laws of England* (1756) (4 vols.).

Bliss, Philemon, *Of Sovereignty* (1885).

Borgeaud, Charles, *Adoption and Amendment of Constitutions in Europe and America* (1895) (translation by Hagen).

Brierly, J. L., "The Shortcomings of International Law," (1924) *British Year Book* 4.

Briggs, Edmund B., "Sovereignty, and the Consent of the Governed," (1901) 35 *Am. L. Rev.* 49.

Broom, Herbert, *Legal Maxims*, 7th Am. ed. (1874).

Brown, Everett S., "The Ratification of the Twenty-First Amendment," (1935) 29 *Am. Pol. Sci. Rev.* 1005.

——*Ratification of the Twenty-First Amendment to the Constitution of the United States* (1938).

Brown, George Stewart, "Irresponsible Government by Constitutional Amendment," (1922) 8 *Va. L. Rev.* 157.

——"The 'New Bill of Rights' Amendment," (1922) 9 *Va. L. Rev.* 14.

——"The People Should Be Consulted as to Constitutional Changes," (1930) 16 *A. B. A. J.* 404.

——"The Perpetual Covenant in the Constitution," (1924) 219 *No. Am. Rev.* 30.

Brown, Raymond G., "The Sixteenth Amendment to the United States Constitution," (1920) 54 *Am. L. Rev.* 843.

Brown, W. Jethro, *The Austinian Theory of Law* (1906).

Brownson, O. A., *The American Republic* (1866).

Bryce, James, *Studies in History and Jurisprudence* (1901).

Burdick, Charles K., *The Law of the American Constitution* (1922).

Burgess, John W., *Political Science and Comparative Constitutional Law* (1891) (2 vols.).

——*Recent Changes in American Constitutional Law Theory* (1923).

——*Reconstruction and the Constitution, 1866-1876* (1902).

Butler, Nicholas Murray, "The Constitution One Hundred and Forty Years After," (1928) 12 *Const. Rev.* 121.

Byrnes, James F., "The Constitution and the Will of the People," (1939) 25 *A. B. A. J.* 667.

Cadwalader, Thomas F., "Amendment of the Federal Constitution," (1926) 60 *Am. L. Rev.* 389.

Calhoun, John C., *Works*, Cralle ed. (1854) (6 vols.).

Cardozo, Benjamin N., *The Growth of the Law* (1924).

Carman, Ernest C., "Why and How the Present Method of Amending the Federal Constitution Should Be Changed," (1938) 17 *Ore. L. Rev.* 102.

Chafee, Zechariah, Jr., Book Review, (1918) 32 *Harv. L. Rev.* 979.

Child, Sampson R., "Revolutionary Amendments to the Constitution," (1926) 10 *Const. Rev.* 27.

Clark, Edwin Charles, *Practical Jurisprudence* (1883).

Clark, Jane Perry, "Some Recent Proposals for Constitutional Amendment," (1937) 12 *Wis. L. Rev.* 313.

Cohen, Hymen Ezra, *Recent Theories of Sovereignty* (1937).

Cooley, Thomas M., *General Principles of Constitutional Law*, 3d ed. (1898).

———"Sovereignty in the United States," (1892) 1 *Mich. L. J.* 81.

———*A Treatise on the Constitutional Limitations Which Rest Upon the Legislative Power of the States of the American Union*, 8th ed. (1927) (2 vols.).

Corwin, Edward S., "Social Planning under the Constitution: A Study in Perspectives," (1932) 26 *Am. Pol. Sci. Rev.* 1.

Coudert, Frederic R., "Judicial Constitutional Amendment as Illustrated by the Devolution of the Institution of the Jury from a Fundamental Right to a Mere Method of Procedure," (1904) 13 *Yale L. J.* 331.

Creekmore, H. H., "The Sprague Case," (1931) 3 *Miss. L. J.* 282.

Cummings, Homer, "Nature of the Amending Process," (1938) 6 *Geo. Wash. L. Rev.* 247.

Curtis, George Tichnor, *Constitutional History of the United States* (1899) (2 vols.).

Dane, Nathan, *A General Abridgment and Digest of American Law* (1829) (9 vols.).

Dewey, John, "Austin's Theory of Sovereignty," (1894) 9 *Pol. Sci. Q.* 31.

Dicey, A. V., *Introduction to the Study of the Law of the Constitution*, 8th ed. (1915).

Dickinson, Edwin D., "New Avenues to Freedom," (1927) 25 *Mich. L. Rev.* 622.

Dickinson, John, "A Working Theory of Sovereignty," (1927) 42 *Pol. Sci. Q.* 524.

Dodd, Walter F., "Adjustment of the Constitution to New Needs," (1936) 22 *A. B. A. J.* 126.

———"Amending the Federal Constitution," (1921) 30 *Yale L. J.* 321.

———"Judicially Non-Enforcible Provisions of Constitutions," (1931) 80 *U. Pa. L. Rev.* 54.

———*The Revision and Amendment of State Constitutions* (1910).

Dowling, Noel T., "A New Experiment in Ratification," (1933) 19
    A. B. A. J. 383.
——"Clarifying the Amending Process," (1940) 1 *Wash. & Lee
    L. Rev.* 215.
Duguit, Léon, *Traité de Droit Constitutionnel,* 2d ed. (1921) (5
    vols.).

Eastwood, R. A., and Keeton, G. W., *The Austinian Theories of
    Law and Sovereignty* (1929).
Eldridge, Seba, "Need for a More Democratic Procedure of Amend-
    ing the Constitution," (1916) 10 *Am. Pol. Sci. Rev.* 683.
Elliot, Jonathan, *Debates on the Adoption of the Federal Consti-
    tution,* 2d ed. (1937 facsimile of 1836 ed.) (5 vols.).
Emerson, Rupert, *State and Sovereignty in Modern Germany* (1928).
Emery, Lucilius A., "The 18th Amendment of the Constitution of the
    United States," (1920) 13 *Me. L. Rev.* 121.

Federalist, The (1788).
Field, Oliver P., "The Doctrine of Political Questions in the Federal
    Courts," (1924) 8 *Minn. L. Rev.* 485.
Finkelstein, Maurice, "Judicial Self-Limitation," (1924) 37 *Harv.
    L. Rev.* 338.
——"Further Notes on Judicial Self-Limitations," (1925) 39
    Harv. L. Rev. 221.
Flack, Horace E., *The Adoption of the Fourteenth Amendment*
    (1908).
Foster, *Minutes of the Rhode Island Constitutional Convention of
    1790* (1929).
Fraenkel, Osmond K., "Constitutional Issues in the Supreme Court,
    1935 Term," (1936) 85 *U. Pa. L. Rev.* 27.
——"What Can Be Done About the Constitution and the Su-
    preme Court?" (1937) 37 *Col. L. Rev.* 212.
Frankfurter, Felix, "A Note on Advisory Opinions," (1924) 37 *Harv.
    L. Rev.* 1002.
Freund, Ernst, "Legislative Problems and Solutions," (1921) 7
    A. B. A. J. 656.
Friedrich, Carl J., Book Review, (1937) 7 *Brooklyn L. Rev.* 266.
Frierson, William L., "Amending the Constitution of the United
    States," (1920) 33 *Harv. L. Rev.* 659.

Gannaway, John W—see Macy, Jesse.

Garner, James W., "Limitations on National Sovereignty in International Relations," (1925) 19 *Am. Pol. Sci. Rev.* 1.

Garrett, Finis J., "Amending the Federal Constitution," (1929) 7 *Tenn. L. Rev.* 286.

Garrison, Lloyd K., "The Constitution and Social Progress," (1936) 10 *Tulane L. Rev.* 333.

Goodnow, Frank J., "Judicial Interpretation of Constitutional Provisions," (1912) 3 *Acad. Pol. Sci. Proc.* 49.

Gray, John Chipman, *The Nature and Sources of the Law* (1909).

Grinnell, Frank W., "Finality of State's Ratification of a Constitutional Amendment," (1925) 11 *A. B. A. J.* 192.

————"A 'Point of Order' on the Child Control Amendment," (1934) 20 *A. B. A. J.* 448, reprinted in 19 *Mass. L. Q.*, No. 5, p. 22.

Hall, James Parker, " 'An Eighteenth Century Constitution'—A Comment," (1912) 7 *Ill. L. Rev.* 285.

Hamilton, Alexander, *Works*, Lodge ed. (1885).

Harrison, Frederic, "The English School of Jurisprudence," (1878) 30 *Fortnightly Rev.* 475.

————*On Jurisprudence and the Conflict of Laws* (1919).

Hart, Albert Bushnell, *Introduction to the Study of Federal Government* (1891).

Hearnshaw, F. J. C., "Bodin and the Genesis of the Doctrine of Sovereignty," *Tudor Studies* (1924) 109.

Hoar, Roger Sherman, *Constitutional Conventions* (1917).

Holding, A. M., "Perils to Be Apprehended from Amending the Constitution," (1923) 57 *Am. L. Rev.* 481.

Holdsworth, Sir William Searle, *Some Lessons from Our Legal History* (1928).

Holst, H. von, *The Constitutional and Political History of the United States*, Lalor translation (1879).

————*The Constitutional Law of the United States*, Mason translation (1887).

Horwill, Herbert W., *The Usages of the American Constitution* (1925).

Howard, Robert L., "Is Our Constitution Adequate for Present Day Needs?" (1937) 23 *Wash. U. L. Q.* 47.

Hurd, John C., *The Theory of Our National Existence* (1881).

Jameson, John Alexander, *Constitutional Conventions,* 4th ed. (1887).

———"National Sovereignty," (1890) 5 *Pol. Sci. Q.* 193.

Jellinek, Georg, *Die Lehre von den Staatenverbindungen* (1882).

Jessup, Henry W., *The Bill of Rights and Its Destruction by Alleged Due Process of Law* (1927).

Johnstone, Frederic Bruce, "An Eighteenth Century Constitution," (1912) 7 *Ill. L. Rev.* 265.

Kaufmann, Wilhelm, *Die Rechtskraft des Internationalen Rechts und das Verhältniss der Staatsgesetzgebungen und der Staatsorgane zu demselben* (1899).

Keeton, G. W.—See Eastwood, R. A.

Kelsen, Hans, *Das Problem der Souveränität und die Theorie des Völkerrechts* (1928).

Klinglesmith, Margaret C., "Amending the Constitution of the United States," (1925) 73 *U. Pa. L. Rev.* 355.

Krabbe, H., *The Modern Idea of the State* (translation) (1922).

Lanier, Alexander Sidney, "Amending the Federal Constitution," (1923) 9 *Va. L. Reg. (N.S.)* 81.

Lansing, Robert, "Notes on Sovereignty in a State," (1907) 1 *Am. J. Int. L.* 105.

Laski, Harold J., *Studies in the Problem of Sovereignty* (1917).

———"The Theory of Popular Sovereignty," (1919) 17 *Mich. L. Rev.* 201.

Lee, Blewett, "Abolishing the Senate by Amendment," (1930) 16 *Va. L. Rev.* 364.

Lewis, George C., *Remarks on the Use and Abuse of Some Political Terms* (1832).

Lincoln, Alexander, "Ratification by Conventions," (1933) 18 *Mass. L. Q.* 287.

Llewellyn, Karl N., "The Constitution as an Institution," (1934) 34 *Col. L. Rev.* 1.

Long, Joseph R., "Tinkering with the Constitution," (1915) 24 *Yale L. J.* 573.

Lunt, Dudley C., "Amending the Constitution," (1930) 23 *Lawy. & Banker* 252 (summarized from the American Mercury).

McBain, Howard Lee, "Or by Conventions," *N. Y. Times,* Dec. 11, 1932, § 4, p. 1:7.

MacDonald, William, A *New Constitution for a New America* (1921).

McGovney, D. O., "Is the Eighteenth Amendment Void Because of Its Contents?" (1920) 20 *Col. L. Rev.* 499.

McIlwain, C. H., "A Fragment on Sovereignty," (1933) 48 *Pol. Sci. Q.* 94.

———"Sovereignty Again," (1926) 6 *Economica* 253.

Machen, Arthur W., Jr., "Is the Fifteenth Amendment Void?" (1910) 23 *Harv. L. Rev.* 169.

Macy, Jesse and Gannaway, John Walter, *Comparative Free Government* (1915).

Maggs, Douglas B., "The Constitution and Recovery Legislation: The Roles of Document, Doctrine and Judges," *Legal Essays in Honor of Orrin K. McMurray* (1935) 399.

Maine, Henry Sumner, *Early History of Institutions* (1888).

Marbury, William L., "The Limitations Upon the Amending Power," (1919) 33 *Harv. L. Rev.* 223.

———"The Nineteenth Amendment and After," (1920) 7 *Va. L. Rev.* 1.

Markby, Sir William, *Elements of Law*, 6th ed. (1905).

Martig, Ralph R., "Amending the Constitution," (1937) 35 *Mich. L. Rev.* 1253.

Mason, Alpheus T., "Mr. Justice Brandeis: A Student of Social and Economic Science," (1931) 79 *U. Pa. L. Rev.* 665.

Mathews, John Mabry, *Legislative and Judicial History of the Fifteenth Amendment* (1909).

Merriam, Charles E., *History of the Theory of Sovereignty Since Rousseau* (1900).

Miller, Justin, "Amendment of the Federal Constitution: Should It Be Made More Difficult?" (1926) 10 *Minn. L. Rev.* 185.

Mitchell, William D., "Methods of Amending the Constitution," (1932) 25 *Lawy. & Banker* 265.

Moore, James William, and Adelson, Shirley, "The Supreme Court: 1938 Term, II," (1940) 26 *Va. L. Rev.* 697.

Morawetz, Victor, A Treatise on the Law of Private Corporations, 2d ed. (1886) (2 vols.).

Morris, M. F., "The Fifteenth Amendment to the Federal Constitution," (1909) 189 *No. Am. Rev.* 82.

Moschzisker, Robert von, "Dangers in Disregarding Fundamental Conceptions When Amending the Federal Constitution," (1925) 11 *Corn. L. Q.* 1.

Musmanno, M. H., "The Difficulty of Amending Our Federal Constitution: Defect or Asset?" (1929) 15 *A. B. A. J.* 505.

Mussman, Michael A., "Is the Amendment Process Too Difficult?" (1923) 57 *Am. L. Rev.* 694.

Needham, Charles Willis, "Changing the Fundamental Law," (1921) 69 *U. Pa. L. Rev.* 223.

Oppenheim, L., *International Law,* 4th ed. (1928).

Pennock, J. Roland, "Law and Sovereignty," (1937) 31 *Am. Pol. Sci. Rev.* 617.

Phillips, Herbert S., "Has the Congress the Power under Article V of the Constitution to Call and Regulate the Holding of Ratifying Conventions Independent of State Legislatures?" (1933) 6 *Fla. St. Bar. Assn. J.* 573.

Picciotto, Cyril M., The *Relation of International Law to the Law of England and the United States of America* (1915).

Pillsbury, Albert E., "The Fifteenth Amendment," (1909) 16 *Me. St. Bar Assn. Proc.* 17.

Platz, William A., "Article Five of the Federal Constitution," (1934) 3 *Geo. Wash. L. Rev.* 17.

Plucknett, Theodore F. T., "Bonham's Case and Judicial Review," (1926) 40 *Harv. L. Rev.* 30.

Pollock, Frederick, *A First Book of Jurisprudence,* 6th ed. (1929).

Pomeroy, John Norton, *An Introduction to the Constitutional Law of the United States,* 10th ed. (1888).

Poore, Ben Perley, *The Federal and State Constitutions, Colonial Charters and Other Organic Laws of the United States,* 2d ed. (1878) (2 vols.).

Potter, Pittman B., "Political Science in the International Field," (1923) 17 *Am. Pol. Sci. Rev.* 381.

Potter, William P., "The Method of Amending the Federal Constitution," (1909) 57 *U. Pa. L. Rev.* 589.

Pound, Roscoe, *Readings in Roman Law,* 2d ed. (1914).

Powell, Thomas Reed, "Changing Constitutional Phases," (1939) 19 *Bost. U. L. Rev.* 509.

Quarles, James, "Amendments to the Federal Constitution," (1940) 26 *A. B. A. J.* 617.

Radin, Max, "The Intermittent Sovereign," (1930) 39 *Yale L. J.* 514.

———"Popular Legislation in California," (1939) 23 *Minn. L. Rev.* 559.

Richman, Irving B., "From John Austin to John C. Hurd," (1901) 14 *Harv. L. Rev.* 353.

Ritchie, David G., "On the Conception of Sovereignty," (1891) 1 *Am. Acad. Pol. Sci. Annals* 385.

Rockow, Lewis, "The Doctrine of the Sovereignty of the Constitution," (1931) 25 *Am. Pol. Sci. Rev.* 573.

Rottschaefer, Henry, *Handbook of American Constitutional Law* (1939).

———"Legal Theory and the Practice of Law," (1926) 10 *Minn. L. Rev.* 382.

Salmond, Sir John, *Jurisprudence*, 7th ed. (1924).

Sandelius, Walter, "National Sovereignty Versus the Rule of Law," (1931) 25 *Am. Pol. Sci. Rev.* 1.

Savigny, Friedrich Carl von, *System des heutigen römischen Rechts* (1840).

Shenton, Clarence G., "The 'Sovereign' Convention of 1873," (1935) 22 *Pa. B. A. Q.* 171.

Shepard, Max Adams, "Sovereignty at the Cross Roads: A Study of Bodin," (1930) 45 *Pol. Sci. Q.* 580.

Sidgwick, Henry, *The Elements of Politics* (1891).

Skinner, George D., "Intrinsic Limitations on the Power of Constitutional Amendment," (1920) 18 *Mich. L. Rev.* 213.

Smith, George H., "The English Analytical Jurists," (1887) 21 *Am. L. Rev.* 270.

Smith, James Allen, *The Spirit of American Government* (1907).

Smith, J. Hopkinson, "Is Prohibition Constitutional?" (1929) 4 *Plain Talk* 415.

Smith, Munroe, "Shall We Make Our Constitution Flexible?" (1911) 194 *No. Am. Rev.* 657.

Special Committee of the American Bar Association, "The Federal Child Labor Amendment," (1935) 21 *A. B. A. J.* 11.

Stephen, Leslie, *The Science of Ethics* (1882).

Stevenson, Archibald E., *State's Rights and National Prohibition* (1927).

Stimson, Frederic Jessup, *The Law of the Federal and State Constitutions of the United States* (1908).

Story, Joseph, *Commentaries on the Constitution of the United States,* 3d ed. (1858).

Taft, Henry W., "Amendment of the Federal Constitution," (1930) 16 *Va. L. Rev.* 647.

Taft, William Howard, "Can Ratification of an Amendment to the Constitution Be Made to Depend on a Referendum?" (1920) 29 *Yale L. J.* 821.

Thayer, James Bradley, "Our New Possessions," (1899) 12 *Harv. L. Rev.* 464.

Thompson, J. David, "The Amendment of the Federal Constitution," (1912) 3 *Acad. Pol. Sci. Proc.* 65.

Thompson, Walter, Book Review, (1938) 32 *Am. Pol. Sci. Rev.* 128.

———Federal Centralization (1923).

Thomson, Meldrim, Jr., "Amending the Constitution," (1938) 42 *Law Notes,* No. 1, p. 9.

Triepel, Heinrich, *Droit International et Droit Interne* (1920).

Tuller, Walter K., "A Convention to Amend the Constitution— Why Needed—How It May Be Obtained," (1911) 193 *No. Am. Rev.* 369.

Uhl, Raymond, "Sovereignty and the Fifth Article," (1936) 16 *Southwestern Social Sci. Q.,* No. 4, p. 1.

Ward, Paul W., *Sovereignty* (1928).

Weinfeld, Abraham C., "Power of Congress Over State Ratifying Conventions," (1938) 51 *Harv. L. Rev.* 473.

Westervelt, George N., "Amend Article V," (1931) 24 *Lawy. & Banker* 166.

Weston, Melville Fuller, "Political Questions," (1925) 38 *Harv. L. Rev.* 296.

Wheeler, Wayne B., "The Constitutionality of the Constitution Is Not a Justiciable Question," (1920) 90 *Cent. L. J.* 152.

———"Is a Constitutional Convention Impending?" (1927) 21 *Ill. L. Rev.* 782.

White, Justin D., "Is There an Eighteenth Amendment?" (1920) 5 *Corn. L. Q.* 113.

Williams, Bruce, "The Popular Mandate on Constitutional Amendments," (1921) 7 *Va. L. Rev.* 280.

Willis, Hugh Evander, "The Doctrine of the Amendability of the United States Constitution," (1932) 7 *Ind. L. J.* 457.

———"The Doctrine of Sovereignty Under the United States Constitution," (1929) 15 *Va. L. Rev.* 437.

Willoughby, Westel Woodbury, *The Constitutional Law of the United States*, 2d ed. (1929) (2 vols.).

———"The Juristic Conception of the State," (1918) 12 *Am. Pol. Sci. Rev.* 192.

———*The Nature of the State* (1928).

Wilson, Woodrow, *Congressional Government* (1885).

———*The State*, rev. ed. (1906).

Woodburn, James Albert, *American Politics: The American Republic and Its Government* (1903).

Wright, Philip Quincy, *The Enforcement of International Law Through Municipal Law in the United States* (1916).

Yawitz, Milton, "The Legal Effect Under American Decisions of an Alleged Irregularity in the Adoption of a Constitution or Constitutional Amendment," (1925) 10 *St. Louis L. Rev.* 279.

Index